Beyond universals
in cognitive development

This Book Is the First in the Series

PATH

PUBLICATIONS
FOR THE ADVANCEMENT
OF THEORY AND HISTORY
IN PSYCHOLOGY

Edited by David Bakan, *York University,*
John Broughton, *Teachers College, Columbia University,*
Howard E. Gruber, *Rutgers University,*
Miriam Lewin, *Manhattanville College,*
and Robert W. Rieber, *John Jay College, CUNY*

This is a series of volumes that display the following features:

▶ understanding of historical aspects of psychological theory
and practice
▶ reflective examination of psychological theory
▶ awareness of the interconnections of psychology and other
disciplines
▶ appreciation of the dialectical and philosophical nature of
our subject matter
▶ frame of reference expressing a grasp of relationships between psychology and the political, economic and social
problems of our times

Through PATH, we hope to publish works of a high scholarly
quality that will avoid a narrow, empiricist approach to psychology. We favor books that avoid the traditions of aliena-
tion, anti-intellectualism, and obscurantism. We want to have
a creative and productive influence on the future of
psychological theory and research.

Beyond Universals
in Cognitive Development

David Henry Feldman
Tufts University

Ablex Publishing Corporation
Norwood, New Jersey 07648

Second Printing 1985.

Copyright © 1980 by Ablex Publishing Corporation.

Printed in the United States of America.

Library of Congress Cataloging in Publication Data

Feldman, David Henry.
  Beyond universals in cognitive development.

  (Publications for the advancement of theory and
history in psychology)
  Bibliography: p.
  Includes indexes.
  1. Cognition in children—Research. 2. Child
psychology—Research. I. Title. II. Series.
BF723.C5F44   155.4′13   79-24338
ISBN 0-89391-029-5

ABLEX Publishing Corporation
355 Chestnut Street
Norwood, New Jersey 07648

To my brother Jerome

Let theory guide your observations, but till your reputation is well established be sparing in publishing theory. It makes persons doubt your observations . . . Charles Darwin

Gruber, H. E. & Barrett, P. H. *Darwin on Man: A Psychological Study of Scientific Creativity.* New York: E. P. Dutton & Co., 1974, p. 123.

That most vicious and Philistine attempt in some quarters to put science in a straight-jacket of barren observation, to draw the life-blood of all science—speculative advance into the secrets of things—this ultra-positivistic cry has come here as everywhere else, and put a ban upon theory. On the contrary, give us theories, theories, always theories! Let every man who has a theory pronounce his theory! This is just the difference between the average mother and the good psychologist . . . James Mark Baldwin

Baldwin, J. M. *Mental Development in the Child and the Race: Methods and Process.* New York: The Macmillan Company, 1895, pp. 37–38.

contents

4

Creativity—Trait versus Process *87*

5

Early Prodigious Achievement,
Developmental Theory and Education *121*

6

The Child as Craftsman *155*

foreword

It has been apparent for some time that the field of child development, especially in relation to cognitive development, has been coasting along on the contributions of Piaget. Some people, like David Feldman, recognize that although the coasting was not in turbulent seas, it had a somewhat fruitless direction that did not bode well for what was ahead. Piaget's mammoth contributions to the effort of establishing the universal characteristics of cognitive development had the unintended consequence of obscuring the simple fact, as David Feldman states, "that most of the energy of most of the people in the world most of the time is not spent trying to achieve universal changes." How does one get a handle on conceptualizing and creatively studying these myriad, nonuniversal human activities? Why, for example, should one study swimming unless one has a very practical goal? Why study (as the author does) map making or child prodigies unless one happens to have a personal interest in them? You do not have to justify such interests but you would not expect many people to share interests that seem narrow and without general import. If you want to feel (or to be regarded as being) in the mainstream of cognitive child development, how can you compare the importance of studying conservation and causality with that of map making and child prodigies? The author of this book gives a clear, simple, bold, and liberating answer: " . . . there are many realms of human activity where achievement is neither inevitable nor does it occur independent from the specific environmental conditions which bear upon it. My basic argument is that these realms of activity are developmental in a meaningful sense and they deserve to be part of developmental psychology's focus of interest." And in this book David Feldman unambiguously and creatively demonstrates the practical and theoretical significance of studying these nonuniversals in terms of developmental processes. As a consequence, the domain of developmental psychology takes on a more complex, exciting, and challenging character.

Of the numerous aspects of the author's stance that I found illuminating, the one I would single out is his view of "the very sticky problem of *transitions*:" the way and pace of the process by means of which an individual is said to progress from one developmental stage (or level) to another. I have never been a partisan of the concept of stage or level because my early professional years were spent administering psychological tests to children, especially those with the label "mentally retarded." I would write what I thought were comprehensive descriptions and analyses of the test performance and behavior of the children, only to find that what people (parents or colleagues) wanted to know was what the IQ was, or the mental age or level, or simply whether the child was retarded or not. I never really learned to respond with equanimity to what I considered at best mischievous and at worst harm-producing questions. Sometimes, I would read from my report that the child had failed an item at one age "level" but had passed other items at higher age levels. We called that "scatter" and some children had a lot more scatter than others. What did it mean that a child's scatter was from the three-year "level" to the nine-year level? What was being obscured by averaging the items passed? After all, we were not administering tests to decide what label to append to the child but rather to provide a basis for formulating an educational program, and to do that one had to be very sensitive to the ways in which the child's behavior and cognitive performance were differentiated. So, when I read Dr. Feldman's critique of the concept of level (or stage), and then his intriguing and instructive studies of map-making behavior in children, it brought back a lot of memories, as well as regret that a book like this had not been available to me.

Dr. Feldman says right out loud that he aims to change the face of developmental psychology. I can assure the reader that far from being an arrogant person, or someone who likes to produce a shock effect, or someone who is captured by an idea and flies into print, Dr. Feldman is a careful, reflective, modest individual in whom this book (the ideas and research it contains) has developed over a period of years. What he is saying to us is neither complicated nor fancy, but if the reader adopts his perspective, he will find that developmental psychology has, in its efforts to establish universal laws, virtually ignored myriad phenomena that are developmental in nature, the study of which has both theoretical and practical significance. For the author, his reorientation of theory leads

him to what goes on in classrooms, and as one might expect from someone who started out in education, the connections he begins to make
between developmental theory and educational practice have a very
convincing ring, as much because of what he proposes as because of how
he demonstrates why past efforts at educational innovation were faulty
and doomed. Few people move from practice to theory to practice as
comfortably and relevantly as Dr. Feldman. That is no small feat these
days when theorists and practitioners appear to be having less and less of
a need for each other.

When Dr. Feldman says he seeks to change the face of developmental psychology, he is not claiming that this book accomplishes that
task. This book is a beginning: a bold statement of position and findings.
It is a challenge to accustomed ways of thinking. It is written by someone
who has the courage to articulate a new perspective that, to my mind, will
give new life to developmental psychology.

SEYMOUR B. SARASON
Yale University

pReface

This book offers a view of cognitive development which, if accepted, would change the face of that field and the larger field of developmental psychology as well. The reader may be wondering why I think such change is needed. The fact is that as a field developmental psychology is one of the healthier and more energetic of the psychological disciplines and cognitive development is a thriving subspecialty. Unlike psychoanalysis in the 1940s when Erik Erikson was writing *Childhood and Society*, developmental psychology seems to be in no need of rejuvenation; it has neither lost its way nor become too rigid. Indeed, it is partly the fact that my discipline is healthy that leads me to believe it may be ready for the major expansion beyond its borders I will be proposing in this book.

My basic point is that the developmental psychology of intelligence has preoccupied itself with the study of *universals*, i.e. achievements which we all will accomplish, and has ignored other equally interesting aspects of cognitive development. There is nothing wrong with an emphasis on universals—quite the contrary. By drawing attention to those qualities that make us part of the human family, by showing that we will all share certain experiences of growth and change, developmental psychology has done its part to help transcend bigotry, prejudice and petty differences among individuals and groups. This is all to the good and might have been the only way that the field could have gotten to the place where it is now. But the fact remains that most of the energy of most of the people in the world most of the time is not spent trying to achieve universal changes. By definition these changes are likely to occur with relatively little effort directly exerted by growing children or those who surround them. Much of the effort that goes into universal achievements may be an unconscious byproduct of other activities and not spent directly for that purpose. Most of the time we human beings occupy ourselves with learning about our culture, the society we find ourselves in including its politics, economics, and other forms of give and take, the traditions and rules that guide and structure behavior, and the many forms of skill and work that are available or required of us. We also attempt to form a notion of who we are and the place we occupy in our family and culture. I will be trying to present a view which sees such enterprises as I have just listed as developmental but not necessarily universal.

Of course a good deal of what I have to say hangs on the meaning I will give to the word developmental, and I will go to some lengths to try to say what I mean by this term. Currently, developmental phenomena are taken to be those which are achieved by all individuals in all cultures over all historical times, independent from the specific environmental conditions which happen to prevail at a given moment in time. Joachim Wohlwill (1973) expresses this view very well. For Wohlwill the important thing about a developmental variable is that it shows progressive change with age, but change that is not brought about by specific conditions in the environment. Variables for which experience is irrelevant (for example balding processes) or variables for which specific instruction is required (for example swimming) are not properly called developmental. Examples of developmental variables in Wohlwill's scheme of things include motor and speech skills, space perception, curiosity, social perception, emotional development and a number of other organismic changes.

What do I mean when I say that many things are developmental but not universal? I simply mean that there are many realms of human activity where achievement is neither inevitable nor does it occur independent from the specific environmental conditions which bear upon it. My basic argument is that these realms of activity are developmental in a meaningful sense and they deserve to be part of developmental psychology's focus of interest. For example, the profession that one chooses to pursue is manifestly not a universal matter. Otherwise all of us might be plumbers. I will try to marshall a case for the fact that many bodies of knowledge (including probably plumbing) are organized into distinctive and conceptually discrete developmental stages or levels. The myriad disciplines, professions, vocations, crafts, hobbies and pastimes are not universal but I believe that they are most assuredly developmental. Not surprisingly I think that Wohlwill's definition is much too restrictive; swimming, I submit, is developmental, not universal but developmental. Essentially I am proposing that the term developmental have its meaning extended to all domains where change can be conceptualized in terms of a series of ever more advanced stages achieved through a process of constructive transformation.

I should add that my attempt to broaden the concept of development is not intended to *exclude* universals from the developmental family. Rather it is intended to place universal achievements into a broader framework. Piaget and his colleagues have certainly shown the value of studying universals in intelligence; others have tried to sketch universal sequences in moral reasoning, social cognition, and the self concept. My hope is to broaden the horizons of the field even as I am compelled to point out its current limitations. Problems that have traditionally been of interest to developmentalists should continue to be of interest to developmentalists; these problems will, though, become a subset of the possible problems that a developmentalist might study. Studying nonuniversals may even inform us about the role of universals in the drama of intellectual growth and the processes through which they are attained.

Beyond the fact that I believe they are there, as the man said of the mountain, of what value are these nonuniversal domains? Two uses for them come readily to mind, one practical and one theoretical. The practical use is to help make developmental psychology more relevant to the professions, particularly those professions that concern themselves with the welfare and growth of children. When I was trained to be a teacher we were not required to take developmental psychology courses; testing, classical and social learning, behavior management—but no development. Even then, and certainly later, I sensed that Piaget and other developmentalists had much to offer practitioners, at least potentially, but somehow the whole field seemed to have missed the point, at least insofar as applications were concerned. Of course it must be said that the field of cognitive development did not really profess to serve the needs of professionals. But the feeling that developmental psychology could offer a great deal to those who work with children motivated much of my own work. If what is presented here is not immediately useful, I hope it is at least a step in the right direction. My attention to possible applications should be particularly evident in the latter chapters.

On the theoretical side my main reason for pointing to nonuniversal developmental phenomena has to do with the very sticky problem of *transitions*. Piaget, the foremost thinker about developmental transitions, acknowledges that his own account is sketchy and incomplete (e.g. Piaget, 1971). I hope that the work presented in this book will make that account more detailed. In fact, it should become clear that in certain respects Piaget has actually prevented himself from making progress on the transitions problem by preoccupying himself with universals. We go into this matter in some detail in Chapter 3, but consider the following point: If development is indeed inevitable (in Piaget's terminology "spontaneous"), then the possibility of studying a negative case is excluded by definition. Since everybody goes through the Piagetian stages and since nothing special in the environment need be done to guarantee that it will happen, whatever transitions occur must occur under virtually any set of environmental conditions. This reduces the possibility of experimental control over the circumstances under which transitions occur, severely constraining empirical work.

With nonuniversal bodies of knowledge, movement through the stages of a field is neither inevitable nor does it occur under all known environmental conditions. Furthermore, individuals vary in the number of stages they achieve from zero to all. For the study of transition processes it is a much better situation to have partial sequences. Chapter 3 presents our empirical work on transitions in a nonuniversal domain and demonstrates the usefulness of such domains for this purpose.

I should say something about what this book does not attempt to address. It does not consider the roots of its theoretical, conceptual and empirical concerns. Other than Piaget and Darwin, only passing mention of other theoretical views occurs. There are of course interesting predecessors of all the ideas discussed here, but to consider these adequately would be a major scholarly work of its own.

The individual chapters are arranged to take the reader from the basic theoretical arguments about expanding the developmental terrain (Chapter 1) and accounting for its various regions over evolutionary time (Chapter 2) to a set of topics that are illuminated by these views. Chapter 3 capitalizes on the assumption that nonuniversal domains share transition processes with universal domains and presents an enriched, elaborated, and extended model of transitions based on conceptual and empirical analyses of the domain of map drawing; this chapter is the most empirical. The topic of creative thinking processes is taken up in Chapter 4, the main point of which is to show that the trait approach to creativity has outlived its usefulness. Creative thinking is conceived as a process of thinking common to all developmental domains and is a natural consequence of transition processes. Picasso's work and Howard Gruber's analysis of Darwin's thinking are used as examples of the application of a developmental process approach to creative thinking.

Chapters 5 and 6 deal with child prodigies and education, respectively. I try in these chapters to show how the prodigy is anomalous with respect to current developmental theories, but may be incorporated meaningfully into theory as expanded in this book. The prodigies chapter also illustrates the heuristics of the theory presented here; I was led to this research deductively from a theoretical structure demanding an explanation of this phenomenon. One consequence of the work with prodigies has been to raise issues and to lead to considerations about the educational process, not only for prodigies but for everyone. Another consequence has been to stimulate a conceptualization of the interplay of forces that entwine to make possible all developmental achievements. This conceptual work has not proceeded very far, but it illustrates how an empirical enterprise (case studies of prodigies) has stimulated conceptual reorganization and led to possible applications as well.

Chapter 6, *The Child as Craftsman*, takes up the relation of developmental theory to education. In it I try to show that an expanded developmental view such as is proposed in this book would be of value to education. The metaphor of the child as craftsman is intended to give expression to matters presented elsewhere in the book in more technical and "scientific" ways.

Perhaps of most direct interest to developmental psychologists is a byproduct of the transitions research reported in Chapter 3. I refer to a reconceptualization of the notion of *stages* in development. Briefly, I have tried to suggest that it makes sense to "remove" stages from inside a child and to think of them instead as existing within domains of knowledge. By taking stages out of the child, so to speak, and placing them within fields or domains of knowledge, it is possible to preserve the usefulness of the concept of stage without falling prey to the pitfalls of earlier views. Surely my view has pitfalls of its own, but these remain for my readers to discover.

It is of course my hope that this book will be most meaningful when read as a whole. For me the work was divided into chapters or research projects or reports only with real difficulty. I recognize that some of the connections among the various chapters are less explicit than they might be; this is so partly because of the length they would add to the book and partly because there are many points still to be worked out. At some later date I plan to share more fully with the reader the evolving system that guides the enterprises summarized here, but that, of course, will be another book.

acknowledgments

I have benefited greatly from association with extraordinary mentors, peers, and friends, and this is a welcome opportunity to acknowledge them—their marks are everywhere in this book. I hope that this finished product provides each of them with some sense of satisfaction and reward for their efforts.

From my student days at Stanford, Pauline Sears, Richard Snow and Robert Sears were particularly willing to tolerate and encourage my sometimes unconventional interests. At Minnesota, Joseph Glick and William Bart were colleagues who shared my passion for cognitive development, and at Yale, Albert Solnit and Seymour Sarason helped keep my educational concerns active and well supported. Seymour has continued to guide and advise me, as the reader can see. Since coming to Tufts, I have found a continuing source of shared purpose and goals as a member of the Eliot-Pearson Department of Child Study. During these years Howard Gruber, whose work I have admired for some time, has become a friend and generous colleague.

I have also had the good fortune to work with a network of fellow scholars on the rocky road to a developmental psychology of education. My good friend and collaborator Gavriel Salomon has shared from the beginning both the excitement and the burdens of the journey. Howard Gardner, Sidney Strauss, and David Olson too, have contributed often and significantly to the enterprise—sometimes it seemed as if we were all writing the same book (or in Gardner's case, books). Gabi Salomon and Howard Gardner urged me to write this book and helped me get through some of the obstacles along the way.

Over the years that the book was written, and for several years before, my collaborators and I have worked with many individuals and have been welcome guests in many homes, schools, institutions and clubs. It would be impossible to adequately thank everyone, but we would be remiss if we did not mention John and Ethel Collins, Avram David, George Kane, Fran Walsh and his charges at the Branford Intermediate School in Branford, Connecticut, the staff and students of the St. Clements Elementary School in Somerville, Massachusetts, and the families of the six children (and of course the children themselves) who are described in Chapter 5.

It has been my happy experience to work with most exceptional students and staff. Constance Stolow and Ellen Reuter have seen this project through its many transitions, unflagging and optimistic about its successful completion. Among many students, two must be singled out for special acknowledgment. Samuel Snyder and Lynn Goldsmith, both of whom I met at Yale, have made, and continue to make, contributions to my work that are so pervasive that it would be impossible to trace them. They are partners in the enterprise, and the fact that they share authorship of half the chapters in the book is only a small indication of their impact. I could not begin to thank them adequately. (I have tried. I married one; the other was already married.) The one I married has somehow managed to integrate the roles of colleague, critic, companion, collaborator, friend and more with grace, charm and dedication; finding her was a remarkable and happy coincidence.

And of course, I must thank my family and friends. My family gave me unusual freedom to explore—and were sometimes surprised at where I have gone! My friends have suffered my idiosyncracies with tolerant good cheer and patience; Bill Byers, Sue Crockenberg, Glenn and Bette Erickson, Diana Garfield, and Shari Kieran deserve special mention.

The members of the PATH group, particularly Howard Gruber and John Broughton, provided just the right combination of support and suggestions for revising the manuscript. It has been a pleasure to work with this group and the good people at Ablex.

Finally, it is a pleasure to acknowledge the support I have received from The Spencer Foundation and its President, H. Thomas James. Since 1974 I have had grants from Spencer on the faith that my work would come to have impact on developmental psychology and education; encouragement from this foundation during these five years has in several senses made this book possible. If it should come to pass that this book makes such contributions, Tom James and the others mentioned here share the credit for them. On the other hand, if there are errors of fact or interpretation found in these pages, God forbid, I accept full responsibility for them.

1
universal to unique–
mapping the
developmental terrain

The primary aim of this chapter is to provide the reader with a relatively brief overview of the frame of reference that has guided our inquiry for the past several years—the idea that developmental achievements range from "universal to unique." Its importance lies in recognizing that there exist developmental domains which are not of the universal variety that have been the stock-in-trade of cognitive-developmental theory. The argument for proposing nonuniversal regions of development is straightforward enough: universal achievements are acquired under conditions so varied that they occur in all environments in all cultures, and while these achievements may be described in rich detail, the nonspecific nature of experience presumed to engender them makes them of limited value in examining the processes by which they are achieved. Moreover, much of what people come to know simply cannot be characterized as universal in this sense. "Nonuniversal" achievements, in contrast, provide us with negative cases (only some individuals acquire them) and demand study of the specialized environmental conditions (such as instruction and available technology) by which they are achieved.

The view we present rests on the untested premise that universal and nonuniversal domains share sufficient common attributes that both may be labeled *developmental*. We explore this premise by examining the assumptions of developmental theory as it now exists and by showing how these assumptions can easily be modified to accommodate nonuniversal developmental achievements. Before turning to this "universal-to-unique" framework itself, we must first consider a matter that is central to our enterprise: the place of stages in theories of development.

STAGES IN DEVELOPMENT

Much debate about developmental theory has revolved around the issue of stages. For some developmentalists a concept of stage is fundamental to the very idea of development. For others, stage is considered an impediment to understanding the nature of development. Whether for or against stages, every developmentalist must come to grips with the place, if any, of stages in the theoretical edifice. In the view which guides the work of this book, developmental stages are utterly central. We hasten to add, however, that the particular notion of stage used in this work is different in certain respects from any previous notion.

When one of us (DHF) was a graduate student at Stanford in the late 1960s, he was taught that the concept of stage was no longer useful—stages could not be tested empirically, were mentalistic and axiomatic, and were of no heuristic value in guiding the work of developmentalists. In particular, the notion of stage was said to be untenable because it assumed a coherent, homogeneous, internal organization that in all likelihood did not exist. Finally, and perhaps most difficult to accept, this internal organization was assumed to transform itself into a qualitatively different organization in some almost magical fashion. Even if such a reorganization as this could possibly take place, the argument went, it would most likely be physiological in nature and thus outside the realm of developmental psychology.

Compelling as these arguments seemed at the time, there remained the intuition that some notion of stage was essential to the developmentalist's work. Kessen had supported this intuition in a paper published in 1962, but just what notion of stage was called for Kessen did not say. In the early 1970s John Flavell (1970; 1971a,b) presented a similar viewpoint, but took it somewhat further. Flavell argued that the Piagetian all-or-none assumption for stage change was neither theoretically tenable nor supported by the empirical data, and he opted for a much more gradualistic, process-based concept of stage. Flavell portrayed the different ideas of stage change with an illustration similar to Figure 1.1.

The first illustration (A) in Figure 1.1 is of an early notion of stages which assumes both an abrupt change from stage to stage and the complete availability of all behaviors for a given stage from the moment of its onset. This notion of stages, which can be found as early as seventh century writings (Aries, 1962), has not been taken seriously in develop-

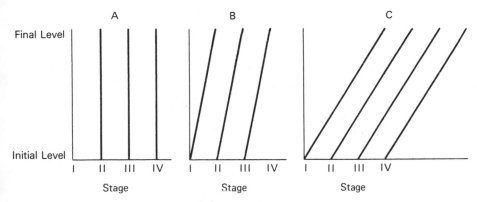

Figure 1.1 A representation of different notions of stage-to-stage movement (adapted from Flavell, 1971b).

mental psychology for some time. Nonetheless, as a caricature of stages, it serves as a useful starting point.

The second illustration (B) is Flavell's rendition of Piaget's view. This model assumes that the *capability* for all behaviors which reflect a stage is available at the moment of transition, but that the actual application of this capability to various problems takes time to unfold. Therefore, there is a gradual increase in the number of, say, concrete operational behaviors until a point is reached when all behavior comes to reflect concrete operations. This may take several years, as is the case with the various kinds of conservation which are acquired between about four and twelve years of age. But, as Flavell was moved to say, Piaget's view that this capability is complete when a single behavior reflecting the succeeding stage first appears is an untested and probably untestable assumption. Furthermore, empirical studies tend to indicate that mental organization is nowhere near as homogeneous or consistent as the Piagetian stage model would imply (cf. Turiel, 1966). Flavell therefore chose to present a much more gradualistic rendering, one like illustration (C), of how transitions between stages might actually occur. In this rendition, behaviors reflective of several stages are present at the same time; behaviors from new stages appear before the development of earlier stages is complete.

The concept of stage that we propose is based on Flavell's notion of stage construction as a gradual process, but to some extent our view takes the stage out of the child's "mind" and represents it as existing instead within a body of knowledge. In other words, when looking for the location of a stage ("Where would you find a stage if you were looking for one?"), theorists have tended to look for it inside a child's head. Piaget, for example, makes this argument:

> We have seen that there exist structures which belong only to the subject, that they are built, and that this is a step-by-step process. We must therefore conclude that there exist stages of development. (Piaget, 1970, p. 710)

While Piaget finds this logic compelling, other theorists have acknowledged that as long as stages are assumed to exist in the mind of a child, it is unlikely that we will ever be able to see what one looks like. Given this problem with traditional stage notions, we have found that concepts of development can be extended in useful ways when stages are defined not as holistic structures, but as levels of achievement within a specific field or domain.

Piaget's tendency has been to treat stages as independent of the content to which they are applied. It is clear, however, that stages of, say, map drawing are not the same as stages of general logical development, even though both are actively constructed by children. Yet by taking the location of a stage to be within a body of knowledge we do not mean to imply that the child does not participate in the qualitative changes we observe or experience in his stage to stage transitions. We do mean to suggest, however, that these successive constructions are linked in significant ways to the specific domains in which they are achieved (see also Turiel, 1977, 1979).

What is gained by conceptually placing stages within domains or bodies of knowledge? Why is it important to stop looking for stages exclusively within the child's head? It is important because critics of stage/developmental approaches have concentrated their arguments on the assumption of an internal, homogeneous, organized set of rules governing behavior (for example, Brainerd, 1977; Gagné, 1968). Charles Brainerd in particular has been unrelenting in his criticism of Piaget's concept of *structures d'ensemble,* the notion that a stage is a structured whole. Most of the empirical data seem to support Brainerd's view; a child at a single moment exhibits behavior reflecting several stages of development. In our own studies of map drawing, for example, it is rare for a child to exhibit reasoning from fewer than three of the six stages. Perhaps an even more compelling argument against a strict Piagetian interpretation of stage is the accumulated evidence that it takes children several years to achieve different concepts belonging to the same stage of development; a minimum of five to six years seems to be required for the acquisition of the various conservation concepts. Given such evidence it is harder and harder to argue that children are in the "same stage" from the appearance of conservation of number (at about four years) to the acquisition of conservation of area (which often does not appear until the early teens).

A critical aspect of the concept of stage we propose is that it does assume a structured whole, but not of the type that Piaget has proposed.

Our notion of a structured whole is conceptually quite different from Piaget's in two significant respects.

First, we do not see structured wholes as ever existing in children's heads. Instead the structured whole represents the idea that a developmental domain can be characterized in terms of a set of idealized stages. The stages are ideal because the behavior of any given child (and the system that generates and governs this behavior) is never as consistent, orderly or stage-appropriate as the hypothetical ideal would predict. "Structures as a whole" therefore represents to us the ideal sequence of achievement in a domain of knowledge that never actually exists except as a model or template against which to gauge the actual behavior of actual children (this point is further elaborated in Chapter 3).

The second difference between our view of structures as a whole and Piaget's is that we do not see stages as restricted only to general, universal cognitive development. Indeed, we will propose that many domains of knowledge and skill may be fruitfully conceptualized as consisting of a set of ideal stages which are mastered in an invariant sequence. While the notion of a structured whole is thus at best loosely descriptive of a child's behavior, it is a powerful tool for conceptualizing the nature of the structure of developmental *domains*. It need not imply that any one person will ever behave exactly according to the ideal or hypothetical set of characteristics which comprises a stage. Such consistency could perhaps be artificially produced by designing a computer program to simulate behavior at a given level for a particular domain— for example, to play chess at the level of an Expert or a Master. The structure of chess (or any of many other domains) could therefore be seen as a series of increasingly sophisticated programs designed to play the game at succeeding levels. But the play of the machine would be much more consistent than any human being's play—and much less interesting.[1]

As does Piaget, we believe that structures are achieved through a "step-by-step" process. For Piaget, though, the incremental nature of the actual construction process contradicts the assumption of wholeness that is supposed to characterize the underlying system even at the first instance of more advanced behavior. Our view transcends this problem by using wholeness as a metaphor for characterizing benchmarks within domains, but not attributing this form of wholeness to the child's cognitive system. As we see it, the construction process is of the structures

[1]As an expression of the view of stage to be taken in this book, the term *stage* itself will be generally used only to refer to universal reorganizations in thinking such as those described by Piaget. For all other developmental sequences the term *levels* is applied. Level is actually intended to be the more general term, with a stage being a particular kind of level, i.e., a universally achieved one. We are indebted to Deborah M. Levene of Tufts for suggesting this convention to us.

themselves, not of their application to various specific contents or problems, and the constructing is never of complete systems in a series of discrete jumps.

ASSUMPTIONS OF DEVELOPMENTAL THEORIES

We believe that, like the ancient all-or-none notion of stages, developmental views such as Piaget's (Piaget, 1968, 1970, 1971) require modification, elaboration and, to some extent, transformation if they are to continue to be useful. Simply reducing the number of assumptions about what can properly be labeled "developmental" accomplishes much of the necessary change. Currently theories of psychological development, it seems to us, share four basic assumptions which are outlined briefly below.

Universal Achievement. Simply stated, this assumption is that there are certain advances in thought which all children will achieve. It has been the major purpose of Piaget's empirical work, for example, to document the common achievements eventually attained by all individuals in all cultures. Piaget and his coworkers have thus attempted to isolate and describe those qualities that make us all cognitively part of the human family. From a developmental point of view, those aspects of thought which make us unique individuals have been of little interest relative to those aspects which we all share and which provide us with a common view of the world (Tyler, 1978).

Spontaneous Acquisition. The achievement of universals is assumed to occur *spontaneously.* By spontaneous the theories do not suggest that these achievements occur in the absence of an environment; this is certainly not Piaget's view. What is meant is that no *special* environment is required to guarantee that an individual will achieve a particular cognitive function or operation. Piaget uses the term "spontaneous" to suggest that children possess intrinsic tendencies to construct a view of the world and that sufficient environmental conditions in all cultures guarantee that, over time, each child will move through all of the stages and achieve all of the basic cognitive operations without specific interventions.

Invariant Sequence. A third assumption is that there are certain *sequences* through which all individual must pass toward some final cognitive system (which in Piagetian theory is called *formal operations*). The steps in the sequence are usually seen as invariant (although not always, see Bart & Airasian, 1974); that is, it is not permissible for an individual to start at any step other than the first one, nor is it permissible for an individual to skip a step in the sequence. One begins at step one (in Piaget's scheme of things, at sensorimotor behavior) and moves through the succeeding steps in a prescribed order (for Piaget the order is: sensorimotor, preoperations, concrete operations, and formal operations). One does not skip stages and one does not move backward in the sequence.

Transition Rules. The fourth assumption of developmental theory is perhaps the most difficult one to describe: there are said to be transition rules governing movement from one stage in a sequence to the next. In principle these transition rules provide an explanation for how earlier steps in a sequence become incorporated into later ones. Stage one, for example, does not simply happen to precede stage two, sharing nothing in common with the latter; this type of description would be closer to a traditional maturationist view. Rather, the developmentalist argues that there are certain ongoing processes or mechanisms by which the steps in the sequence are first achieved and later reorganized as subsequent steps emerge. The fuel for these processes or mechanisms is the existing organization itself which is not only used as the basis for future steps, but which eventually comes to demand its own reorganization as it attempts to deal with the world's complexities.

The integration of earlier steps or stages into later ones through a set of transition processes is often referred to as *hierarchical integration.* A stage is not lost as the child moves to the next step in the sequence, but rather is transformed. The initial set of acquisitions and abilities is integrated into the succeeding set and in some important sense becomes part of it.

These are the four assumptions that seem to characterize most developmental points of view—universality, spontaneousness, sequentiality, and hierarchical integration through transition rules. These assumptions reflect the fact that developmental psychology has concentrated on understanding those changes in the child's behavior that occur without special environmental intervention. However, to provide a unifying set of principles for all of human intellectual development, cognitive-developmental theory has tended to ignore changes in thinking that fail to meet all four of the above assumptions, i.e., changes that are not inevitable, or do not occur spontaneously, etc.

These assumptions have restricted the range of issues that have been viewed as "developmental," and therefore fitting for further study. Piaget, for example, has referred with derision to the preoccupation among American psychologists and educators with speeding up movement through the sequence of cognitive stages as "the American question," which he takes to miss the basic point of his theory. If one intervenes into the process then it is no longer "development" in Piaget's scheme of things. Similarly, trying to draw implications from Piaget's theory for curriculum formation is problematic because it seems futile to contrive a curriculum to provide conditions under which universal stages are achieved. These ways of thinking will be achieved naturally in any case. Therefore, to make contributions to curriculum development we may be inspired by existing developmental points of view, but for the time being we must seek guidance from elsewhere to build those specific curricula.

NONUNIVERSAL DEVELOPMENTAL DOMAINS

In light of the constraints of current cognitive-developmental theory, we propose to extend the theory in the following ways: by accepting only two of the four assumptions of the theory as is and modifying the other two assumptions by limiting their application. We continue to accept sequentiality and hierarchical integration as necessary characteristics of developmental domains, but we would limit the use of universality and spontaneousness as criteria for distinguishing developmental phenomena.

We propose that there are domains of knowledge acquisition that are truly developmental but have not been included in current theoretical treatments of cognitive development because these domains are neither universal nor spontaneously achieved. These nonuniversal domains are not necessarily mastered at the highest (or even initial) levels by all children in all cultures, nor are they achievements which can be acquired spontaneously, independent of the environmental conditions prevailing in a particular culture at a particular moment in time.

To provide some sense of the kinds of knowledge that nonuniversal domains might encompass we suggest the following provisional categories—these categories fall along a continuum from acquisitions that are universal to ones which are unique. We have already spoken of universals; they are the focus of developmental theory as we know it. As we move from universal achievements (such as conservation) to types of knowledge which fewer individuals will acquire, we begin to move along a continuum from universal to uniquely organized domains of knowledge (see Figure 1.2). These nonuniversal categories represent regions of cognitive achievement which satisfy the requirements of sequentiality and hierarchical integration, but which also require some form of outside intervention to facilitate acquisition.

Our aim here is to sketch major landmarks so as to convey the

Figure 1.2 Developmental regions from universal to unique.

general lay of the developmental landscape rather than to specify details of the terrain. Our purpose is much like that of the early explorers of this continent who first charted the overall characteristics of the country and only later detailed the particulars. The difference is between noting that "there are some high mountains to the northwest" and that "the highest mountain in the northwest sector is 15,600 feet." In this same vein, we see the different regions demarcating the universal-to-unique continuum as provisional and approximate. They are not intended to suggest precisely where each region falls, nor even to provide clear boundaries between the various regions. With these remarks made, we now briefly describe these nonuniversal domains.

Cultural

There exist domains of knowledge that all individuals within a given culture are expected to acquire; these domains comprise the region of the continuum which we call cultural. Examples of cultural domains include reading, writing and doing arithmetic, understanding and drawing maps, and understanding one's political and economic systems. The expectation is that every child in the cultural group should be able to achieve a certain level of mastery of the designated domains, although not necessarily the highest level in each.

Obviously the domains which are important to master will vary from culture to culture, as will the level of expected achievement within them. Equally obviously, for certain domains (such as mathematics) achievement at some level will be expected in many cultures, while for others (such as knowledge of democratic principles) achievement will only be required in some. Still other domains (e.g. certain religious observances, or techniques for navigation in sailing canoes) may appear as necessities in but a few.[2]

Discipline-Based

At the next major landmark are developmental domains that are based on mastery of a particular discipline. In some discipline-based domains

[2]We should note that we do not use the terms domain and culture (or society) in a specialized or technical sense, but simply according to their everyday meanings. While anthropologists, sociologists, and others are more exacting in their use of these terms (cf. Geertz, 1973), our use of them here is conventional rather than technical.

9

such as chess or aviation, the different levels of mastery and the criteria for their attainment are clearly and explicitly established (e.g. Expert or Master level play in chess). For other domains (such as medicine, carpentry, or political leadership) the levels of achievement arc less clearly defined. One difference between cultural and discipline-based bodies of knowledge is that fewer people learn discipline-based domains than cultural ones. Primarily, however, the differences between these two regions lie in the extent to which the individual can exercise choice in selecting a domain to master and the extent to which one comes to share a distinctive way of thinking about the intricacies of the domains regardless of one's particular culture. Discipline-based thinking cuts across cultural boundaries; otherwise there could be no international chess tournaments or other forms of intercultural communication or competition within a discipline. As with cultural domains, instruction and a technology are part of the domains of this region.

Idiosyncratic

Still less frequently attained than discipline-based domains are those which lie in the idiosyncratic region of the continuum. Most idiosyncratic domains are probably actually subareas of a discipline, craft or profession. Not very many individuals within a culture will necessarily (or should necessarily) achieve a given level of expertise within such domains. Idiosyncratic domains represent one's specialty, one's *metier*, the particular work that a person chooses to master in a particular way. Idiosyncratic though one's specialty may be, the process of mastering these kinds of domains is nonetheless a developmental one. If an individual elects to study mathematics he must begin at the beginning of mathematics and advance through its levels, progressing from novice mathematician to expert to master mathematician.

One of the most striking kinds of examples of idiosyncratic development is the child prodigy. Here we see youngsters who seem to connect with a domain in a most unusual way, almost as if they were pretuned to express their individuality through this one special field. Part of what is so compelling about performing at a very high level at a very young age is the apparent reciprocity between child and field. One gets the impression that such children were somehow destined to select a special domain by powerful natural and cultural forces. No matter how powerfully specialized or awesome a child's achievements may be, however, child prodigies move through the levels of their field to become specialists more or less as others do. What is so different about them is that they move at such an extraordinarily rapid rate. We shall consider the matter of child prodigies in more detail in Chapter 5. More typical

idiosyncratic specialties are the particular subareas of a discipline practiced by adults, e.g., open heart surgery, Elizabethan music, Maserati
repairs, patent law, ice sculpture, etc.

Unique Achievements within Domains

Finally, moving as far from universal achievements as we can, we come
to the region of unique developmental achievements. These represent a
form of organization within a domain that has never before been accomplished in quite the same way. There is, to be sure, a certain axiomatic sense in which all behavior is unique, including all developmental
changes; it is in the same sense that each of us is a unique physical
organism. The kind of achievement we discuss here, however, goes beyond this sort of uniqueness. We propose that individuals may at times
fashion out new levels of organization within a domain or, in the most
extreme cases establish a new or radically altered domain by transcending the constraints of an existing field or discipline to establish a major
new order. Those unique achievements that reorganize a body of knowledge are identified in our scheme as *creative* ones. From the many unique
reorganizations of knowledge that occur, a small number which are perceived as particularly useful may eventually become incorporated into
domains which enjoy wider popular exposure (see Chapter 2).

By including unique reorganizations in thinking, we have extended
the range of developmental phenomena from universally mastered domains of knowledge to unique reorganizations of existing domains. But
note that while all creative advances in thought are in some sense unique,
not all unique advances should be called creative. Creative advances
result in substantial new contributions to bodies of knowledge; most
unique advances, in fact, do *not* do this and therefore are not considered
here as creative.

ENVIRONMENTAL CONDITIONS
FROM UNIVERSAL TO UNIQUE:
CATALYSTS FOR REORGANIZATION

Flavell (1971a) observed that universal achievements emerge "assuming
that the organism is a neurologically intact human being and assuming a
normal human environment" (p. 122, emphasis in original). About this
"normal human environmental" Flavell says the following:

> I have trouble thinking clearly about the "normal human environment"
> part . . . . It seems to imply that there must be invariant features common
> to a wide range of . . . environmental objects and events . . . these higher

order, invariant features which any and all possess constitute necessary nutriment or "aliments" for . . . development . . . . I personally take as a major objective for our field [i.e. developmental psychology] the search for possible *universal* outcomes of human cognitive development . . . which are common to all normal people in all societies . . . The [environmental] contributions to their genesis must consist of the aforementioned invariants of human experience . . . . The [role of the environment] . . . is subtle and hard to conceptualize, but its conceptualization is a necessary task. (p. 122)

Flavell clearly sees the role of environmental conditions in bringing about developmental change as a neglected but important topic. We offer a few suggestions below in the hope of moving toward a richer understanding of the conditions under which developmental advances take place. Not surprisingly, we extend Flavell's mandate to environmental conditions associated with nonuniversal as well as universal achievements. Our aim is to suggest some of the environmental conditions which may give rise to qualitative shifts in levels of development, whether they are universal or unique.

Universal Conditions

The environmental conditions that help to stimulate the acquisition of universal bodies of knowledge seem to be of two types: human conditions and nonhuman ones. An example of a nonhuman universal condition is the redundancy present in the physical environment, which leads the child to discover that the world consists of permanent, three-dimensional objects. Piaget has given considerable attention to such happenings, plotting sequences in the acquisition of the object concept, space, time, casuality, etc. (e.g. Piaget, 1952, 1954; Piaget & Inhelder, 1948). Surely the fact that objects have weight and substance, that they drop to the ground, that they stand in topological relationships to one another, must provide experience necessary for building an adequate conception of the physical world. Also, regularities in time—changes during days, weeks, months, and years—are surely among the conditions that lead to temporal representation, causal inference, categorization, etc.

While nonhuman conditions are usually external to the individual, human conditions include internal qualities of the changing individual as well as conditions created by social interaction with others. The facilitating effect of social interaction has been confirmed by recent research in moral judgment and conservation. This facilitation is particularly effective where a child at a lower level of development is confronted by others whose moral judgments are at the next higher level of the domain (e.g. Blatt & Kohlberg, 1973; Kohlberg, 1973; Kohlberg & Gilligan, 1974). Other researchers have demonstrated similar facilitating effects of social exchange with respect to the acquisition of conservation (e.g. Murray, 1972; Silverman & Geiringer, 1973) and map drawing (Levin, 1978).

These findings are consistent with Piaget's view that social interaction does not play a direct causal role in determining the nature of thought. Rather, in the course of social contact the child is confronted with a series of physical and social perspectives other than his own. Such conflicts are thought to motivate the child to seek a resolution of the disparate views, or what Piaget (1923) called "verification" in his early work. By generating cognitive disequilibrium, the desire for change is energized:

> What then gives rise to the need for verification? Surely it must be the shock of our thought coming into contact with that of others, which produces doubt and the desire to prove .... The social need to share the thought of others and to communicate our own with success is at the root of our need for verification. (p. 204)

Social interaction thus leads to motivation for the transformation of cognitive structures. In particular the desire to communicate with others and to have others accept one's views seem to energize the change process.

Other universal human conditions are more internally located. These include physical, perceptual, and neurological consistencies in response as well as regularities in bodily processes that may be related to time (e.g., sleep patterns), space (e.g., one's own movement and locomotion), and causality (e.g., crying), in much the same manner as are external patterns. Little more need be said about these universal conditions but that we know too little about them and we should know more.

Cultural Conditions

By definition, conditions that serve as catalysts for universally achieved thought patterns are available to all individuals in all cultures.[3] We believe that there are, in addition, sets of less pervasive conditions limited to members of particular cultures which give rise to mastery of the levels of cultural domains. Patterns of achievement and nonachievement for cultural domains are more varied than for universal ones. Perfectly normal members of a society may not achieve basic competence in all

---

[3]It is true that there are instances where universal catalysts do not result in the formation of the related competencies, but these cases seem to involve organic causes (e.g., blindness, deafness), serious emotional disturbance (e.g., autism), or some devastating trauma (perhaps the result of an accident or an illness e.g., stroke, or the side effects of medical procedures).

culturally valued fields, even in domains where competence is taken to be a critical aspect of cultural membership. Thus, the opportunities for investigating naturally occurring differences in cultural conditions and for examining the possible effects of intervention are potentially much greater than for universal conditions. One type of cultural condition has its roots in what Bruner (1971, 1975) has called culturally evolved "amplifiers" of human capacities. These amplifiers *carry* and *preserve* the knowledge that constitutes cultural domains of thought. The number and variety of cultural amplifiers is staggering: all of the symbol systems, models, tools, technology, and artifacts as well as the variety of cultural institutions and their products are examples (Gardner, Howard & Perkins, 1974; Olson, 1974; Salomon, 1974, 1979).

A second set of powerful cultural conditions is the array of techniques involved in the *transmission* of knowledge. While observation and imitation of an adult may be sufficient to acquire some of the simpler cultural skills such as bathing (Bruner, 1972), most such skills are acquired "nonspontaneously," that is, planned instruction using specialized techniques is requisite to their mastery. To be sure, schools and formal instruction by trained teachers have not existed for very long in human history, and much of what is learned about cultural domains may be acquired through other forms of cultural intervention (Bruner, 1972). Nonetheless cultural institutions, particularly schools, have been of major importance in introducing the child to the valued amplifiers of the culture, as Bruner has emphasized. Of special interest are the ways that instructional processes stimulate transformation and change in intellectual organization (e.g. Scribner & Cole, 1973). Despite centuries of experience we still know very little about why instruction works sometimes and not others, or about why some techniques affect some children positively and others negatively (Olson, 1972; Salomon, 1979).

Even one of our foremost thinkers about the nature of instruction, Jerome Bruner, frankly acknowledges that he has relatively little to say about the specific cultural conditions that might give rise to particular achievements. To the extent that he has written about this issue, Bruner's analysis tends to be in terms of general "cognitive conflicts" that must be stimulated as a precondition for intellectual advance. But as he notes, "the rub is that there are many cognitive conflicts . . . that do not lead a child to grow" as well as ones that do stimulate change (Bruner et al., 1966, p. 4).

David Olson's recent work also considers the role of formal instruction in the development of knowledge and skill. In some of this research he focused on the concept of "diagonality" (Olson, 1970), or how the child learns to recognize and/or construct diagonal lines under varying instructional conditions. Olson has investigated with special care how the medium through which a concept is presented affects how well the child understands that concept (e.g., drawing, talking about, or building diagonals on a checkerboard). From this initial set of problems Olson has taken up the broader issue of why instruction works at all (Olson, 1972). Of particular importance in his view is that there are media-specific qualities in the transmission of knowledge (Olson, 1974). While the underlying information or knowledge conveyed by various media may be the same (e.g., instructions presented via spoken words, sign language, or the printed page), they may not be equally effective in imparting that information because of fundamental differences in the media themselves (Salomon, 1979). The particular medium that carries the information has a structure of its own which is in part independent of the information it carries. If the knowledge transmitted through that medium is to be received, the child must be able to comprehend the structure of the medium along with the knowledge it conveys.

It follows that one fundamental purpose of instruction is to impart not only knowledge about the world but also skill in the utilization of various media. Noting that different cultures present the child with different information-carrying media, Olson (1970) has even defined intelligence as "skill in a cultural medium" (p. 193). Acknowledging that little is known about the processes through which skills in particular media are acquired, Olson speculates about the possible sources of skill in Euclidean geometry as an example:

> It is likely that the child's acquisition of skill in this medium has its beginning in such things as representational and geometric drawings, and building with blocks. As these skills are specific to our culture, people in other cultures or subcultures not sharing this medium can be expected to perform more poorly, as do, in fact . . . Kenyan children. (1970, p. 195)

Most cultural achievements require some form of instruction and, by virtue of being subject to modification and experimental control, provide a way to study conditions under which progress from level to level takes place. When more universal forces are at work, however, this is not a feasible strategy. The process of mastering cultural domains, then, is a layered one. The child's goal is to acquire some body of knowledge which is presented to him through some medium. In order to obtain the information, the child must first develop skills at extracting it from the medium in which it is embedded (Salomon, 1979).

Cultural conditions, then, tend to be those which directly instruct the child or which facilitate the acquisition of skills in a medium, facilitating (in Bruner's terms) the acquisition and use of a valued amplifier of human capabilities. As we have noted, though, we know very little explicitly about how this acquisition process works. If cultural domains are developmental, then it should be possible to learn something about how they are acquired by focusing on the environmental conditions prior to, during, and after a new level has been achieved. With this type of information we would then be able to specify which types of intervention might induce the cognitive conflicts that are likely to result in developmental advances and which are not.

In sum, cultural environmental conditions are different from universal conditions in that they are created, husbanded, preserved and passed on by members of a culture. Many of these cultural conditions are transmitted through various media which have been evolved to amplify and extend human capabilities. They help organize and integrate the more spontaneously evolving concepts and ensure the acquisition of culturally valued knowledge that cannot be transmitted solely in the context of action. Tools, techniques and models of aspects of reality are some of the ways in which knowledge becomes part of the cultural environment that is presented to the young.

Discipline-Based Conditions

Discipline-based environmental conditions may be distinguished in a number of ways from the other conditions discussed so far. In contrast to universal and cultural conditions, disciplined conditions help catalyze the acquisition of more advanced levels within a domain which are typically achieved by only a relatively small subset—sometimes a tiny subset—of the members of a given culture. On the other hand, disciplined conditions share with universal and with some cultural conditions the property that they are effective in facilitating such advance in practitioners from any culture. Professionals, students of an art or a craft, scholars and tradesmen share with colleagues in other countries and in other cultures many of the skills and capabilities that are characteristic of their discipline. Needless to say there are also distinctive qualities to the expression of these skills; American Indian jewelry and Yemenite jewelry are both jewelry, but one would rarely be mistaken for the other.

It should be evident that disciplined conditions and cultural conditions overlap insofar as the exposure to certain discipline-based domains is available in many cultures. For example, there have been poets and musicians in virtually all known cultures; yet few in any culture will actually become poets or musicians themselves. We wish to focus for the moment on these and other disciplines whose acquisition would typically be considered optional within a given culture, i.e., where mastery is not necessary for participation in the culture.

Unfortunately, except for a few recent attempts in the field of the visual arts (e.g., Gardner, 1973; Getzels & Csikzentmihalyi, 1976) little is known about what makes a discipline a discipline, let alone how people advance through it. Our assumption that the acquisition of disciplines is sequential and hierarchical implies that they have distinct stages or levels of achievement. Master practitioners of the discipline might well be able to specify these levels (see Chapters 5 and 6). A paper appearing in a recent issue of the journal *Cognition* presents the sort of research that our conception of disciplined conditions seems to suggest. Hatano, Miyaki and Binks (1977) studied the performance of expert abacus users for evidence that the techniques of calculation made possible by the device were eventually internalized by the users. Ten subjects at various levels of skill were given calculation problems with and without an abacus and were also asked questions both mathematical and nonmathematical in nature during their work. Imitative finger movements among abacus users of intermediate skill when solving problems without an abacus suggested that the technique of calculation utilized in the abacus was in the process of being "interiorized." Advanced users reported that they had used finger movements at an earlier time but no longer needed to do so. The "mature stage" users were also not disturbed in their calculations by prohibition of finger movement, nor by asking them to tap rhythmically, while "intermediate stage" subjects were. "In other words, abacus operation tends to interiorize into mental operation through a transition stage wherein the mental operation is not completely independent from the motor system and abacus-simulating finger movement gives important support" (p. 53). As the authors suggest, their results are quite suggestive of the development of levels of performance within this discipline, but "longitudinal studies are necessary to establish that individuals must make these qualitative changes" (p. 53). While mastering the abacus may not be the most compelling discipline to study, it does seem to meet our criteria as a discipline-based body of knowledge, and the results suggest that there are levels to the discipline that include qualitatively different ways of calculating.

A discipline has the effect of organizing reality, of suggesting certain possibilities and of foreclosing others. It becomes a set of controlling conditions in a person's psychological environment (Salomon, 1979). Indeed, the meaning of the term "discipline" implies that one's way of thinking, of organizing reality (or part of it) takes on a distinctive and traditional form as a consequence of acquiring that discipline. Moreover, individuals do not restrict their disciplined thinking to those problems which comfortably fall within the domain itself. When a disciplined way of constructing reality has become too confining, "breakthroughs" may be achieved by practitioners from other fields who apply a somewhat different perspective to long-standing unsolved problems (Kuhn, 1962; Ghiselin, 1952).

One of the advantages of studying developmental levels within a discipline is that most subjects are adults who can more readily reflect upon their experience (not always, of course; see Chapter 5). A second advantage is the likelihood that achievement of the levels within the discipline are compressed in time relative to the acquisition of broader cultural or universal domains; that is, more levels are covered in a smaller amount of time. In many disciplines one can, of course, continue reaching new heights for a lifetime, but the basic sequence of acquisition may not take as long as the acquisition of universal logical structures. This in turn offers the possibility of studying stage and sequence issues without some of the problems associated with more general developmental domains.

Metahobby. As a way of beginning to investigate further the nature of discipline-based bodies of knowledge, one of us (DHF) has given students at Tufts an unusual assignment; its purpose is to examine whether several fields are indeed developmental and are structured according to qualitatively different levels of achievement. The assignment is called "metahobby." The students (about 150 to 175 have participated thus far) are required to begin a hobby that they have always wanted to learn but have not had time to try. Their assignment for the semester is to spend a reasonable amount of time learning how to do something challenging with which they have had little experience. The only constraint is that the hobby they choose has to be sufficiently difficult that they are unlikely to master it fully in a semester's time. They are instructed to reflect upon the experience in a journal and try to relate their experience to developmental theory. And of course the "theory" these students learn is, more or less, the same one that is contained in this book.

It is impossible to tell the extent to which ideas about development are imposed upon the student's experience. The impression which emerges, however, is that the imposition, while no doubt a factor, is surprisingly minimal. Amazingly, almost all of the students thus far have been able to conceptualize their metahobby projects in terms of developmental levels and developmental transitions which seem quite plausible and natural. The metahobbies have ranged widely—belly dancing, ethnic cooking, sculpture, skiing, auto body work, calligraphy, radio braodcasting to name only a few. The range is remarkable but the common threads are, from our point of view, even more impressive. There is a real sense that the students' analyses are not simply a relabeling of experience. The notion of developmental levels and transitions within the variety of discipline-based domains selected seems to make a profound difference to these students as they reflect on their experiences. In other words, the approach does seem to lead to a different and fruitful frame of reference for organizing and understanding intellectual development, particularly in the nonuniversal domains that can be called disciplines.

Idiosyncratic Conditions

In the sets of environmental conditions considered thus far we have emphasized: (a) the importance of experience in the physical and social worlds, (b) cultural conditions and formal instruction, and (c) the meaning of acquiring a discipline. Moving from the universal domains, individual (internal) conditions become more crucial to the process of development in terms of both selecting domains to be mastered and responding to the available forms of instruction. Here, we focus on an even more restricted set of conditions which seem to have a unique personal flavor. The hallmark of these idiosyncratic achievements is the complimentarity between a field of endeavor and a set of individual predispositions or talents. As mentioned earlier, in some sense all individuals do what they do in unique ways, so there is an idiosyncratic aspect to all activity. However, *idiosyncratic conditions play a particularly crucial role when an individual has already progressed from novice to apprentice, to journeyman, to craftsman, to specialist, to expert, and is perhaps able to develop a singular expertise or preeminence in a field.* This progression conveys the development through levels we have in mind as an individual moves toward idiosyncratic expression within a domain. Obviously, when one has reached the most advanced level of a field, he or she shares with few others—or even no others—an individual way of organizing that field. Even when an individual never reaches the more advanced levels of a specialty, his approach or technique may be highly idiosyncratic.

The distinctive quality of idiosyncratic accomplishment in a domain is the extent to which achievement is a function of a highly specialized, joint set of personal and environmental conditions. Here the subtle interplay of individual and environment seems to reach its full expression. Perhaps the most telling examples illustrating such reciprocity between individual and field are to be found among child prodigies. Fascinating questions about sequence, mastery, the effects of instruction, predisposition to a field, etc., tumble forth once the child prodigy has been provisionally admitted to the fraternity of developmentally lawful happenings. A paradoxical aspect of the prodigy's achievements is that they seem to arise with a minimum of formal tutoring, running counter to other cultural and discipline-based conditions which require prolonged and systematic exposure. These aspects of early prodigious achievement are less mysterious, however, when prodigies are conceptualized as examples of idiosyncratic developmental achievement for, as we shall see in Chapter 5, prodigies are actually no less (and perhaps more) dependent than others on appropriate environmental conditions for their achievements.

Another topic which, like early prodigious achievement, has tended to fall outside the boundaries of cognitive developmental theory is *creativity*. The same forces that lead us to extend developmental phenomena to include esoteric work within a discipline also impel us to consider creativity. Since creativity is discussed in detail in Chapter 4, however, here we will only mention that in accounting for creativity we must also extend our conception of developmental achievements since nontrivial creativity occurs only when a unique developmental advance within an idiosyncratic domain has been achieved.

Unique Conditions

For other developmental advances the fact of achievement is relatively straightforward to document. These reorganizations in thought are responses to reasonably well understood problems, problems for which criteria of mastery and accomplishment are known. When a practitioner reaches the limits of his craft and yet continues to struggle with a problem that cannot be solved satisfactorily or an intention which cannot be suitably expressed, the likelihood of a unique reorganization seems greatest. In its more substantial forms a unique advance is made possible by truly transcending what has gone before, by appreciating fully the traditional importance of a problem and by sensing the limits of a known paradigm for dealing with it (Kuhn, 1962). By applying a combination of distilled experiences and knowledge to an unsolved problem an individual or group of individuals may move beyond the limits of existing knowledge in a way that changes their view of a field and reorganizes their way of thinking about it. This reorganization, if communicated to others, may become an important environmental condition itself, contributing to the achievement of the new level or reorganization by other individuals who have advanced to an idiosyncratic level of accomplishment in the domain compatible with the change. In other words, unique advances are most likely to themselves become incorporated into critical environmental conditions for facilitating developmental advances by others. By studying creative processes and products within this framework we may be able to understand better the conditions that give rise to unique developmental advances both remarkable and mundane.

CONCLUSION: RELATIONS AMONG DEVELOPMENTAL DOMAINS

The universal-to-unique continuum represents the idea that many domains may be identified as developmental without having to be universally acquired. These different regions of nonuniversal cognitive endeavor meet the two key assumptions of sequentiality and hierarchical intergration that we have suggested are necessary for a domain to properly be called developmental. The continuum itself is defined in part by differences in the kinds of environmental conditions which lead to each type of achievement and in part by the decreasing frequency with which advanced levels of each domain are achieved, i.e., by a set of regions which vary from achievement by virtually all individuals to achievement by perhaps a single individual, as in the case of powerful creative insights. Despite these differences, the regions of the continuum are similar in terms of the processes for advance from level to level within a domain. We would argue that the means by which individuals effect advances within domains of knowledge—the mechanisms of transition—are much the same for universal bodies of knowledge as they are for unique ones.

Once we have begun to make these conceptual links among the different regions of development and their domains, we are left with a number of questions. For example, are universal achievements prerequisite to all or only to some nonuniversal developmental achievements? Are universal domains the set from which all other domains are fashioned? Do the domains within the regions themselves constitute some form of a developmental sequence or are they organized in some other way?

In terms of the sequence of prerequisite functions it seems obvious enough that some of the universal achievements are necessary for cultural or more idiosyncratic pursuits to occur. Yet it does not appear that *all* universals need be acquired before *any* cultural mastery may take place. We are far from knowing, of course, but a reasonable guess at this point follows closely the line of argument put forward by Flavell (1971b). This guess is that achievement of at least certain elements of universal domains must precede initial mastery of aspects of cultural domains, but that there may also be parallel development in these two regions of thought. The same is true for cultural domains with respect to disciplined, disciplined with respect to idiosyncratic, and idiosyncratic with respect to unique achievements.

Reaching the end or final level in a common domain is not prerequisite to beginning the process of mastery of a less common one, but it does seem likely that one cannot begin the latter until one has mastered at least some aspects of more basic, commonly achieved bodies of knowledge. It is not necessary, for example, to have grasped the full use of formal logic and reasoning to begin to learn to read, nor is it necessary to have mastered reading in order to begin to play the violin. It is necessary, however, to know that symbols can stand for things or ideas (a cognitive universal) in order for reading (whether words or music) to make any sense at all. And one can begin to play the violin only if one has been introduced to that part of cultural knowledge that makes violin playing possible. In a similar vein, Howard Gardner (1973) has argued that producing graphic art requires concrete but not formal operations and the Kohlberg group (Kohlberg, 1969, 1971) sees concrete operations as necessary for various levels of moral judgments or reasoning to occur.

When we ask the question about whether the domains in the less idiosyncratic regions of the continuum are included somehow in those of the more individualized regions, we face a thornier set of problems. In some sense and virtually by definition all other domains are dependent upon universal bodies of knowledge. Yet cultural domains are not really a subset of universal domains. While both are developmental in the sense that we use the term, cultural domains do not seem reducible to universal ones; there are universal aspects to cultural (and all other domains), but cultural domains also have their distinctive qualities as well. Cultural domains, however, do provide a set from among which disciplined, idiosyncratic and unique domains are fashioned. Perhaps this change from noninclusion in the case of universals to inclusion when we consider only the different regions of nonuniversal achievement is due to the increasing importance of individual qualities of mind and temperament in the selection and mastery of the more idiosyncratic domains. In fact, when we think about unique achievements we tend to think of them less as independent bodies of knowledge and more as unique *aspects* of an idiosyncratic domain (except, of course, in the extreme case of creative genius where a new domain may itself be fashioned). These rare instances of unique creative achievements are the cutting edge of new knowledge, some of which may even eventually become universal.

Thinking of a dynamic relationship between unique achievements and universal ones makes it possible to consider how the universal changes we have discussed come to achieve their status. A unique set of conditions gives rise to a unique mental reorganization of a domain in one or more human beings. If that reorganization is communicated or expressed in an effective way, it becomes a dark horse candidate for status as a universally important domain of knowledge. Thus a speculation can be offered: over evolutionay time *every* developmental advance may have once been a unique developmental advance. The unique advances of one generation have the potential to become critical environmental conditions for succeeding generations. It is this historical and evolutionary aspect of the universal-to-unique framework that is the focus of the next chapter.

2
unique to universal–
the role of novel behavior
in the evolution of knowledge

Our purpose in this chapter is to further elaborate the universal-to-unique continuum by proposing another link among its various developmental regions. This is the link forged by time. The domains in the different regions share a common history, for they all originated from novel ideas—that is, they all began as novelties from the unique region of the continuum. Through the process of "cultural incorporation" of novel ideas described in this chapter, the various domains themselves may extend along the continuum, becoming bodies of knowledge to be mastered by larger and larger segments of the culture.

Each new body of knowledge begins as a unique reorganization of ideas by one or a few individuals. As these ideas become organized and reorganized, they are incorporated into the larger network of ideas. Over time, some sets become domains of knowledge and may begin to extend from the unique toward the universal regions. How far a domain moves toward the region of universal achievements (or whether it moves at all) is a function of the number, quality, stability, and utility of reorganizations it undergoes and also of the effectiveness with which these potential advances are communicated to others. Movement of a domain along the continuum is also a function of the extent to which the knowledge contained in a given domain becomes crucially important in some way to larger numbers of individuals over time.

The notion that a domain, once formed, may extend from the unique region of the continuum into one of the more universal regions reveals a number of characteristics of the continuum itself which are explored in this chapter. Perhaps the most important is that as a given domain develops, it may occupy a number of different regions along the continuum at various points in its history. This, in turn, suggests that domains located in different regions may represent expressions of the same processes of incorporation but at different points in the histories of the domains. Thus, universal and nonuniversal domains not only share attributes of having developmental levels and transition processes, but also share the common underlying process of cultural incorporation. What differs among the domains in different regions of the continuum is the span of time that this process has been operating and the importance (as of that moment) of the domain for human cultures.

NOVELTIES IN THOUGHT

A few years ago we asked a prominent Yale psychologist working within the Pavlovian tradition what research, if any, could be found in the literature of experimental psychology dealing with the issue of novelty in thinking. After a few moment's pause to consider the question, he replied that as far as he knew there really was not any recent work on the topic. He mentioned a few experiments from the 1940s having to do with problem solving and insight, making and breaking mental sets and so on, but said that on the whole nothing of any real significance had appeared in the literature during the past thirty years. He added by way of an exclamation point that there was more than enough to do just trying to understand predictable and mundane responses; as far as he was concerned, the science of psychology was by no means advanced enough to consider the problem of new responses.

We grant that rigorous experimental work on novelty in thought is well into the future, at least in the sense that our friend meant it. As the reader will see, some of the research reported elsewhere in this volume (especially in Chapter 3) begins an empirical line of study on the appearance and effects of simple novelties on individuals learning to master a particular cultural domain. However, for the present chapter, it would matter little if there were no work yet of an empirical sort; some important issues regarding the effects of novelties can be fruitfully discussed even though we are still in the dark about how novelties in thought come about. So for this discussion we take for granted that novelties in thinking somehow occur. It is what happens after they occur that is of interest. We are not so much concerned with what happens to the individual bringing about the novelty (this is the business of Chapter 4), but rather with what happens to the body of knowledge of which the new idea becomes a part.

Considering the effects of a novelty on an existing body of knowledge allows us to propose a plausible account of the origins and history of the universal-to-unique continuum. For the purposes of this discussion, a novelty in thought represents any idea (or ideas) that may have the potential to catalyze a reorganization in a body of knowledge. Not all novelties have equally powerful impact on their bodies of knowledge, of course. Novel thoughts can range from relatively trivial to relatively important in terms of their immediate or eventual impact on the domain.

Viewing the production and incorporation of novelties as part of a process of evolution within bodies of knowledge creates an interesting change in the character of the universal-to-unique continuum. With the addition of this notion, the continuum changes from a set of relatively stable categories or regions as presented in Chapter 1 to a representation of a dynamic process which has been captured at a particular moment in time. The domains which occupy the different regions may differ with time as they become more and more relevant to the functioning of the larger community, extending toward the universal of the continuum. New elements are continuously entering the system at the unique end, and these become potential catalysts for reorganizing domains. Over time it may become increasingly important for some bodies of knowledge to be understood and mastered by more and more members of a culture. These will be refined and simplified so that they can be more effectively communicated. As this happens the domain itself develops, extending from the unique and idiosyncratic regions of the continuum toward the more universal ones. Each domain of the continuum may thus be seen to be more ancient than its neighbors to the right and more recent than its neighbors to the left. Over eons of time the novelties in thinking produced by countless individuals and shared with countless other individuals have been winnowed down to those that remain as the accumulated knowledge passed from generation to generation.

Novelties that effect changes in existing bodies of knowledge (or establish entirely new realms of endeavor) are to be our focus of interest—i.e., we are concerned with novelties that have significant impact. More frequent, but of less interest here, are advances which allow individuals to reconceptualize various domains of knowledge for themselves. While they are related, novelties that transform domains of knowledge and novelties that transform individuals' understanding of existing domains are not precisely the same. Thus, novelty can be considered within two contexts, both of which are "historical" in some sense. First, novelty may be judged in relation to the previous experience of an individual. Every behavior is novel to some degree as it never exactly replicates earlier ones, but we also judge novelty in terms of how unprecedented a given behavior is for a particular individual.

The second context within which novelty is judged is the field (or fields) of knowledge; we call this the context of the domain. Often the individual believes his behavior to be novel in relation to both contexts when in fact it is only novel in relation to his own experience—this is a form of egocentrism. Egocentrism of this type is typical of the universal congitive changes that characterize development during the course of childhood. The changes allow the child to see new vistas opening as he develops more and more powerful cognitive structures, and he often feels as if he were the only person to ever have experienced the attendant alterations in thought and perception. And these changes unquestionably do reveal new vistas for the child, even though the adult knows that they are actually familiar views to fellow travelers of more advanced years.

From the point of view of a six-year-old child the experience of reorganizing a universal domain, say seeing the conservation of a continuous quantity problem for what it is—a sleight of hand played on us by our own perceptual systems—may be as powerful relative to his own developmental level as evolving a new explanation for ion exchange in chemical reactions may be to a chemist. The six-year-old's insight, however, has no direct implications for the domain, nor for the universal-to-unique continuum. It does assure us that yet another child has achieved yet another advance in his thinking, and this may mean that later on when he has mastered the levels of his specialty he may produce something of significance for his field. But a child's achievement of concrete operational thought has no direct implications for the future of the domain of logic. In contrast, a new explanation of ion exchange might stimulate a reconceptualization of certain chemical processes, and would thereby become a candidate for inclusion in the evolving body of knowledge about chemistry.

A Puzzle

As a domain extends toward the universal region of the continuum its transmission depends less on special attention from agents of the culture such as parents, teachers, priests, mentors, family members, older peers, etc. And yet earlier, as the domain became more important for the culture, *more* attention had to be paid to make sure that as many members of the society as possible mastered its knowledge.

It is not clear just what accounts for the fact that certain kinds of knowledge are eventually acquired without specific environmental intervention, when at an earlier time a substantial amount of attention had to be paid to ensure their transmission. It seems that individuals must at some point have evolved a predisposition toward acquiring universal bodies of knowledge (for example, time, space, and logic) and that this predisposition is now part of the biological inheritance of every human being. We know that by the time a domain has reached universal status it must be possible for virtually all of us to spontaneously acquire the valued knowledge. This suggests that the environmental conditions which support the acquisition of that knowledge are sufficiently varied and readily available that everyone will naturally encounter some of these conditions in their transactions with the environment.

This, to be sure, is a very different pattern from what seems to happen in nonuniversal domains. Unlike universally acquired domains of thought, the acquisition of nonuniversal bodies of knowledge is not necessarily supported by powerful tendencies which are part of one's biological heritage. These bodies of knowledge cannot be acquired through the normal, everyday experiences which seem sufficient for catalyzing the acquisition of universal domains. For those domains which extend into nonuniversal regions of the continuum, cultural resources must be brought to bear to teach them in some deliberate, systematic manner.

Lamarckian as it may seem, the capability to acquire certain levels of knowledge for certain domains must eventually become transmissible from generation to generation by some biological process. For example, some time long ago someone (or some few individuals) must have discovered the concept of number. Explaining this concept and illustrating its importance to one's peers, and later one's children, would have been no small feat. Now an understanding of the notion of number is quite a basic cognitive achievement, and provides the foundation for an understanding of mathematics and other domains (Gelman & Gallistel, 1978). We cannot yet begin to explain how a domain shifts from cultural to universal, that is, how it changes from a domain that is mastered only with the aid of some specific form of instruction or other intervention to a domain for which individuals are predisposed to master its contents without any deliberately imposed intervention. Nor can we explain how the original creative insight, say that the number of objects in a collection remains the same regardless of the physical shape of the collection itself, initially comes about. For now we must take these processes as given and direct our attention to those aspects of transformation and change about which we can say something more specific.

By doing so we follow a tradition perhaps best exemplified by Darwin's work. Darwin's thoughts about evolution rested upon the notion of variation despite the fact that he was never able to describe the mechanisms that produced it. Once presented, however, his notions about evolution guided the search for the mechanisms of variation. If we can show how novelty affects the process of developmental change, perhaps others will be stimulated to search for a plausible mechanism to explain how a novelty in thought is produced in the first place (Gruber & Barrett, 1974).

Since we have mentioned Darwin, we should note that much of our thinking about novelty and its effects on bodies of knowledge has profited from drawing analogies to biological evolution. The role of novelties in the process of extension of bodies of knowledge from unique to universal seems to us analogous to the roles of gene mutation and recombination in biological evolution. This line of speculation is not unprecedented, having been advanced as a model for the evolution of scientific thought (Campbell, 1974, 1975; Popper, 1959).

The basic outline of the argument is that novel thoughts are subject to "selection pressures" which are similar in some ways to those that operate in biological evolution. This similarity allows one to think of novel ideas as fuel for a mechanism for changing the structure of bodies of knowledge over time, and for influencing the importance of the domain for a culture. We do not embrace this argument without reservation; indeed some have argued that it is a precarious position to take (cf. *American Psychologist*, 1975, *31*(5), pp. 341-384). With full appreciation for the limitations of such an analogy, we hope to show that the comparison of variation, selection, assimilation, transformation, and maintenance in biological evolution provides a fruitful way to think about the role of novelty in the evolution of bodies of knowledge.

THE ANALOGY TO BIOLOGICAL EVOLUTION

It seems to us that selection and "incorporation" of novelties into domains of thought which, in turn, come to be mastered by larger and larger segments of the culture may occur by a mechanism analogous in some ways to that of natural selection. This analogy has been suggested before in several contexts. As noted above, Campbell (1974, 1975) and Popper (1959) have used the analogy in discussions of the progress of scientific knowledge. Also, thirty years ago the neurophysiologist R.W. Gerard (1946) proposed the analogy of novelty to mutation, invoking "imagination" as a cognitive process equivalent to the spontaneous alteration of genetic material:

> Imagination, not reason, creates the novel. It is to social inheritance what mutation is to biological inheritance; it accounts for the arrival of the fittest. Reason or logic, applied when judgment indicates that the new is promising, acts like natural selection to pan the gold grains from the sand and insure the survival of the fittest. Imagination supplies the premises and asks the questions from which reason grinds out the conclusions as a calculating machine supplies answers. (p. 227)

Gerard thus compares imagination to mutation and reason to selection, arguing that some novel ideas which are candidates for inclusion in a body of knowledge eventually prove to be useful and some do not. It is the role of reason, or judgment, to decide which are which. In biological evolution, selection works through a reproductive advantage for those individuals who display certain behaviors (or physiological or morphological characteristics). In the evolution of bodies of knowledge, selection works through the active incorporation or rejection of novel ideas into domains of knowledge; the impact of the selected novelty is to make the knowledge carried in the domain more important to the culture at large. Some initially novel ideas or behaviors influence a field of knowledge in such a way that their inclusion becomes important for the further development of that field and these further developments may, in turn, make it important that more and more members of the culture learn some of the contents of the domain.

It is likely that at least since the beginnings of human tool use some novel ideas and behaviors have been recognized as important and valuable. New contributions have been incorporated into existing bodies of knowledge and skill and, when integrated into an ongoing tradition, have become part of the accumulated knowledge and wisdom that we identify as part of culture. On some basis that we do not fully understand decisions are made by parents, educators, clergy and others that certain information must be passed on to future generations through socialization and instruction. Other knowledge is judged less important and less effort is made to ensure that it will be transmitted.

While there are interesting similarities between the processes by which novel ideas are incorporated into the knowledge base of a culture and by which physical and behavioral characteristics are selected, they are also different in important ways. These differences also merit our attention. For example, the two differ strikingly in the mechanisms by which change occurs as well as in the speed with which changes are effected.

Biological evolution is an extremely slow process spanning many generations; it operates at the level of the individual organism by favoring certain individuals with slightly higher rates of reproduction and survival of offspring. In contrast, cultural evolution may proceed at a far faster rate; a new discovery or idea can revolutionize a field of knowledge in a matter of a few years. Furthermore, the selective advantage conferred by novelties is more likely to occur to groups rather than to individuals and through mechanisms that are quite distinct from those considered to be normally involved in biological evolution. These differences notwithstanding, processes of biological and cultural selection are not totally distinct. Indeed, they are inextricably intertwined.

For example, Dobzhansky (1962) and others (e.g. McClearn, 1972; Wilson, 1975) have noted that it is naive to maintain that cultural achievements occur only after biophysical evolution is complete—the two processes occur reciprocally. In a related vein, Cavalli-Sforza and Feldman (1973a, 1973b) have begun developing a quantitative model for genetic inheritance that includes a cultural component. They suggest that cultural factors contribute to the phenotypic development of each individual, primarily through the influence of parental phenotypes on the child. Although conceptual and empirical work relating cultural to biological change is not widespread, there does seem to be increasing recognition within the biological research community of the necessity to consider those cultural factors that may affect the course of biological evolution.

THE ROAD FROM UNIQUE TO UNIVERSAL

Figure 2.1 re-presents the universal-to-unique continuum, adding several features regarding the effects of novelties. Most unique reorganizations of domains by individuals fail to impact on a wider audience. This may happen for a variety of reasons. Such novelties may not be communicated to others or perhaps are communicated ineffectively, expressed in terms that are idiosyncratic, obscure or arcane, may be of no real interest, or may be just plain wrong; these constitute the category of noncreative novelties in Figure 2.1. By "noncreative" we simply mean that a particular novelty, however unusual, daring, expressive, satisfying or individually meaningful, does not contribute in any significant way to others' understanding of a field. Because they are not perceived as useful, noncreative novelties simply tend to fade out of existence, as the culture makes no effort to ensure that they are acquired by members of the society.

Only a small proportion of the novelties that are produced are creative; once expressed, they are recognized as useful by other individuals and are adopted by them. Creative novelties thus contribute to

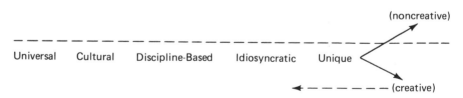

Figure 2.1 The universal-to-unique continuum illustrating extension of a domain after creative reorganization.

the accumulated knowledge of a field. A unique novelty begins its trek toward universality at the point when it is perceived as creative—when individuals other than its originator find it to be a useful idea, when it fills a gap in existing knowledge, or when it opens up new avenues of thought. Only a tiny number of novel thoughts are ever perceived as useful at all, even a tinier number continue to be useful for very long, and even a smaller number yet become continuing parts of an evolving field. For every plausible atomic theory developed there must have been many more explanations of the composition of matter that were eventually discarded.

When a novelty becomes a significant part of a domain or body of knowledge, its fate and the fate of the field of which it is a part become linked. When the novelty stimulates a reorganization in the body of knowledge as a whole two events take place. The domain is reconsidered and re-evaluated within the larger culture, and the novelty sheds its uniqueness as it becomes integrated into the domain—even while transforming it.

Figure 2.2 illustrates the proposed relationship between time and domains occupying various developmental regions. Universal

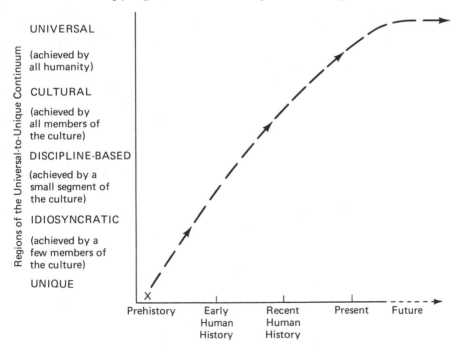

Figure 2.2 History of a developmental novelty from first occurrence (X) to extension into the universal region.

achievements have been part of the human cognitive repertoire longer than cultural, discipline-based, idiosyncratic and unique ones; Figure 2.2 plots the history of a single developmental achievement that has become universal. It may take a very long time for a novelty (and its domain) to extend into the cultural and universal regions of achievement, if this actually occurs at all.

The speed of incorporation and extension does not necessarily *have* to be slow, although this may be the rule, particularly as the domain extends into the cultural region. An example where communication of a novel achievement was relatively rapid and its assimilation into a body of knowledge almost immediate was Linus Pauling's presentation of the structure of RNA:

> During the summer of 1937 I devoted a good part of my time, perhaps half-time for a few weeks, to the attempt to find a way of folding polypeptide chains that would account for the x-ray pattern of keratin. I worked a little on the problem during succeeding years, and, of course, we had a large program of experimental investigation of simpler substances, amino acids, and peptides, going on. I think that it took me about a day to discover the alpha helix in the Spring of 1948, when I settled down to work on the problem again.

David Olson comments:

> Yet in the space of a brief scientific report, which could be read in about 15 minutes, he was able to describe his discovery to the scientific community. What had taken Pauling years to learn took colleagues and students only minutes. (both quotes from Olson, 1972, p. 9)

If a novelty transforms a body of knowledge and skill in the way that Pauling's certainly did, it is likely to be incorporated into the field almost immediately. Other sets of ideas, also novel, will be discarded or ignored if they are not perceived at the time as valuable. The long period of obscurity of Mendel's formulation of particulate inheritance illustrates how novel reorganizations may fade if they are not perceived as important for a body of knowledge.

If, upon incorporation of the novel idea a field of knowledge becomes more valuable, complete, interesting, or germane to some aspect of living or knowing, it may be deemed important that larger and larger numbers of individuals learn about it.[1] Thus, depending on the perceived significance and communicability of the reorganized domain, a society may place greater emphasis on becoming proficient with the new knowledge; this is typically accomplished through instruction.

For example, in the 40 years or so since computers were invented

---

[1] It should be evident that very little is known about the factors that contribute to the "perceived significance" of an idea at a particular point in time. This problem is of course worthy of the most careful study.

hundreds of people in this country have learned how such machines operate and many thousands have learned to use them to perform calculations. This latter group (which includes the authors) is able to make use of the computer as a tool without having to know its theoretical underpinnings or its more technical aspects. This has been made possible by increased communicability of knowledge and better instruction in how to use the tool. Other (more specialized) professionals who learn the technical aspects of computer use not only can keep current machines functioning but can try to improve their design. Because knowledge about computers is perceived as important for some segment of the society (and also for the smooth and efficient functioning of the society itself), it becomes the task of the culture to find ways to instruct key individuals to use the technology of computers.

Some bodies of knowledge may become so integral to operating successfully within a society that virtually all members of the group are expected to achieve competence in these domains; these were called cultural domains in Chapter 1. In Western societies simple arithmetic and communication skills (e.g., reading and writing) are examples. Such capabilities as these may have once been achieved by an exceedingly small "educated" proportion of the human population, but over time they have become so basic that they are integral to cultural membership. As the technology and pedagogy of a body of knowledge become more powerful, more varied ways to achieve mastery are made available, and more and more members of the society can acquire the valued knowledge. A program like "The Right to Read" is a recent example of an attempt to extend the tool of reading to a greater number of members of this society.

The circumstances under which various epistemological advances or achievements are found valuable (become "selected for") are not well understood. It is possible that for bodies of knowledge which have become very valuable to the culture—those that all members of the society must learn—pressures to acquire the knowledge take place at both the individual and the cultural level. Pressures may be brought to bear against those individuals who have difficulty developing these critical abilities by identifying them as "abnormal" in some way; possible forms of such pressure could be ostracism, ridicule, segregation into institutions. Pressures on the society may lead to efforts to devise more ways to transmit the knowledge, resulting in a wider range of environmental conditions supporting the mastery of the domain. At some point along the way biological processes may "take over" by selecting against those individuals who do not seem to be predisposed to acquire the valued skills through the range of environments available (and adequate for most people). In practice, this may mean that there is selection (in terms of reduced fitness) against those who do not seem "educable" with respect to the desired ability (Dobzhansky, 1970). Selection would operate against those individuals who did not possess a predisposition to construct the skill from the existing environmental inputs.

It is possible that cognitive abilities which are initially nonuniversal might become part of the human biological program by a process that Waddington (1953, 1957) has called genetic assimilation. This is a mechanism by which a characteristic which is initially expressed only by certain individuals in response to certain changed environmental conditions becomes programmed into the genomes of more and more members of succeeding generations; the characteristic changes from being environmentally induced in a few members to becoming biologically programmed and elicited in many individuals without special exogenous treatment. Wilson (1975) has suggested that human social behaviors may have evolved in this way. Whether by Waddington's mechanism or some other, a major change in the manner of transmission of knowledge takes place when a domain extends into the universal region.

Simply put, our argument is that the selection of novelties over evolutionary time occurs at every point along the continuum from unique to universal; in the few most successful instances, the novelty (and its attendant domain) travels the entire route. In the process, there is a shift from deliberate, systematic instruction to transmit the body of knowledge to a spontaneous (most likely biologically supported) predisposition in the individual to construct the knowledge from his or her everyday experiences in the environment. Although most novel ideas at the unique end of the continuum never become part of the universal human repertoire, a small number that are valuable for one purpose or another will be incorporated into the body of knowledge and will begin to extend into the more universal regions of the continuum. This incorporation process does not have to be a conscious one in the same way that biological selection is neither conscious nor deliberate. Novelties in thought which are likely to be valuable in the sense intended here are expressed in the form of various tools, technologies, communication skills, and conceptual models that members of a culture learn to use. Given sufficient importance for human adaptation, a few novelties will eventually become part of the human program, as common across cultures as within them.

PROGRESS OF NOVELTIES OVER TIME

To carry the discussion of incorporation a bit further we consider additional aspects of the process. Emphasizing the dynamic aspect of development draws attention to the fact that any description of intellectual skills and capacities can provide only a "stop-motion" picture of intellectual development. We cannot know for sure what bodies of knowledge our species will develop in the future, nor precisely what human abilities existed in the past; we can, however, speculate about the history of knowledge based on our assumptions about its dynamic character.

Figure 2.3 is an attempt to convey the sense of continuous movement and ongoing change that emerges when a temporal component is added to the universal-to-unique continuum. Our earlier illustration (Figure 2.2) showed the hypothetical history of a developmental novelty which has become universal. In that example we assumed that the first appearance of the novelty must have occurred many thousands of years ago for the incorporation process to have had time to do its work. Consider for a moment the fact that novelties in thought are occurring all the time, novelties that are unique in only a statistical sense as well as those that are truly creative. Sometimes novelties occur which transform ideas from trivial to practical. For example, Leonardo DaVinci had invented the bicycle except for a mechanism that transfers energy from pedals to wheels. What was perhaps a whimsical notion became a practical one with the achievement of a technological advance (i.e. a pedal-drive mechanism), although many years later.

Figure 2.3 simulates histories of developmental novelties which appeared at various points in human history, including the present. The leftmost curve is the same as in Figure 2.2; it indicates the history of a

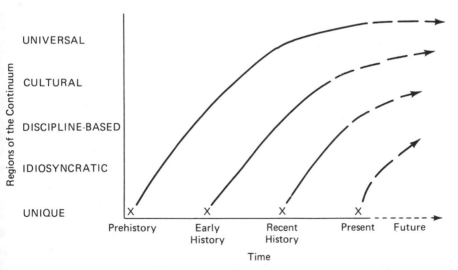

Figure 2.3 The extension of novelties (and their domains) as a function of the historical era in which the novelty first appeared (X).

developmental novelty that appeared at some early point in history and that subsequently extended into the universal region of achievements. The other curves show the progression of unique achievements which occurred later in human history. The process of cultural incorporation—of communication and selection—begins anew for each novel behavior or idea. If the novelty is valuable, it begins the long journey from unique to universal, from unusual to common expression, from environmental to biological transmission. The ellipses are included in this figure to suggest that the entire process is a continuing one. However crudely, Figure 2.3 tries to capture the dynamic quality of the process of cultural incorporation.

In the idiosyncratic and unique regions of the continuum a relatively large amount of planned intervention is required for the achievement of more advanced levels of mastery of the domain. At all points along the continuum, however, the role of environmental conditions on the acquisition of knowledge is crucial. What changes as the domain extends toward the universal region is the "naturalness" of the environmental input and the proportion of individuals mastering the body of knowledge. The amount, variety, and quality of instruction carried on in a culture is an indication of the number and variety of unique developmental achievements that have become requisite to full participation in the social life of the culture.

HOW MIGHT NOVELTIES OCCUR?

In his mid-twenties, Charles Darwin signed on as the naturalist for the HMS "Beagle" and spent the next five years sailing around the world gathering notes on the variety of natural forms he encountered. It was this voyage and his response to it that made manifest Darwin's dissatisfaction with the creationist explanation of how the earth came to be populated by living matter. Darwin saw a plausible alternative to the theory that a Divine Creator had produced the enormous variety of life forms he encountered during his voyage. For example, in the Galapagos Islands Darwin saw a multitude of avian species that seemed peculiarly suited to their unusual and varied environments; it occurred to him that reciprocal relationships between environments and the kinds of organisms populating them must exist, and that these very relationships might explain the origin of new species (Gruber & Barrett, 1974).

Although we have taken no voyage comparable to Darwin's, it occurred to us that the variety of human inventions seems in its own way as overwhelming and inexplicable as the infinite variety of life forms that Darwin saw. Just as Darwin rejected Divine intervention as an explanation for the relationship between organisms and environments, we were compelled to see novelty as the natural consequence of individuals' intellectual interactions with their environments rather than as a miraculous and inexplicable cognitive gift.

As to how the individual actually *produces* novelty, while we do not know very much about it, two requirements seem crucial to the process: a new insight into some aspects of the problem (Feldman, 1974; Henle, 1975), and a reorganization of a field as it exists, which allows the individual to produce new combinations of already available elements (Bruner, 1962). This union of insight and reorientation toward old facts is one which has been documented by many inventors, and will be taken up in greater detail in Chapter 4. Familiar examples are Watson and Crick's construction of an intertwined pair of spiral staircases, which in turn stimulated them to seriously consider a double helical structure for DNA, and Kekulé's dream of a snake turning to bite its own tail, which led him to consider a ring structure for the benzene molecule rather than a chain.

Considering these two requirements of insight and reorganization in terms of our analogy to biological evolution, an "insight" might represent genetic mutation or reorganization, and the reevaluation and reordering of existing knowledge might refer to selection processes favoring the new genetic structure. It is important to recognize that there are limitations to the amount of change or novelty that a system can sustain in either biological or cultural evolution. Those genetic mutations which are radically atypical generally result in such drastic dysfunctions of the organism that it does not survive. Furthermore, some genetic reorganizations (inversions, for example), seem to be far more frequent than expected by chance, while others apparently cannot physically occur (Dobzhansky, 1970). In like manner there are clear limitations on the degree to which a body of knowledge can be successfully extended or reorganized. Those discoveries that move so far beyond the current state-of-the-art of a field are often considered unintelligible and dismissed as useless or even crackpot. While such ideas do not cause the "death" of an entire body of knowledge or render a person nonviable in the same way that certain mutations or recombinations of genes do, novelties in thought which are too far in advance of their time may "die off," sometimes to be "resurrected" at a later point in time when they fit more closely into the prevailing paradigm of a domain. Leonardo's fantastic inventions, Aristarchus' computation of the earth's circumference (Thrower, 1972), and the Arab invention of algebra, are examples of novelties that were available long before any widespread appreciation or practical need for them existed. They are examples of a mismatch between the appearance of a novelty and a society's readiness for cultural selection and incorporation. Only those discoveries which make sense to others and which are comprehensible extensions of existing knowledge will have a chance of reorganizing their associated domains and being incorporated into more universal regions of cognitive achievement.

Human invention can thus be viewed as having much the same place in the evolution of bodies of knowledge that gene mutation and reorganization have in the evolution of biological characteristics. Novel behavior assumes great importance because it represents the most powerful psychological force in the formation and evolution of human cultures, particularly in the evolution of cultural bodies of knowledge. Without the continued production of novel ideas, the diversity of intellectual endeavor which it ensures would disappear. Mayr (1970), Dobzhansky (1970), Clarke (1975) and others have argued that the maintenance of genetic diversity is extremely important for the evolutionary success of any species; an underlying flexibility is essential in order to survive and adapt to changing environmental conditions. This seems to be no less true of ideas than it is of genes.

The message seems clear. Diversity both within and across bodies of knowledge should be valued and encouraged, or as Clarke (1975) has expressed it: "We should, perhaps, ask for polymorphisms in our institutions to match the polymorphisms in ourselves" (p. 60). Maintaining diversity of intellectual endeavor seems of paramount importance, since often what is required for survival is change that responds to uniquely human dilemmas. It can be assumed that within limits a society producing a greater number of usable novel achievements will be better off than a society producing fewer, for it will have the capability for continued evolution and may be better able to respond to changing environmental conditions.

CONCLUSION

Young Charles Darwin was overwhelmed by the variety he found in nature. We are overwhelmed by the variety of achievements and inventions that we have found in human thought. That we would find Darwin's explanation for the evolution of species a fruitful analogy to pursue in making sense of the evolution of bodies of knowledge should not be surprising. And Darwin was not unaware of the possibility of our analogy; Gruber and Barrett (1974) have shown that from the very outset Darwin included man and his unique mental powers in his musings about evolution. Our discussion of novelties is in keeping with this Darwinian tradition; it is an attempt to make human behavior more comprehensible by considering it as part of a natural process. Where there are living beings there is novel behavior; when these living beings are human some of their novel behaviors catalyze reorganizations in culturally valued bodies of knowledge. This is a most startling fact of mental life. The function of novelty in human behavior is to provide the raw material for the evolution of developmental domains, of bodies of knowledge and skill.

In this chapter we have proposed that, over time, novel ideas may become incorporated into the mainstream of human thought so that what is a unique achievement today may be a universal one in the far-flung future. Whether or not this observation turns out to be true in some scientifically defensible sense, it leads to some interesting implications for developmental psychology. The view of the place of novelty in the evolution of knowledge offered in this chapter leads to the proposal of plausible time bound relationships among domains of knowledge at all points along the universal-to-unique continuum (cf., Chapter 3). These connections remain to be made fully explicit, but the sense of the extension of domains over time from unique to universal should be clear.

It can be reasonably said of Darwin's insights about evolution that they lessened the remarkableness of humanity when man became simply another expression of a natural process rather than a special creation of God. Similarly, it can be said that our discussion of the evolution of knowledge may also detract from man's "special place" in nature. By viewing the production of novelties as a normal aspect of human behavior they lose some of their mystery, as do the individuals who produce them. On the other hand, the processes through which novel thoughts are expressed become even more remarkable as they become more comprehensible.

It is perhaps accurate to say that in the future, when we reflect upon creative works, greater credit will go to the countless individuals who have contributed to and husbanded the smaller, cumulative achievements of earlier generations, but who themselves never shared center stage with those fewer, more remarkable individuals responsible for major new syntheses or discoveries. While the view offered here may detract a bit from a *specific* individual's achievements, it seems to us to enhance the overall achievement of humanity.

Our guess is that the dynamic process of evolution of domains of knowledge sketched in these pages makes things a little less mysterious but no less awesome. It is as if Loren Eiseley (1946), in discussing the incredible improbability of life existing on other planets in anything like the form it does here, had added cultural as well as physical factors to his equation. He did not, but the case for human uniqueness and creative accomplishment is, if anything, strengthened by the observations put forward here. We cannot help but believe that Eiseley would have agreed.

3
ınɒıvıɒual ɒevelopmental tʀansıtıons— a fılm metaphoʀ

In Chapter 2 we were concerned with the fate of a cognitive novelty after it had occurred and had begun to be communicated to others. The purpose there was to present a plausible history of the universal-to-unique continuum: where it came from over eons of time, what kinds of cultural selection processes might have governed its growth and where it might be headed in the future. We did not worry a great deal about how *individuals* came upon novel ideas. Yet it is of course true that every novel idea must come from the mind of someone. In this chapter we examine the general set of processes that govern the production of new ideas. These processes are sometimes called *transition mechanisms* because their function is to transform mental organizations (Flavell, 1971b; Kessen, 1962; Langer, 1969a, 1974). As we noted in Chapter 1, an assumption about the universal-to-unique continuum is that fundamentally similar transition mechanisms govern movement in all of its regions. In this chapter we illustrate these transition processes with reference to relatively mundane reorganizations in thinking; in Chapter 4 we will look at the more powerful reorganizations which may contribute to our store of knowledge. Reorganizations in regions of the continuum other than the unique may be less dramatic than those which revolutionize whole bodies of knowledge, but they reflect a set of processes that are occurring continuously during an individual's lifetime—in all kinds of transitions.

We chose an analogy in Chapter 2 based on biological selection processes to express and explore ideas about the history of the universal-to-unique continuum. For somewhat similar purposes we elect

41

here to use the device of metaphor. The metaphor pursued in this chapter is that of a motion picture film. Ideally, we would like to have a camera able to record every individual reorganization in every region of the developmental continuum. Needless to say we have no such camera, but if we did we would probably begin by focusing on one region, or perhaps even select a single domain within that region so our enterprise would be less overwhelming. This is (metaphorically speaking) what we do in this chapter. We attempt to shoot two films of transitions in a single domain—map drawing. While the images thus produced do not reveal the actual mechanisms that govern reorganization, they do reflect the consequences of this process in rich enough detail to guide the search for more adequate accounts of the mechanisms themselves. In tracing the sequence of transition states as a child moves from level to level in map drawing, we will glimpse (a) the *conditions* that give rise to novelties, (b) the *changes in organization that seem to accompany* novel behavior, and (c) the *consequences* that follow from getting a foothold in the next level of the domain.

Before we get too far into the discussion, we want to assure the reader that our efforts are based on data gathered on children's map drawing over the past several years. What we present therefore is not a flight of metaphorical fancy—although we confess that there are fanciful aspects to it—but rather an attempt to use the idea of a motion picture film to organize our data and to guide theory construction.

The first film uses group data to construct a sequence of steps in the transition process that is consistent with theory as we understand it and predicts reasonably well changes in map drawings for individual children. The second film takes a closer look at some more subtle changes that give rise to the general picture constructed with the group data.

Not surprisingly we choose to focus our efforts on capturing certain specific changes in map drawing that seem theoretically important. In the first film our metric is a shift in "modal level," an approximation to the traditional definition of stage and stage change. The second film examines specific changes in the map drawings, for example, from representing buildings "straight on" to representing them in consistent 90° perspective, i.e. from above. This kind of change reflects movement to a more advanced level of spatial representation. If 90° perspective is the first problem that the child has solved at a higher level, this kind of change comes as close as anything in our data to what seems to be meant by a developmental "novelty." Taken together the two views of change in children's map drawings aid our understanding of developmental transitions as continuous transformations in the organizational state of the child's mind.

Before we present our two films, it is necessary to place them in their proper theoretical context. For this purpose we will review some of the thinking of Piaget and others in the cognitive-developmental tradition about the problem of developmental change. We will assume that the reader is familiar with the basic ideas in Piaget's system (for those unfamiliar with Piaget's work, we recommend Cowan, 1978; Flavell, 1963, 1977; Ginsburg and Opper, 1979; or Gruber and Vonèche, 1978). A second purpose in reviewing Piagetian and neo-Piagetian research on developmental change is to introduce some of the concepts, measures and techniques used in gathering the data upon which our film efforts are built.

PIAGET ON CHANGE: AN OVERVIEW

It was Piaget who is credited with discovering that child thought is not simply an imperfect copy of adult logic, but rather a series of qualitatively different "logics" each consistent within itself, but different from adult thought. Moreover, Piaget argues that these stages in cognitive development are neither biologically programmed nor given by the environment, but instead are *constructed* or created by children as they actively attempt to understand the world. They cannot be given by the environment because at times they are factually incorrect (preschoolers often believe that the moon follows them around, that the wind is alive, and that dreams come in through the window at night). Nor are they innate because these "wrong" ideas are later given up. To illustrate the process of construction, Piaget tells this story about a mathematician friend of his:

> When he was four or five . . . he was seated on the ground in his garden . . . counting pebbles . . . . He put them in a row and he counted them . . . up to ten . . . and started to count them in the other direction . . . . Once again he found ten. He found this marvelous that there were ten in one direction and ten in the other direction. So he put them in a circle and counted them in both directions and found ten . . . . So he put them in some other direction and . . . in some other arrangement and kept counting them and kept finding ten. There was the discovery that he made. (Piaget, 1964; in Gardner, 1978, pp. 231-232)

And exactly what was discovered? Piaget asserts that it was neither a property of pebbles (i.e., not given by the environment) nor a property of his friend (i.e., not biologically given), but instead a property of the action of ordering: specifically that the sum is independent of order. An action, then, clearly requires something to act on and someone to do the acting. In the absence of either there is no knowledge created or constructed; in the coordinated presence of both there is cognitive development.

Within Piaget's framework every action (or perhaps transaction is a more descriptive term) has two aspects: adaptation and organization. Adaptation, which refers to the interplay between a child's cognitive system and his experience, in turn has two complementary aspects: *assimilation* and *accommodation*. Assimilation refers to "taking in" the environment and relating it to existing mental models, while accommodation is noticing aspects of experience which are *not* easy to interpret with existing models and changing the models to effect a better "fit." Roughly speaking, assimilation is the "molding of experience to fit the mind" and accommodation is the "molding of the mind to fit experience." Each process operates only in conjunction with the other; neither ever operates in total isolation. Organization may be understood as the strictly internal parallel to adaptation. Not only do the cognitive models assimilate and accommodate to each experience, but they also assimilate and accommodate to each other. The results of this "mutual assimilation and accommodation" among mental models are coherent, well organized ways of thinking. Piaget calls them *les structures d'ensemble* or "structured wholes," and for him they are a defining characteristic of cognitive developmental stages.

Structures d'ensemble are at the heart of Piaget's theory. The child is neither a blank slate nor a solipsist but rather a *scientist*. He is constantly building models of the world and testing those models against his experience, often in ways that facilitate changes in the models themselves. These changes, Piaget argues, are universal, invariant and spontaneous. Each successive set of models is a coordinated mental system that grows out of, enriches and incorporates aspects of previous stages to generate a more powerful and more satisfying overall system.

Conditions Giving Rise to Change

Why is it that cognitive systems change? *How* do they change? *When* do they change? For Piaget the why question is not a question at all. Asking why cognitive systems change is much like asking why a fish swims or why lungs breathe. Swimming is part of what it means to be a fish and breathing is part of what makes a lung a lung. Swimming and breathing are two functions which help to define fish and lungs respectively. From Piaget's biological perspective the motivation to function is not a separate force which requires separate explanation, but rather a part of the inherent nature of the structure itself. It is the nature of fish to swim, of lungs to breathe, and of cognitive structures to change. Thus for Piaget the why question is really contained in the how question, and the answer to the how question lies in describing structures and functions.

The structures in Piaget's framework are of course the stages which characterize human cognitive development from infant sensorimotor intelligence through adult formal operations. The functions most directly related to change are assimilation and accommodation. How do assimilation and accommodation facilitate development? Simply stated, every assimilation is accompanied by a complementary accommodation, and every accommodation is cognitive growth which makes possible new assimilations, further accommodations, and so on. This dynamic interplay of assimilation and accommodation is called *equilibration* and is seen by Piaget as the fundamental mechanism of cognitive developmental change. When appropriately discrepant, new or unexpected experience upsets equilibrium (upsets the balance of assimilation and accommodation), facilitating cognitive activity aimed at restoring equilibrium and leading to intellectual development. In this "dialectical" fashion, new intellectual abilities solve old problems and also make possible the appreciation of new ones in a dynamic, never-ending process.

While we have not directly addressed the when question, Piaget would probably argue that the answer is implicit in the above discussion. Structures are likely to change when they are in disequilibrium, when the assimilation/accommodation balance is upset. And this is about as far as Piaget goes in detailing the specific conditions giving rise to change. To be sure, if one is concerned with only those changes which are universal, invariant and spontaneous, then describing the stage sequence and declaring an inherent, progressive force toward the final stage might be considered an adequate treatment of the change process. But because we are concerned with changes that are neither universal nor spontaneous, we see a more elaborate treatment of disequilibrium as crucial to our work (see also Langer, 1969a, 1969b, 1974; Strauss, 1972; Turiel, 1969, 1974). We have found it useful to distinguish at least three aspects of disequilibrium: one related to adaptation (external), one related to organization (internal) and one which Langer (1969a) has called the "energetic parameter" of disequilibrium.

External Disequilibrium. When a child confronts and tries to deal with an environmental event, adaptation occurs. If the child's current models of the world permit interpretation of this experience with relative ease, i.e., if it can be assimilated without significant changes in the models themselves, the cognitive system remains in relative equilibrium. If it is too discrepant to be processed at all, the child will ignore it as best he can. In contrast, there sometimes occur situations where an event is sufficiently novel such that no readily accomplished interpretation is possible within the bounds of the existing cognitive system. If this discrepancy is recognized and responded to, the result is external disequilibrium. We call it external disequilibrium because the source (the "perturbation" in Piaget's terms) is external to the child. The disequilibrium itself, of course, derives from the interplay of child and environment, from attempts at adaptation.

Thus, external disequilibrium arises from experiences which are sufficiently discrepant to facilitate significant accommodation and restructuring of a child's cognitive system. Exactly what constitutes "sufficient discrepancy" and "significant restructuring" are very difficult and largely unresolved issues. Typically, providing an experience which requires thinking skills characteristic of a more advanced developmental stage, followed by evidence that the child begins to reason at that stage, are criteria for restructuring taking place. Many Piaget-based training studies use this approach and criteria such as these (see Brainerd & Allen, 1971, or Flavell, 1970 for reviews).

Internal Disequilibrium. In contrast to external disequilibrium with its focus on adaptation and child/environment interplay, internal disequilibrium refers to the child's intellectual organization itself. It reflects what might be called contradiction or competition among the child's alternatives for dealing with experience. For example, logical inconsistency between two cognitive rules or models, if recognized by the child, would be an instance of internal disequilibrium.

While Piaget has written about internal equilibrium, internal *dis*equilibrium has not received as much attention. This may be in part because internal disequilibrium is somewhat difficult to reconcile with Piaget's notion of *structures d'ensemble*. A stage is a structured whole, so the argument goes, and because children are "in" stages, their mental organization should reflect that same unity of process and product. Variations in consistency, *les décalages,* have been called by Piaget (1971) a "negative" aspect of development, a nuisance to him in his search for universal, integrated structures. But such variation need not be a negative quality, particularly when considered as a possible impetus for the child to build new cognitive systems. About this possibility we will have more to say later on.

The Energetic Parameter. An obvious difficulty in moving from the world of theory to the world of children's behavior is that even the most cleverly encouraged putative contradictions between child and environment, or among child-produced responses, may not be noticed—let alone be used—in the creation of new structures. Therefore, recent treatments of disequilibrium and developmental change have begun to emphasize the child's realization that "something here doesn't quite fit." Langer (1969a) calls this realization the "energetic parameter" of disequilibrium and describes its importance as follows:

Here the concern is with the affective character of disequilibrium between mental acts as a source of cognitive reconstruction . . . . Piaget presents evidence that suggests the child must be cognitively "ready" to assimilate contradictory information and *to feel that something is wrong,* if there is to be any cognitive reorganization and development. (p. 30, emphasis added)

The idea of wanting to make things fit as a source of motivation for intellectual achievement appears often in the psychological literature; it is generally called *intrinsic motivation* (see Deci, 1975, for a review of related work). Most approaches, including Piaget's, emphasize the importance of "optimal discrepancy"—neither too little nor too much—but nowhere in the literature is there much detail about how to arrange this match (Hunt, 1961). Finer grained analysis of internal, organizational aspects of a child's developmental state, we believe, may provide a way to predict the set of conditions that will energize the child's system and prepare it for progressive developmental change. Our vehicle for approaching these issues empirically has been children's map drawing.

MAP DRAWING: A NONUNIVERSAL DOMAIN

Map drawing is an especially appropriate domain with which to begin the study of nonuniversal domains and the conditions under which their stages or levels are achieved. Although Piaget and Inhelder (1948) used map drawing to study universal aspects of spatial reasoning development, there is considerable evidence that modern cartographic skills are acquired neither universally nor spontaneously, and mapping techniques are undeniably a creation of culture. Yet research by Piaget and others (e.g., Feldman, 1971; Feldman & Markwalder, 1971; Snyder & Feldman, 1977) does indicate that map-drawing ability progresses through a hierarchical and invariant sequence of levels. Map drawing, then, is an example of a culture-linked, nonuniversal developmental domain, one which has evolved from a discipline-based domain to its current cultural status over the last five or six centuries. In the fifteenth century few individuals could read geographic maps and even fewer could construct them (McLuhan, 1964). Today, the basic principles of modern cartography are easily communicated, and maps have become commonly available in many cultures (though the science of cartography remains a discipline and retains its esoteric aspects).

Additionally, the production of a map calls upon a variety of spatial and logical-mathematical skills—for example, topological, projective, and Euclidean concepts and how to use them to represent geographical features. As a task which requires the coordination of these concepts, map drawing may be used to diagnose both the developmental level of several different sets of skills as well as their integration into a representational system. For this reason Piaget and Inhelder (1948) in a book on spatial reasoning development used a map-drawing task to summarize the trends they had noted on other tasks:

> In practice, the construction of a [map] entails (1) the selection of a particular point of view, together with certain pictorial conventions intended to express it . . . . (2) A system of co-ordinates—whose function should be self-evident—along with the implied concepts of straight lines, parallels, and angles. (3) Reduction to a specific scale, which entails the concepts of similarity and proportion. Hence the construction of a map incorporates in a single entity all the concepts examined [in the previous 13 chapters] and at the same time shows how they are related to one another. (p. 426)

In studying a map drawing, then, we are able to gather information about the child's developmental level in handling numerous aspects of this domain—perspective, spatial arrangement (e.g., a system of coordinates), proportion, and the symbolic (i.e., pictorial) conventions through which they are expressed. From that same drawing we can also evaluate the way in which these several aspects are coordinated into a representational system.

Finally, before describing the map-drawing task we have used in our research, we note that mapping may be considered to be one of the categories of cultural conditions mentioned in Chapter 1 and also similarly described by Piaget and Inhelder (Inhelder & Chipman, 1976). Learning to draw a good map involves using shared conventions for representing, organizing and communicating the features of a geographical landscape.

Mapping, then, is a symbolic model for representing and transforming parts of reality, a cultural amplifier in Bruner's terms (cf. Chapter 1). It is a system of rules and procedures which draws on a variety of spatial and logical skills, requires their integration and coordination, and does so in a way which could hardly occur spontaneously.

A Map-Drawing Exercise

The mapping exercise we have used requires the child to draw a map of a miniature village landscape, one similar to the small models used by Piaget in his research. Since our work gives greater attention to symbolization that did Piaget's, the landscape model we use is constructed from relatively realistic model railroad paraphernalia rather than from the more stylized trees, buildings, etc., used by Piaget and Inhelder (see Figure 3.1). The children draw only with a pencil on an eight and one-half inch square paper, which we provide.

In their study of maps produced by similar procedures, Piaget and

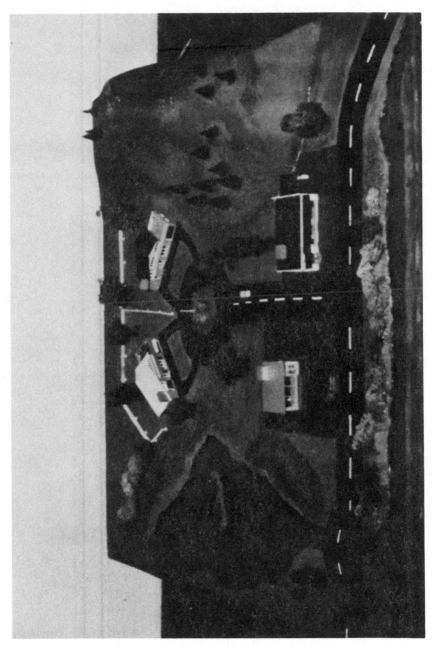

Figure 3.1 The landscape model photographed from about 45°.

Table 3.1
Levels of Spatial Reasoning Development
as Revealed in Map Drawing
(adapted from Piaget & Inhelder, 1948)

Level 1: No spatial correspondence except for a few elementary proximities

Characterized by child's inability to distinguish between spatial proximity and logical resemblance or between spatial separation and logical difference. Yields objects on map which do not appear on model and objects on model which are not represented on map. Arrangement appears virtually arbitrary.

Level 2: Partial coordination

Characterized by recognizable but inconsistent logical and numerical correspondence. Spatial correspondence often confounded with logical resemblance or limited to small groups of proximal objects and isolated left-right relations without an overall spatial plan. Representation limited to one dimension (i.e., uses frontal view) with detail and proportion essentially unrelated to model.

Level 3: Midway between partial and beginning of general coordination

Characterized by inconsistent coordination, i.e., reasonable logical and numerical correspondence but with a mixture of perspective (e.g., frontal, 45°, 90°) and viewpoints, in poor but recognizable proportion to model. Larger groups of objects now linked together to produce primitive overall representations of model, often with "photograph-like" detail.

Level 4: Beginning of general projective and Euclidean coordination

Characterized by items in good logical and numerical correspondence and arranged according to a crude two-way system of reference (i.e., width and depth) with a consistent 45° or 90° perspective. A legitimate two-dimensional representation of the model often with some evidence of abstraction, but with as yet inaccurate scaling—relative sizes of objects often proportional, but distances (especially heights in the 45° perspective) remain distorted.

Level 5: Mastery of distances and proportions

Characterized by complete coordination of logical and numerical with spatial correspondences. Although not formally scaled with metrics and fractional reduction, an adequate diagrammatic representation of the model. A consistent 90° perspective with clear evidence of abstraction and symbolization.

Level 6: The abstract plan with metric coordinates

Characterized by complete coordination, totally accurate scaling, a consistent 90° perspective, and use of abstract symbolization.

Inhelder describe the development of map drawing as the successive coordination of two sets of correspondences between a model landscape and the map: (1)LOGICAL-MATHEMATICAL correspondences concern the way in which logical classes of objects (e.g., houses, trees, etc.) and numerical collections (e.g., *three* houses, *ten* trees, etc.) are represented. As we shall see, a given drawing may emphasize shared logical qualities without regard to number, include both logical and numerical correspondence or, at the most primitive level, be essentially devoid of either logical or numerical correspondence. (2) SPATIAL correspondence concerns the representation of objects as they are integrated within an overall spatial framework, i.e., how well the sizes and distances on the model are maintained on the child's map. On a good map the objects correspond both logically and numerically and are arranged so that spatial relationships are properly maintained as well. The successively more sophisticated attempts to achieve this coordination have been cast by Piaget into a six-stage developmental sequence. An adaptation of that sequence (Table 3.1) guides our scoring procedures. Figures 3.2 through 3.7 provide examples of map drawings generally representative of each of the six developmental levels outlined by Piaget.[1] The maps reproduced in Figures 3.3 through 3.6 were drawn by children in our studies; those in Figures 3.2 and 3.7 have been modified somewhat for illustrative purposes.

The *level one* map in Figure 3.2 shows primitive logical correspondence to the landscape model; there are some trees and buildings represented as well as some crisscrossing lines which might be roads or perhaps a road and a river (which do intersect on the model). Numerical correspondence is entirely absent, and spatial relationships are limited to elementary proximities such as the crisscrossing lines, the buildings on the ends of what could be a road, and the large, centrally located circular object. The trees are represented in a vertical line indicating that logical resemblance has here completely overridden spatial correspondence. In short, while there is enough in the way of correspondence to suggest that this is a map of the landscape rather than a picture that has been simply made up, we can say little more than that. The young map maker producing a level one drawing has only begun to grasp the idea that a map and the place being mapped must somehow correspond.

The major advance of map drawing at *level two* (Figure 3.3) is that there is evidence of logical, numerical and spatial relation between landscape model and map. However, they tend to be treated in relative isolation with first one aspect being emphasized, then another. The ability to integrate the separate sets of correspondences simultaneously is poorly developed. For example, Figure 3.3 shows the hill, lake, and river each marking an edge of the map, but only the river marks the appropriate edge. Similarly, the bridge is part of the road, but the river does not pass under it; instead the road seems to go on right into the lake! There are some trees on the hill and some more in other places, but both numerical and spatial correspondence are imprecise. There are build-

---

[1]We say "generally representative" of each level because none of the examples is a "pure type." Each of these maps is predominately at one level and shows more characteristics of that level than of other levels, but all exhibit aspects of several levels or what Piaget has called *décalage*.

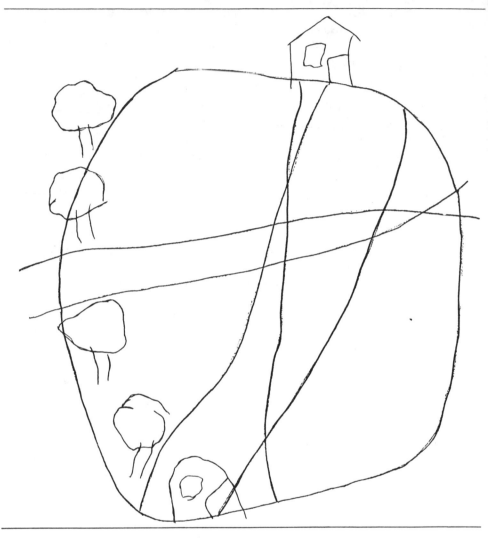

Figure 3.2 A level one map.

ings in only three of the four quandrants, and they are represented identically and idiosyncratically. The central rotary is missing entirely, and while each house is surrounded by a fence, there are two separate fences rather than a shared one as on the model. Finally, the map is largely in "front-on" perspective, almost as if one were standing on its bottom edge, and proportion is poor—notice that one of the vehicles and several trees are shown as large as the bottom-most building.

As logical, numerical and spatial correspondences begin to be

Figure 3.3 A level two map.

coordinated at *level three* (Figure 3.4) larger groups of objects become linked in an overall spatial plan. Thus, if the miniature landscape were an actual hamlet you could use a level three map to find your way around. However, you would often be surprised by the actual distances between things, their real sizes once you found them, and you would find that some things mapped are not present, as well as others present but not mapped. Still, as Figure 3.4 shows, things found would be relatively easy to identify because of the photograph-like detail in which they are often represented. While proportion remains inaccurate in that it does not correspond well to the model, it is more real to life than the rather incredible proportion characteristic of level two (e.g., these houses may not be this size, but this size is a reasonable one for real-life

53

Figure 3.4 A level three map.

houses somewhere). Piaget describes level three as "transitional" between partial and general coordination and the drawing in Figure 3.4 does reflect some of the inconsistency characteristic of the transition. For example, the two buildings on the right side are roughly in proportion, as are the two on the left side. But when all four buildings are considered together the proportion is poorer—the two houses in the upper part of the landscape, for example, should be the same size. Similarly, the two areas of elevated land are placed at appropriate corners of the lake, but are shown inside the lake rather than along its edges as they really are. Finally, we note a mixture of perspectives (some 90°, some 45° and some "front-on") as well as some inconsistency in viewpoint (e.g., parts of the fence are seen from the front and other parts are seen from one side). In sum, a level three map maker seems to recognize the purpose of a map and is able to coordinate bits of appropriate information in some rough form. He or she does so, however, inconsistently and idiosyncratically, without applying representational conventions. A level three representation often looks more like a picture than a map.

A *level four* map (Figure 3.5), in contrast, is marked by more consistent coordination of logical, numerical and spatial relationships. The overall spatial plan incorporates improved arrangement of objects, more appropriate proportion and more accurate numerical correspondence. In short, a trip around this hamlet guided by a level four map would include far fewer surprises than with the level three drawing. Most of the

Figure 3.5 A level four map.

mixture between partial and general coordination is gone. There is but a single viewpoint and except for some "incidental" features (e.g., trees, vehicles, etc.) the map is drawn from a consistent 90° perspective. A level four map, then, conveys better information because it does so in a more efficient, more consistent way. Improved scaling and placement render the full, photograph-like detail we noted in level three less necessary for positive identification of objects. What something looks like is redundant with where it is—if where it is relative to other things is represented with some accuracy. Even so, there is only a partial loosening of the "pull of perception" toward realistic representation. A level four map incorporates little in the way of the domain's symbolic conventions; abstraction is typically limited to what is inherent in a realistic 90° perspective. While drawings at this level are not as "picture-like" as those at level three, neither are they as abstract and symbolic as those at more advanced levels. In sum, a level four map has many of the characteristics of a rough aerial photograph which, after all, is a common first step in the construction of a modern map.

Figure 3.6 shows a *level five* map drawing, one which clearly merits the label of a geographic map. There is complete coordination of logical, numerical and spatial correspondences; spatial arrangement and proportion, though not mathematically exact, are quite good, and for most practical purposes this representation is a serviceable map. In addition to increased accuracy, level five begins to incorporate more systematically the conventions of the domain. Relevant information (e.g., where and what an object is) is differentiated from largely irrelevant information (e.g., exactly what it looks like) and the former is represented in a more efficient, more abstract manner. Labels and/or icons substitute for the realistic presentation of detail more common at the earlier levels, and the conventional use of 90° perspective is adopted.[2] In sum, a level five map does everything a level four map does, but does it more consistently, more accurately and with greater utilization of the domain's abstract conventions. A level five map maker seems to know quite well the purpose of a map, knows which information is relevant to that purpose and is beginning to adopt the conventions which make its abstract representation possible.

The *level six* map drawing shown in Figure 3.7 requires little comment. The two principal improvements over the level five example are accuracy, which approaches perfection, and increased use of abstract symbolization. While a few labels remain, the icons characteristic of level five have been replaced by more arbitrary symbols in conjunction with a key. Gradations in elevation, for example, are indicated by means of

---

[2]While the pine trees in Figure 3.6 may seem to violate the consistent 90° perspective, our interpretation of these is that they are stylized representations, or icons, intended to identify the object and its location, not a realistic "front-on" perspective.

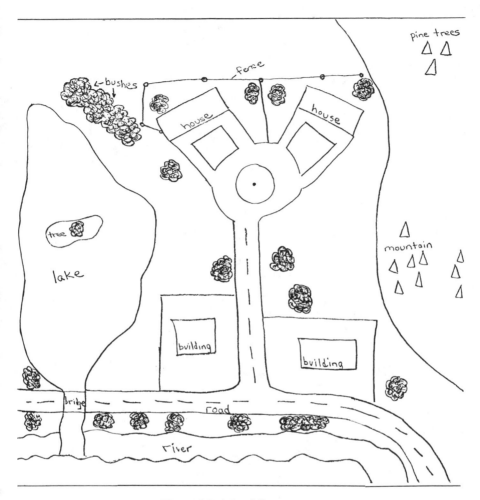

Figure 3.6 A level five map.

topographical contours, a sophisticated use of an abstract convention. While the mapping task we have presented is a relatively crude one in comparison to the vast array of complex information which can be incorporated in modern maps, the ability to draw a level six map indicates real appreciation for and considerable skill in applying the fundamentals of cartography.

DEVELOPMENTAL STATES

Having now described the six idealized levels of map drawing, we move to a consideration of transition processes as revealed in the actual drawings produced by groups of children. In Chapter 1 we argued that

57

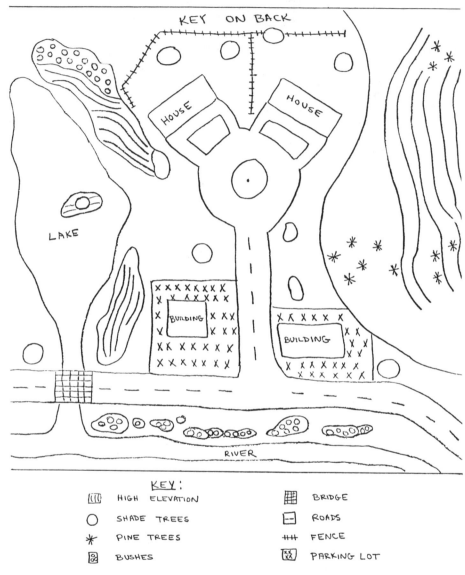

KEY ON BACK

HOUSE

HOUSE

LAKE

X X X X X X X X
X X X X X X X
X X BUILDING X X X
X X X X X
X X X X X X X X
X X X X X X X X

X X X X X X
X X X X X
BUILDING X X
X X
X X X X X X
X X X X X X X X
X X X X X X X X

RIVER

KEY:

〔〖 HIGH ELEVATION		▦ BRIDGE
○ SHADE TREES		⊟ ROADS
✳ PINE TREES		╫╫ FENCE
▨ BUSHES		〔✕✕〗 PARKING LOT

Figure 3.7 A level six map.

developmental stages do not exist in the minds of children; instead, we suggested that <u>developmental *levels* exist in the psychological structure of domains.</u> Having removed stages from children, we also <u>removed children from stages</u> and placed them instead in developmental *states*. A developmental level, then, is not a representation of a child's overall cognitive system. Rather it is one idealized system for dealing with certain kinds of knowledge which, in conjunction with other such systems or parts of systems, can be used as templates against which to gauge the child's intellectual repertoire—his or her present developmental state. Once the notions of developmental level and developmental state are thus established, we can begin to test the extent to which children do or do not conform to the ideals. Moreover, we can also explore how the various developmental states are transformed from one system to another, including the internal conditions under which a new level begins to appear.

The focus of Piaget's work on map drawing was to classify children as being "at" or "in" an overall developmental stage. While it is certainly possible to describe map drawings—and therefore children—as generally representing one stage more than others (as we have just done in the preceding section), our experience with maps and children is that such typologies do not reflect children's actual performance: no two maps judged to be at the same stage are identical, nor does any child ever produce a "pure" map representing a single stage.

In contrast to Piaget, the premise for our studies was that the variability normally present in children's map drawings would lead us to a more powerful conception of transition mechanisms (Feldman & Snyder, 1977). Rather than classifying each map as belonging to a single developmental stage, we divided the domain of map drawing into the four spatial concepts and skills that Piaget and Inhelder identified in their own research: (a) spatial arrangement, (b) proportion, (c) perspective, and (d) symbolization. Building upon the general Piagetian stage descriptions, we were able to construct four parallel sequences of developmental levels, one for each of the sets of concepts just mentioned.

Our experience also indicated that for a given child, different features of the miniature landscape tended to be represented at different levels. Roads and other flat surfaces, for example, were represented in 90° perspective before buildings were. And while virtually all the children's maps included the lake, far fewer represented the proper number of trees. We therefore separated the specific topographical components of the landscape model into four "feature clusters," where each cluster is a set of items which shares logical and/or physical properties. A scoring procedure was developed (see Snyder, Feldman, & LaRossa, 1976) such that a trained judge could evaluate the developmental level at which each spatial concept was applied to each of the four feature clusters. In addition, the judge evaluated the level at which each spatial concept had been applied overall to the "map as a whole." This procedure yields a total of 20 developmental level classifications for each map: (4 feature clusters + 1 map as a whole) × (4 spatial concepts) = 20. The general developmental levels are presented in Table 3.1; the spatial concepts and feature clusters scored are summarized in Table 3.2.

Table 3.2
Spatial Concepts and Feature Clusters
Used in Scoring Map Drawings

SPATIAL CONCEPTS (adapted from Piaget & Inhelder, 1948)

  I. ARRANGEMENT—emphasizes topological concepts in lower levels and Euclidean concepts, i.e., systems of coordinates, in advanced levels.

  II. PROPORTION—emphasizes Euclidean concepts, i.e., similarity

  III. PERSPECTIVE—emphasizes projective concepts

  IV. SYMBOLIZATION—emphasizes pictorial conventions

FEATURE CLUSTERS

  A. *Buildings*—easily identifiable logical class; regularly shaped; obvious third dimension, but relatively easy to represent.

  B. *Hill, bridge, island, other elevated land*—among major features of model; relatively large, irregularly shaped; three-dimensional; more difficult to represent.

  C. *Lake, river, roads, driveways, parking lots*—major flat surfaces of model; easily represented.

  D. *Trees, fence, motor vehicles, flagpole, bushes*—relatively small, more "incidental" features of model; obvious third dimension; relatively difficult to represent.

  E. *All-inclusive score*—the map as a whole.

Applying our scoring procedure to a single map drawing permits us to obtain data on four aspects of spatial reasoning as they are applied to five sets of problems in mapping. When the twenty developmental level classifications are plotted in histogram-like form (see Figure 3.8) we

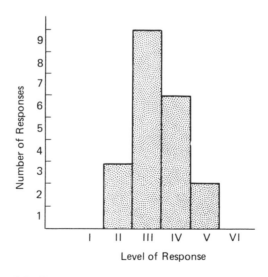

Figure 3.8 Illustration of a "configuration" of responses to the Map Drawing Task.

have a schematic representation of a child's developmental state with respect to map drawing—we call it a "configuration." Configurations tell us about variation in a child's behavior across developmental levels—the relative sophistication of each spatial concept and the consistency with which it is applied to various features of the landscape model. Additionally, a set of calculations can be applied to each configuration to yield a variety of quantitative indices related to internal and external disequilibria.

Modal Level

Typically the majority of a child's responses fall at one developmental level; this we call the modal level. The remaining responses are usually distributed more or less widely but almost always with decreasing frequency at levels one step from the mode, then two steps removed and even three steps away in some cases (see Figure 3.8).

Modal level is an index of central tendency or a best estimate of the child's most commonly used organizational structure. It is the basis for a qualitative classification of the overall map into one of the six developmental levels, an evaluation akin to the ones Piaget made on the basis of clinical judgment. As an estimate of a child's usual way of thinking, modal level is useful in research on external disequilibrium. External disequilibrium arises from a comprehensible but problematic discrepancy between a child's usual way of thinking and his recent experience. One way to express the degree of discrepancy (too little? just right?) is in terms of the difference between the child's modal level and the level of the events he or she encounters in the environment. Thus, researchers (ourselves included) have explored the effects of different interventions aimed at levels *below* the child's mode, *at* the modal level and one or more levels *above* the mode. While results are not entirely consistent, it is fair to say that experiences above the mode have generally facilitated developmental advance, whereas experiences below the mode have usually resulted in little change (e.g., Arbuthnot, 1975; Kuhn, 1972; Snyder & Feldman, 1977; Turiel, 1966, 1969).

Modal level, however, is a relatively crude estimate of a child's developmental state when used alone, and while we sometimes refer to "level three children" for the sake of convenience, there are often significant differences among children who share the same modal level. Additional aspects of developmental states, especially the distribution of other responses around the mode, provide valuable information not captured in the modal level measure.

Level Mixture

The tendency for children to exhibit responses indicative of more than one developmental level (Piaget's décalages) has been termed by other researchers "stage variation" (Turiel, 1966, 1969), "structural mixture" and "transitional reasoning" (Strauss, 1972), and "level mixture" (Snyder & Feldman, 1977). Level mixture (as we will call it) has theoretical import because of its relation to internal disequilibrium. In contrast to external disequilibrium (structure/environment discrepancy), internal disequilibrium is thought to arise from discrepancies or inconsistencies within the child's internal system itself; hence its relation to level mixture. As an index of the amount of competition among elements in a child's intellectual repertoire, level mixture reflects general instability in the system (Strauss, 1972). The degree of instability reflected in level mixture provides a useful measure of readiness for developmental change, i.e., of disequilibrium.

A potential source of instability and thus readiness for advance is the increased likelihood that children with greater degrees of level mixture will produce contradictory responses in a series of related tasks. For example, in some situations a child may exhibit logical or concrete operational solutions to problems, while in other similar situations preoperational or intuitive strategies may be applied. Because level mixture reflects the presence of thinking at several different developmental levels, the likelihood of moving back and forth between two conflicting strategies (and presumably the chance of developmental advance) is greater than if mixture were minimal. A number of researchers have demonstrated this positive relationship between level-mixture or level-mixturelike measures and change: in classification of objects (Kuhn 1972), map reading (Markwalder, 1972), map drawing (Snyder & Feldman, 1977), conservation of area (Strauss & Rimalt, 1974), and moral reasoning (Turiel, 1969). Presumably, past a certain point, increases in level mixture are unrelated or inversely related to advance, but this remains to be tested empirically.

In our own empirical work we quantify level mixture in a child's map drawing according to a procedure suggested by Turiel (1969). The number of responses at each developmental level is multiplied by the number of steps separating that level from the mode; these products are then summed and divided by the total number of responses. Level mixture thus adds a measure of variability to the indication of central tendency provided by the modal level estimate. There remains to discuss another measure which provides still finer discrimination among transition states.

The Bias Index

Just as there are differences in level mixture among children with the same modal level, there are differences among children who share both mode and degree of mixture in their map drawings. For example, in the extreme case of two mirror-image configurations, perfectly symmetrical patterns of response occur but on opposite sides of the modal level (Figure 3.9). While the two configurations in Figure 3.9 are indistinguishable with respect to mode and level mixture, common sense suggests that they represent two quite different types of developmental states. The bias index was devised to capture this difference (Snyder & Feldman, 1977). Bias focuses on the distribution of nonmodal-level responses: a greater number of responses above the mode is designated *positive* bias; conversely, a greater number of responses below the mode is termed *negative* bias.

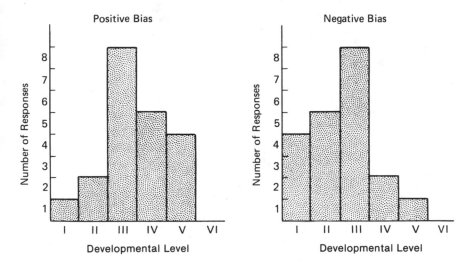

Figure 3.9 Illustration of positive and negative bias profiles.

To ground the notion of bias in our conceptual framework, recall that Strauss (1972) equates level mixture with "transitional reasoning." While variation in use of developmental levels is certainly indicative of transitional reasoning, the bias index speaks directly to a most pertinent question: transitional between what and what? Bias distinguishes those children moving toward strengthening a currently existing modal level (negative bias) from those children moving away from the current mode and toward the succeeding developmental level (positive bias). This difference between being on the way into a modal level and on the way out of one relates to the question: how much discrepancy, i.e., how much external disequilibrium is just right for inducing change? It suggests that intervention experiences *at the modal level* might be most appropriate for stimulating advance in negative bias children (who still respond to a variety of situations with strategies less advanced than the modal level), while positive bias children would be expected to profit more from experience at levels above their mode (because these more complex strategies are already emerging). In the empirical tests we know of, positive bias, in concert with experience at levels above the mode, was strongly related to advance in modal level (Levin, 1978; Snyder & Feldman, 1977).

Elaboration and Consolidation

Our conceptual analysis of how modal level, level mixture and bias in various combinations describe phases of developmental transitions has by and large been confirmed by results from the experimental studies mentioned above. These results suggest that development proceeds through alternating periods of internal equilibrium and disequilibrium, as well as through periods of "elaboration" and "consolidation," which are related but not identical to the equilibrium/disequilibrium states (cf. Flavell & Wohlwill, 1969). As new higher-level cognitive skills emerge, level mixture (i.e., internal disequilibrium) increases and continues to increase while these new skills are elaborated or extended to a wider range of situations. The process of elaboration then becomes reflected in a positive bias index. As the application of these newer skills becomes the child's usual approach to problems in the domain, an advance in modal level occurs and is followed by a period of decreasing level mixture (i.e., less internal equilibrium) as the system consolidates around the new mode. The process of consolidation is signaled by a negative bias index, and when completed, the system is prepared for creation of a still more advanced level as the cycle begins once more.

When a child begins to consolidate a new, more powerful system, there is typically a tendency to overapply it (Langer, 1969b). The application of well-consolidated skills to new situations will tend to reveal new problems which require the creation of still higher-order skills for their solution. Thus a developmental state, even a well equilibrated one, does not remain stable for long, but rather moves in a dynamic cycle from one state of disequilibrium to another, with periods of stability and consolidation setting the stage for the emergence of more sophisticated cognitive strategies (Piaget, 1970).

By this time the reader may have begun to sense that our description of various transition states is leading up to a proposed sequence of phased changes in the child's system for representing space in map drawings. This sequence is the plot of our first film, an empirical illustration of a provisional sequence of states of transition in children's map drawings over a three-year period.

DEVELOPMENTAL STATES AND DEVELOPMENTAL TRANSITIONS THROUGH A LONG-RANGE LENS

We began our study of map drawing by collecting maps from 96 fifth graders, scoring them by the procedures described earlier and calculating modal level, level mixture and bias for each child's drawing. The 63 children who exhibited modes at level three were split into positive and negative bias groups and also divided by level mixture (i.e., amount of internal disequilibrium). The children were then assigned to interventions which presented different degrees of external disequilibrium: instruction with map drawing techniques at the child's modal level, one level above or two levels above the child's mode. Our results [detailed in Snyder & Feldman (1977)] are easily summarized: the bias index was the most powerful and consistent indicator of progressive developmental change—positive bias children advanced in modal level nearly three and one-half times as often as did negative bias children. Instruction at levels higher than the pretest mode also increased the frequency of modal level advance. The effect of level mixture was less easily interpreted. The findings upon which we began our "film" of transitions, however, are best captured by outlining more specifically the patterns of change observed in three different groups of children.

1. Consolidating children (those with negative bias) typically did not change modal level, but did move from consolidation to elaboration (from negative to positive bias) following the interventions.
2. Elaborating children who had received instruction at their modal level also did not change modes, but did retain a positive bias index.
3. Elaborating children receiving instruction at levels higher than their mode tended to advance in modal level and at the same time shifted from elaboration to consolidation (from positive to negative bias) at the succeeding developmental level.

These patterns of change suggested that a more systematic examination of intermediate steps in the process of transition from one modal level to the next would prove useful. Might not this accomplishment be profitably described in sequential terms itself? Toward this end we collected additional maps from all available children two years after the original study and again one year later. The two- and three-year-follow-up groups included 76% and 70% of the original children; no further instruction in map drawing had been provided during this time.

Figure 3.10 presents a protocol of one child's performance on our map-drawing exercise over the three year period. The first three configurations come from the intervention study just described and reflect pretest, posttest, and delayed posttest performance respectively. The fourth and fifth configurations show maps collected in the follow-up

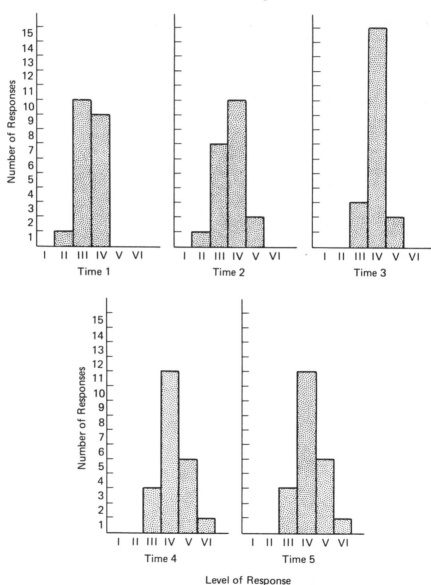

Figure 3.10 Five configurations for a single child over three years time.

studies. Configurations, then, are like snapshots or "still frames" reflecting a child's cognitive system with respect to the domain of map drawing at a particular point in time. The process of taking repeated snapshots over time provides a more dynamic representation, a "film" of how the sequence of transformations in these developmental states may occur. Of central interest is the study of how particular developmental modes are built up or *strengthened* and then torn down or *weakened* as they gain or lose responses.

Elaboration and consolidation both key on the strengthening of developmental levels. Elaboration is the extention of newly acquired skills to a wider range of situations. Consolidation is the strengthening of "older" abilities until their application becomes routine. We therefore define consolidation as the strengthening of levels below the current mode, while elaboration refers to the strengthening of levels above the mode. Since the elaboration process strengthens levels above the mode, however, levels below the mode are concomitantly weakened. Our operational definitions of elaboration and consolidation rest on the straightforward assumption that development is generally progressive. Thus, on the average, abilities at lower levels will tend to have been part of the cognitive repertoire longer than abilities that have emerged at higher levels. Similarly, the emergence of a new mode indicates that this higher level has now become the child's typical way of dealing with problems; it thus seems a reasonable marker for the end of elaboration and the beginning of consolidation. We assume also that positive bias indicates an overall tendency toward elaboration, while negative bias denotes a tendency toward consolidation. Finally, we take the degree of level mixture to be an index of instability, with higher mixture indicating relatively greater instability.

Even with these operational definitions of stability, instability, elaboration and consolidation, however, the classification of changes within individual protocols remains a difficult task. To provide a general picture against which to gauge each child's changes, we have combined and transformed the individual protocols into a more manageable set of group composites. First, the immediate and the delayed posttest configurations for each child were averaged since these were separated by only five weeks during which no map drawing instruction occurred. We reasoned that their combination offered a more reliable representation of the children's knowledge of map drawing at a point in developmental time than did either single drawing. Second, using the pretest configurations from the intervention study, children were separated into four groups distinguished by various combinations of level mixture and bias: (1) a low level mixture group, (2) a middle mixture/positive bias group, (3) a high mixture/positive bias group, and (4) a middle level mixture/

negative bias group.[3] The data from those children in each group who had received instruction at levels above their mode were then combined and the percentage of all responses falling at each developmental level was calculated. Four histograms were plotted for each group to show the changes in map drawing performed over the three-year period: pretest, posttests, first follow-up (two years later) and second follow-up (three years later).

Oversplicing

With but four "frames" for each group and three years for development to occur, our filmmaking efforts were somewhat limited. To increase the number of frames we adapted the film editor's technique of splicing. Figure 3.11 presents an example of our method, which we call *oversplicing*. Oversplicing involves following one group of children from pretesting onward until one of their subsequent histograms could be superimposed on the pretest histogram of a second group. Matched points in developmental time may then be compared to check the success of the overlapping splice and the film is able to continue to trace the course of development beyond a group's last histogram by following a second group, and so on.[4] In Figure 3.11 for example, histograms (b) and (d) show the point at which two groups were "joined"—the similarity in shape of histograms is striking. Histograms (c) and (e) are also part of the overlap. While the comparison here is somewhat less striking, it is still reasonably clear; the patterns of performance of the two groups changed in quite similar ways. Histogram (f) shows the second group at a later point in developmental time—our assumption, of course, is that subsequent testing of the first group would have eventually produced a histogram very similar to this one. Applying the oversplicing technique to the data from the four groups described above yielded a six-step film of progress from one modal level to the next (see Figure 3.12).

How well do the data fit the kinds of changes we expected? Recalling that level mixture reflects the degree of stability or instability in the system and that the bias index distinguishes elaborating systems from consolidating ones, it can be seen that the group data, when spliced together this way, outline a sequence of developmental transition phases which is remarkably congruent with the theoretical account presented

[3]There were too few high mixture/negative bias children to permit reliable interpretation of progress in this group.

[4]The "over" in oversplicing thus refers to the "overlap," the period of developmental time shared by both groups in the splice. It thus contrasts this method with simple splicing (as in a cross-sectional design) and a true film (which requires a longitudinal study). In some respects, then, oversplicing is similar to cross-sequential methodology (cf. Schaie & Strother, 1968).

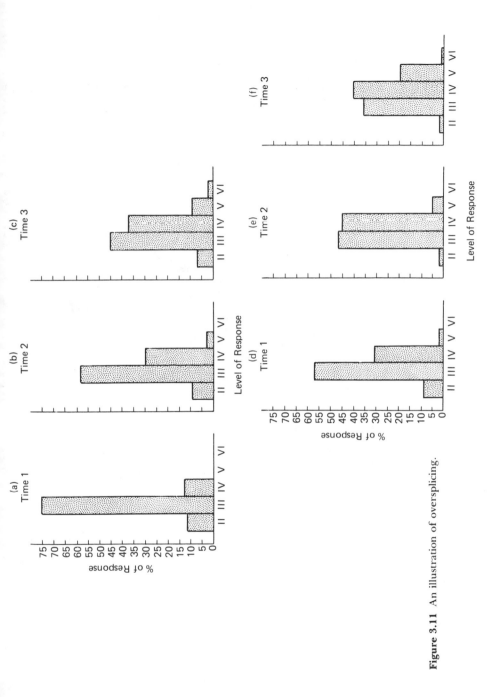

Figure 3.11 An illustration of oversplicing.

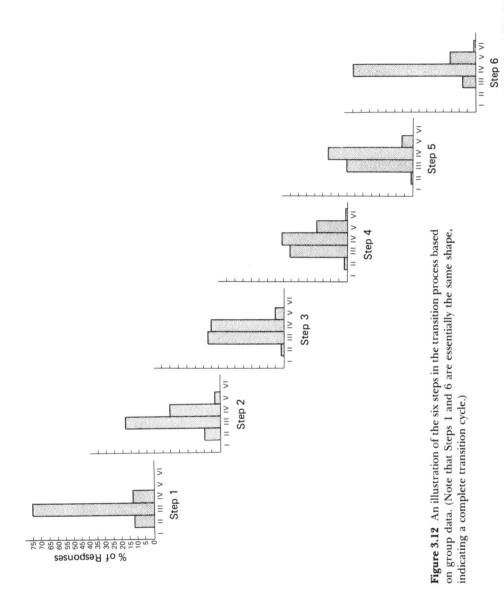

Figure 3.12 An illustration of the six steps in the transition process based on group data. (Note that Steps 1 and 6 are essentially the same shape, indicating a complete transition cycle.)

earlier. We begin at Step 1 with a state of high stability and high consolidation around the modal level (the "zero" level as a reference point). Step 2 shows increased instability (i.e., higher level mixture), a weakening of the mode and of the minus 1 level, and concomitant strengthening of the plus 1 and plus 2 levels. This process of elaboration has yielded a clear positive bias index. At Step 3 we see continued elaboration—the plus 1 level is now nearly as strong as the mode—and with it a further increase in instability. Together these suggest that the system is ripe for modal level advance.

Step 4 shows the most important event (at least traditionally) in the process of developmental transition—a new modal level has emerged. Concurrent with the appearance of the new models continued high level mixture, but with a shift from positive to negative bias. These suggest a relatively unstable developmental state, as would be expected in the case of a newly-achieved mode, but consolidation of that new mode will strengthen it as development proceeds. At Step 5 the consolidation process is clearly underway. Both extremes of the configuration have weakened, while the more central "minus one" and modal levels have strengthened to produce increased stability (i.e., lower level mixture). Finally, at Step 6 the film "loops" back on itself; once again we see a state of high stability and high consolidation, but this time at the succeeding developmental level. These six "scenes" provide some empirical support for our theoretical speculations about the succession of states that characterize movement through a developmental transition.

To determine whether the four group composite sequence shown in Figure 3.12 reflected the sequence of changes for the individual groups themselves, we checked each group's sequence of steps against the composite. The changes made by each group over the three-year period of the study are summarized as follows:

Group 1: Low level mixture	Step 1—Step 2—Step 2—Step 3
Group 2: Middle mixture/positive bias	Step 2—Step 3—Step 4—Step 5
Group 3: High mixture/positive bias	Step 3—Step 4—Step 4—Step 4
Group 4: Middle mixture/negative bias	Step 5—Step 6

Except for repeating steps, all groups conformed to the sequence generated by the oversplicing technique. There are of course dangers in this kind of analysis. All the children in the study began at modal level three, all children received some instruction in map drawing, and each group was composed of children who had received one of three different treatments. Also, many of the same protocols used to construct the film were then used to "test" it. Additionally, the histograms are group composites which do mask to a certain extent individual variation in the transition process (but see below). Still the sequence is more than hypothetical; it is revealed in the data. The suggested sequence of states is not only plausible but follows from theory. The alternation of phases of relative equilibrium and relative disequilibrium, the periods of elaboration and consolidation, the systematic changes in stability are all consistent with the theoretical account. In the next section we again examine the plausibility of the film sequence by assessing the extent to which individual children conform to predictions based on the group data.

Individual Changes

Having constructed a broad film sequence to highlight (if in somewhat idealized form) the phases involved in advancing from one modal level to the next, we began the task of reviewing the changes made by individual children to see how well they agreed with the group-based data. In order to accomplish this we sought to formalize the sequence of transition states in a set of possible *principles* through which developmental states change (see Table 3.3). The heart of the transition process as we see it is the alternation of periods of elaboration and consolidation.

The bias index and level mixture together define these two developmental states, with positive bias and higher mixture indicating elaboration, and negative bias and lower mixture indicating consolidation. Elaboration prepares the system for modal level advance; thus a shift from negative to positive bias precedes an advance in modal level. Modal level advance, in turn, signals the transition from elaboration to

Table 3.3
Proposed Principles of Developmental Change as Abstracted
from the Group-Based Film

A. *Consolidating systems—Negative bias:*
   1. Level mixture generally remains constant or decreases until a shift from negative to positive bias occurs.
   2. A shift from negative to positive bias precedes an advance in modal level and may
   2. be accompanied by an increase in level mixture suggesting the beginning of elaboration.

B. *Elaborating systems—Positive bias:*
   1. Level mixture generally remains constant or increases until bias shifts to negative.
   2. Positive bias is maintained until a modal level advance occurs.
   3. A modal level advance is accompanied by a shift from positive to negative bias and may also be accompanied by a decrease in level mixture suggesting the beginning of consolidation.

C. *Modal level:*
   1. Modal level does not revert to lower levels.
   2. Modal level advances only one level at a time.

---

consolidation and should therefore be accompanied by a shift from positive to negative bias and perhaps a decrease in level mixture. Finally, modal level changes are progressive and are limited to one level at a time.

Comparing these principles as outlined in Table 3.3 to the changes observed in the configurations of the individual children yielded a 75% incidence of agreement between predictions and data.[5] Of the 134 possible changes, 100 of them were in accord with the predictions of how developmental states should change.

To summarize the results of our group-based film effort, we have constructed a sequence of phases of transitions based on the Piagetian equilibration model which emphasizes the role of disequilibrium. Using histograms showing performance over time, our "film" illustrates the intermediate steps in moving from one modal level to the next and to some extent tests the plausibility of our conceptual analysis of change processes. Principles of change in developmental states derived from the group-based film yielded good agreement with changes in individual children's map drawings, thus further supporting our sequence. In the next section we apply an even finer-grained lens to these data; we begin to examine level-to-level movement of individual responses from children in the sample, adding texture to the system-wide changes we have observed thus far.

A LOOK AT TRANSITIONS
THROUGH A CLOSE-UP LENS

The crucial conceptual advance that made the second film possible came about because of an almost trivial technical change in the way we represent level mixture. One of us (DHF) was preparing for a colloquim at Tufts and was deciding which among many possible tables and figures to present. It was important to say something about level mixture, both because it was an idea which was not widely enough circulated and because it was so central to the way we thought about internal disequilibrium. Level mixture as first introduced by Elliot Turiel is usually represented as a histogram showing the percentage of a child's responses that reflect various developmental levels.

The histograms we had been using were based on raw frequencies,

---

[5]In applying the principles to changes in level mixture, "remains constant" was operationally defined as change of less than eight points of mixture in either direction. The empirical basis for this range is plus or minus less than one-half a standard deviation as calculated on our sample. Also, as was the case in constructing the group-based film, the two posttests for a child were combined to represent a single point in developmental time.

not percentages (see Figure 3.8). In order to prepare the more standard level-mixture histograms it was necessary to count the number of responses children had made at various map-drawing levels. Doing this was rather tedious. To make the counting easier, horizontal lines were drawn through the columns. This small modification made for convenience sake has turned out to be extraordinarily important for our work. Almost instantly it became clear that each of the individual responses that made up the columns in the histogram reflected the child's solution to a specific map-drawing problem. In other words, we discovered that it is possible to consider not only the number of responses at a given developmental level, but also that *each response is itself distinct and identifiable*. For example, the spatial arrangement of buildings is a specific problem with which the child must deal, achieving a solution at a certain developmental level. As long as the child's solution to this problem is not obliterated by simply counting it as a member of a column of other responses, the movement of this response across levels can be tracked over time. This movement can also be compared with changes in solutions to other specific problems over the same time interval.

Psychological Elements

The realization that each of the twenty separate indicators of map-drawing ability could be tagged and their movements traced led us to produce configurations like that in Figure 3.13.[6] The individual responses were termed "psychological elements" because an element is the typical term used to refer to the individual parts of a cognitive structure. A structure is often defined as a set of elements governed by a set of rules, a definition compatible with our purposes.

Our elements were called psychological because they exist only as a result of a child's actual attempts at spatial representation. For example, drawing a map of our model landscape requires that the buildings be arranged on paper in some fashion, but it is only when a child actually attempts to arrange the buildings that the "element" exists. Arrangement as a spatial concept thus occurs only when a person attempts to do it; it is not an abstraction that exists apart from a child's activity, but is dependent on the child's attempts to deal with particular spatial problems.

To have conceptualized the domain of map drawing as twenty psychological elements would have served little purpose if our empirical work had not been longitudinal. A Turiel-type level mixture histogram

---

[6]Since each element is an identifiable response the term histogram is somewhat misleading, as histograms represent frequencies only. We therefore have called these representations of developmental states "configurations."

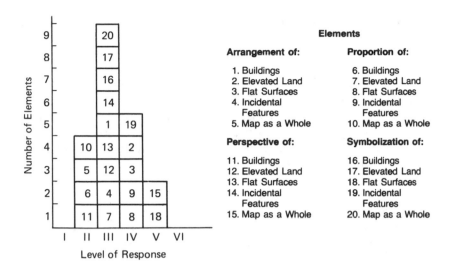

Figure 3.13 The twenty "elements" of the domain of map drawing. (Note that the vertical position of each of the elements within a level is arbitrary, i.e., it has no meaning. There were for this child at this time 4 Level II responses, 9 Level III responses, etc.)

and a configuration of psychological elements say much the same thing about the child's psychological state at a given moment in time. The advantage of analyzing psychological element movement becomes clear, however, when a longitudinal series of protocols is available showing different points in development for individual children. Here the opportunity exists to trace the movement of specific elements over time. This kind of analysis has led to conceptual and empirical advances in our understanding of developmental transitions, particularly those aspects of transitions having to do with novelties, which are defined here as the appearance of an element at a level unprecedented for a given child.

To illustrate why this is so we must again consider the notions of décalage, resistance, and their relation to novelties. For Piaget the basic intellectual capabilities of a stage are constructed all at once. The first appearance of reasoning at a new stage signifies that the child's "competence" to reason in this manner is basically complete. A novelty, then, is an initial behavioral manifestation of an overall internal shift in structure. Although Piaget assumes internal consistency, he acknowledges inconsistency in performance. The various conservations, for example, are achieved over several years, but formally they are seen to require the same underlying logic. Décalage is Piaget's label for this phenomenon of delays in the appearance of behaviors, and resistance is his explanation for décalage. Some problems or tasks are said to be more resistant to the application of logical structures than others. Therefore, easier problems emerge from competence to performance more quickly than the more resistant ones. But these resistances are not relevant to a theory of transitions because transitions occur in the realm of competence, according to Piaget (1971).

Our view of transitions as a series of element movements leads to a radically different interpretation of novelties and a different notion of structure as well. Instead of a transition occurring all at once, we assume that transition is an ongoing process of partial structural transformation (cf. Flavell, 1971b). We make no assumption that an overall structure is somehow in place when the first behavior reflective of that new level appears. There is therefore no specific point at which a transition has occurred; transformation is occurring continuously. Resistances of different contents are also not irrelevant; the overcoming of resistances reveals some of the workings of the system in the child's head. The system that makes possible this repertoire of responses is the child's "structure" at that moment.

For Piaget a transition has occurred whenever a novel behavior appears in sturdy form, reflecting the existence of a more advanced stage. For us a novelty is only one (albeit an important one) of many changes in a system which are suggestive of the organization of the child's cognitive functioning at that point in time. The difference is subtle but important. Piaget's conception of transitions leads to no obvious empirical test, since structure is assumed to be complete at its first behavioral manifestation; our view of psychological elements is testable, and we have begun to examine it empirically. (It should be noted, however, that our use of novelty here captures only some of the meaning of novelties as described in Chapter 2).

Once the domain of map drawing had been represented in terms of the twenty psychological elements, a provisional definition of a developmental transition became possible, to wit: *a developmental transition is the transformation of any set of psychological elements making up a structure such that each element advances one level.* This definition is illustrated in Figure 3.14. As the reader can see, the shape of the configuration in Figure 3.14 is unchanged from Time 1 to Time 2. Each element has moved one level in advance of where it was at Time 1. As the simplest, most straightforward definition of a developmental transition, Figure 3.14 specifies what happens to each element of a structure (in our sense) when a developmental transition occurs.

While we do not believe that this illustration necessarily shows inner workings of transitions, the definition offered here is a useful template against which to gauge our findings. For example, we suspected that elements do not always move one level at a time. We already knew in fact that some aspects of map drawing moved more rapidly

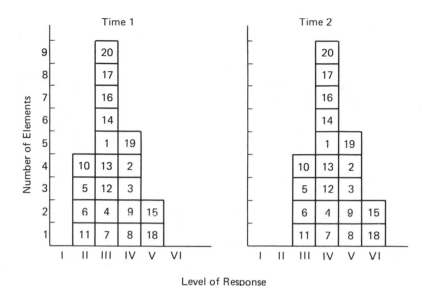

Figure 3.14 Illustration of the formal definition of a developmental transition: All elements move + 1 level.

forward than others, i.e., covered more levels than others over the same unit of time. We also knew that some elements tended to move backward as well as forward (Feldman & Snyder, 1977).

The true complexity of the problem of specifying "lawful" movements is not readily apparent. Even taking the simplest model of transitions, as in Figure 3.14 where all elements move forward at the rate of one level per unit time, there are nearly 2500 trillion sequences of element movement in map drawing that could lead to the same result.[7] If differences in the number of levels covered and the direction of movement are added to the system, the number of sequences is still larger. If we do allow for these more varied movements among elements, as both theory and our empirical results indicate is the case, a more accurate (and even more complex) model of transitions emerges. But with the method of tracking psychological elements and their movements over time, we are able to begin to study transitions at a level of detail sensitive enough to chart some subtle aspects of the transition process.

Some Movements and Positions

A perfectly consistent map drawing would yield a configuration showing a twenty-element stack at one level and no elements at any of the others. Many types of deviations from this "ideal" could be studied, but we

[7]The actual number of possible sequences is 20! or 2,432,902,008,176,640,100.

77

focused on two sorts of unusual movements and two unusual positions of elements. The two movements were: forward more than one level, which we called *leaping,* and backward more than one level, which we called *deep reversion.* The two positions that first attracted our attention were those at the extremes of the configuration. At the extreme left or lower bound we studied elements which seemed to lag behind the rest of the configuration; these were termed *laggards.* At the extreme right or upper bound we noted with obvious interest the appearance of an element at a developmental level beyond anything the child had exhibited previously—a *novelty.* We expected that elements at the extremes would be the least stable and would therefore be more likely to leap and deep revert, if for no other reason than because they were the least well integrated into the overall configuration. In general we found that the system of map drawing is a stable one; between any two points in time almost two-thirds of the elements did not move at all. And when there was movement, almost two-thirds of the elements moved forward, and one-third backward.

Not surprisingly, we center the present discussion around an examination of novelties. For the purpose of studying novelties we analyzed the four maps drawn by each of 48 children between their fifth and seventh grade years.[8] By examining a child's configuration of elements prior to, at the time of, and subsequent to the appearance of a novelty, we were able to carry out the first empirical study of the conditions under which a developmental novelty occurs and to examine the consequences of a child's having achieved this kind of developmental advance (Feldman & Snyder, 1977). An example of a child's protocol including a developmental novelty is shown in Figure 3.15, where the novelty appears at Level VI (Time 4). Because a novelty was defined as a single element appearing at a developmental level unprecedented for that child, it was necessary to know something about its history. As Figure 3.15 shows, the novelty appears only in the fourth protocol, making it possible to infer with some confidence that no element had previously appeared at this level. Situations similar to this one in other children's protocols enabled us to study the movement of novel elements both before and after they become novelties.

What have we learned about novelties? First of all we know now that (at least in map drawing) novelties are not common; they occurred only in roughly ten percent of the configurations. We have also learned that novelties tend to occur more frequently among some elements than others; this suggests that certain "contents" of the domain are regularly at the vanguard of developmental change, while others are relegated to

[8]At the time of this writing, analysis of element movements from the fourth to fifth map was just beginning.

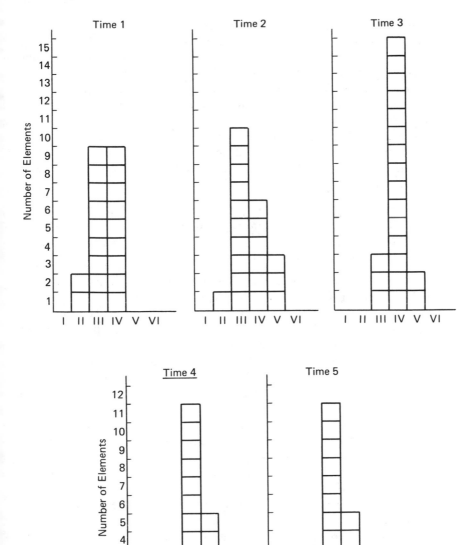

Figure 3.15 Protocol for a child in the longitudinal study showing changes in map-drawing configurations over three years with a novelty shown at Time 4.

bringing up the rear. In map drawing it appears that the concepts of symbolization and perspective are more likely to yield novelties (more than 70% of the novelties reflected these two spatial concepts) while arrangement and proportion were less likely (about 30%). Thus, when a child first apprehends a higher developmental level, he or she begins to advance the cognitive structure more commonly with some elements than others.

We have also started work on other problems in structure/content relationships prior to, at the time of, and following the appearance of a novelty (Feldman & Snyder, 1977). We have begun to answer questions such as these:

From where (in a configuration) does a novelty typically come?

What are the effects on the rest of the elements in a configuration when a novelty appears?

What happens to a novelty after it has appeared?

Novelties, as it happens, are frequently leapers. This means that the element which is to become a novelty tends to leap out of the middle of a configuration to take its place at the leading edge. For novelties, leaping occurs more than seventy percent of the time, while for other elements the frequency of leaping is only about four percent.

As discussed earlier, the element that becomes a novelty has a specific identity; it reflects a certain spatial concept applied to a specific map drawing problem. What of the fate of those other elements that share a spatial concept or a map-drawing problem with the novel element? Suppose, for example, that our novel element is *perspective of buildings*. What happens to the other elements that also deal with say, perspective of trees, or of roads? What seems to occur is that the novelty has a strong "pulling" effect on other elements sharing its spatial concept and a somewhat less strong pulling effect on elements dealing with the same map-drawing problem or feature (in this case the feature cluster of *buildings*). Figure 3.16 shows how a novelty "pulls" other elements sharing its spatial concept. An element that shares a spatial concept with a novelty is likely to move forward with a probability of about .60, while other elements move forward at a rate of about .30 during the same time interval.

Finally, we may ask what happens within a configuration after a novelty has appeared? Here our results are sketchy, but we have found some fascinating leads. Perhaps most striking is the fact that novelties are relatively unstable; they tend to *revert* back one or more levels after their appearance. Almost 80 percent of the novelties reverted at least one level during the next time period, and 56 percent showed deep reversion (they reverted more than one level). This rate of deep reversion is re-

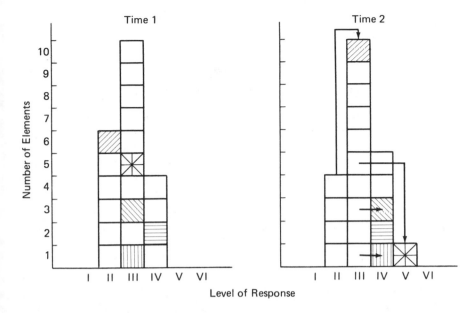

Figure 3.16 "Pulling" effect of a novel element on other elements sharing its spatial concept. Also shows "leaping" of a novelty.

markable when compared with the overall reversion rate for all elements, which is about fifteen percent for all reversions and only 1.6 percent for the more pronounced deep reversions.

From results such as these we have begun to piece together a picture of the role of novelties as catalysts in the transition process. Novelties seem to leap out of the middle of the pack to take their place at the highest level of a configuration. Novel elements also exert a pulling influence on other elements sharing the same spatial concept. Once a novelty appears, it often subsequently reverts back into the configuration, almost as if the child found the new level a bit too heady a brew and decided to be somewhat more conservative so as to regroup cognitive forces.

Also of interest in our analysis was an examination of elements reflecting certain contents that may play other roles in the transition process. We saw, for example, that novelties tended to come from among elements involving the spatial concepts of perspective and symbolization. We also found that spatial arrangement provided a high percentage of the deep reversions, and laggards more often than not reflected a map-drawing problem related to proportion (see Feldman & Snyder, 1977). As we continue to unravel the mysteries of the structure-building process, we will have to learn more about these specific spatial reasoning problems because of their potential special roles in developmental transitions in the domain of map drawing. With the techniques for tracking element movement, it is now possible to study these matters empirically.

ON THE MEANING OF MOVEMENTS

We would of course like to specify precisely which elements move and why they move as a configuration is transformed from level to level, but the complexity of the task remains staggering. At some later point we would hope to integrate our observations of single element movements into the more global view of transition states that was the outcome of our group oversplicing enterprise. For now we are limited to juxtaposing the two views. Still, it seems appropriate to comment in a preliminary way on the relationships we perceive between types of element movements and some traditional issues relevant to developmental transitions.

There is ample speculation in the literature about backward movement—what we have called reversion—as part of the transition process. Heinz Werner (1957) is the theorist who has perhaps been most explicit about this aspect of development and Jonas Langer (1969b), a theorist in the Wernerian tradition, has elaborated upon Werner's views. Both Werner and Langer stress the idea that development is not all progressive, but that preparation for movement to a more advanced level of functioning may well include some "dedifferentiation" or temporary reversion to earlier levels. "Regression in the service of the ego" (Kris, 1958)) is the phrase that expresses somewhat the same notion within the psychoanalytic tradition. We use the term reversion rather than regression because, like Strauss (1972) and Turiel (1974), we believe that the individual's overall developmental organization does not move backward. More plausible from our point of view is that various elements in a generally forward moving configuration are drawn back temporarily in order to consolidate a level or enhance elaboration of an emerging level. The term reversion seems to us to capture this aspect of backward movement better than the term regression.

Rapid forward movement, similar in some respects to leaping and novelty, also has a time-honored place in the developmental literature. Perhaps the idea of *readiness* best captures this notion. Given an individual with a certain set of capabilities at a certain point in time, we can predict relatively rapid progress if the appropriate conditions are met. Most earlier views of stage-to-stage progress also partook of this notion. Piaget's *structures d'ensemble* is often interpreted as precipitous movement from one state to the next, although recent discussions of the stage issue (particularly Flavell, 1971b; Gruber & Vonèche, 1978; Piaget, 1975) place less emphasis on this idea. It is now our interpretation that Piaget means his notion of stage advance to be taken only in a most metaphorical way. Perhaps it is accurate to say that for Piaget a new stage is *glimpsed* at the appearance of a novelty, but the full range of capabilities must be constructed and consolidated over an extended period of time. This way of dealing with the issue might even eventually resolve the paradox between *structures d'ensemble,* which seems to demand rapid movement of an entire set of elements, and gradual transition, which is more likely to be what actually happens, even in Piaget's view of things (Gruber & Vonèche, 1978).

To summarize, a novelty does seem to signify the first solid behavior reflecting a new, more advanced level. This new level, however, has only a foundation and a few joists; it is far from complete at the appearance of the novelty. This may be what Piaget means by *décalage*; although the child has apprehended a more advanced level of thinking, he has done so only in a limited area of the domain. It follows that a novelty, once it has appeared, may be drawn back into the center of the configuration because the child has no way to integrate this new-found apprehension into his already well established ways of thinking within the domain. But the fact that a new, more advanced solution reverts to an earlier level or is abandoned under countersuggestion, does not (contrary to Piaget) necessarily mean that "mere learning" has taken place. Our data suggest that an essential part of the transition process seems to be reversion of novel elements; reversion thus may be seen as integral to development. The significance of reversion may lie less in the fact that it represents a failure to resist countersuggestion (as Piaget has argued) than in understanding where in the transition process the reversion takes place. Under some conditions reversion may indeed indicate "mere learning," under others it may signify development at work.

To push this line of speculation one step further, we would expect that the appearance of a novelty in the sense it is defined in this chapter, signifies something like the occurrence of "insight" in problem solving, but it is not clear just what happens following this insight. There seem to be two possibilities, and these may manifest themselves in different ways in terms of element movement. One possibility is that the novelty is the "missing link" in an almost complete structure. Once this link is in place, the structure coalesces, becoming more complete and irreversible. Piaget seems to suggest something very much like this when he reports that a child who had solved a problem of recurrent reasoning exclaimed: "Once one knows, one knows forever and ever!" (Piaget, 1971, p. 5). A second possibility, one which seems more plausible, is that a novelty is probably not the final truss in a well evolved structure, but rather the first hint that a grand new structure will be built in the future. Indeed, if it were possible to conduct an interview at the exact moment when a novelty appeared, we would predict finding a child who is both exhilarated and anxious, excited and troubled. And we would expect on this basis that novelties would be rather short-lived behavioral phenomena, not the stable, irreversible, unshakable reasoning of a newly achieved, well consolidated structure.

Unfortunately, we do not have data on the reactions of children to the appearance of a novelty in their own thought. It does seem, however, that the event which makes a structure unshakable is probably not a novelty, not a single element pushed beyond the prior boundaries of a configuration. The "once one knows, one knows forever and ever" phenomenon, we believe, is more likely to be precipitated by moving a lagging element up so that the mode becomes really well consolidated, achieving a stable equilibrium state. A novelty on the other hand is more likely to be an ephemeral, fleeting insight, a glimpse into the future.

We confess that these speculations about the meaning of various element movements go well beyond our data. Nothing presented here can yet reveal the true meaning of a novelty, nor the function of laggards, nor the significance of rapid forward and backward movement. But the techniques described in this chapter show that the study of specific movements among specific elements adds fine grain to the broad picture of transition states presented earlier.

REFLECTIONS OF TWO NOVICE FILM MAKERS

In this chapter we have tried to deal with issues of individual developmental change through two "films" of the transition process. Since we see change as a continuous process of transformation, we chose to feature two traditional indicators of qualitative advance: modal level shifts and developmental novelties. A modal shift is as close as we could come to a measure of "overall stage change." We wanted to construct a sequence of changes in developmental state that would lead up to, include, and then follow a shift in this most frequent level of response. We produced a set of six phases of transitions that did just that. Following a modal level advance, this film would simply be rewound and run again, but with the whole configuration having advanced to the next level.

By distilling from these data a set of principles governing developmental transitions, we could account for changes among nearly three-quarters of the individual children in our sample; not bad for a first try. Still, these children were the same ones who provided the group data upon which the sequence was built. We would have more confidence in the accuracy of our scenario if we had another set of map drawings with which to test this sequence. We are working on this, but in the meantime we must be content with what seems to us a respectable first outing. Obviously there are many more subtle changes that occur between modal level shifts than are reflected in our six frames. It must be something like an actor finding that his or her best scenes ended up on the cutting room floor.

As a complement to this necessarily general picture, we moved in for a closer look at specific movements among the psychological elements that comprise a child's map drawing. The kind of movement that has interested us most is the developmental novelty, the first appearance of reasoning at a level unprecedented for a child. We were able to trace the conditions preceding and following the appearance of novelties in individual children's protocols. While we cannot yet say why a novelty does what it does, we can at least begin to shed a little light on the matter.

It seems that novelties leap out of an elaborating configuration, pulling a number of other "like-minded" elements with them to more advanced levels. It also seems that novelties frequently revert back into the middle of a configuration after they have made a first, dramatic appearance. We are not sure why this is so, but it may well have something to do with the child consolidating his gains before taking too great a further risk. A novelty seems to show the child what is possible, to set a new but somewhat dangerous carrot out in front of one's cognitive donkey; but then the carrot jumps back on the wagon and somehow helps move the rest of the load.

We have obviously just begun to explore this enormously complicated but fascinating process called developmental transitions. By studying a relatively slow-moving, stable domain like map drawing, we have been able to capture on "film," if only in grainy, jerky and primitive scenes, some of the movements of cognitive systems as they proceed from level to level. Future efforts will necessitate refinement of our tools and techniques for studying both the general and the more specific aspects of transition processes. This will undoubtedly require that we branch out into other domains as well as study map drawing, but we would not, after all, want to become type-cast after only two films.

4
CREATIVITY –
TRAIT VERSUS PROCESS

This chapter explores relationships among creativity, intelligence, and education within two broad traditions in psychology. The first of these traditions, which has often been referred to as a "trait" approach to human behavior, attempts to establish the existence and organization of enduring human qualities. The second approach concerns itself more with "processes" than with traits and aims to explain *how* people perform intellectual and creative acts. The main objective of the chapter is to demonstrate that the traditional trait concept of creativity has certain inherent conceptual limitations that may be fruitfully overcome by taking a process view; the process view to be offered was inspired by Piaget's description of developmental processes and grew out of my efforts at studying developmental transitions.

It may seem paradoxical for a theory like Piaget's which attempts to establish universal sequences in intellectual development to have inspired a conception of creativity, perhaps the most unique of all human activities. The relation between these two kinds of achievement becomes much clearer, however, if considered in terms of the framework presented in Chapter 1, which places the two—universal and unique—along a continuum of developmental advances. It is postulated that unique intellectual advances are similar to universal ones in that they share some of the same processes of acquisition and change. It was, in fact, in coming to grips with the full range of "novelties" in cognitive development—Piaget has called them "the great mystery of the stages"—that the commonality among creative works and other forms of intellectual advances first began to appear comprehensible and even necessary and obvious.

To illustrate just how different these two regions of achievement—universal and unique—are typically perceived to be, let me describe a "natural experiment" that occurred in a developmental psychology class I taught at Yale. The students (about 100 of them) were viewing a film on intellectual development (Kagan & Gardner, 1972) in which a Piagetian conservation-of-liquid experiment was being shown. In the midst of showing a six-year-old child working on this task, the scene flashed to still photographs of Albert Einstein, Freud, Newton, and then Piaget himself! As the first photograph appeared the students broke into spontaneous laughter. The juxtaposition of Einstein and a six-year-old pouring water from one jar to another was apparently just too much, and the students quite reasonably seemed to find the two images incongruous and amusing. I am not sure what the film makers had intended to suggest by this cinematic device, but I think the reaction of my students was probably typical. Their laughter increased with each new photograph, until they guffawed with delight when *le patron* Piaget appeared.

What were my students laughing about? The film might have been trying to draw the viewer's attention to the fact that the processes of discovery are universal, that the child performing the conservation task might become an Einstein or a Freud, or that different problems are challenging at different points in time. Each of these notions, of course, has some merit, but what was it that struck the students as being so amusing? Were they amused by the juxtaposition of novice and genius? Since the film moved rapidly to another scene there was little opportunity for reflection, and it is impossible to tell in retrospect what was happening.

I believe that the effect of the cinematic link between "Everychild" and Einstein stimulated opposing sets of meanings in a pleasing and delightful manner; similarities and differences were played off one against the other (Koestler, 1964). Whether intentional or inadvertent, this little episode draws attention to the fact that the analogy between Piagetian stage advance and creativity is not an obvious one. When it is drawn, it must be drawn with the realization that it goes against common sense. Common sense says that Einstein was a preeminent thinker, sharing very little in mental organization and mental capacity with anyone, let alone with a six-year-old nonconserver.

The discrepancy between a great, even monumental intellectual achievement and an earthy, mundane one was sufficiently great for the prominent evolutionist George Gaylord Simpson (1974) to discard a Piagetian interpretation given to Darwin's achievements by Howard

Gruber (Gruber & Barrett, 1974). In order to appreciate fully the differences between achievements that have substantial impact beyond one individual's insight and those achievements that do not, it is therefore necessary to examine the universal-to-unique continuum more closely. In this chapter, then, we shift our focus from novelties that seem to signal reorganization in cultural domains to novelties at the extreme of the continuum that reorganize whole domains themselves.

TRAIT AND PROCESS

Since one of the objectives of this chapter is to present a view of creative intellectual processes as distinguished from traits, some of the more salient features of the trait approach to creativity should be noted, as it is in terms of these features that processes and traits are compared.

A trait approach has guided most empirical research in creativity (Nicholls, 1972). A trait view, first of all, emphasizes increasingly precise study of differences among individuals. J.P. Guilford, the father of the trait approach to creativity, stated the position clearly in his 1950 presidential address to the American Psychological Association:

> I have often defined an individual's personality as his unique pattern of traits. A trait is any relatively enduring way in which persons differ from one another. The psychologist is particularly interested in those traits that manifest themselves in performance; in other words, behavior traits . . . . Creative personality is then a matter of those patterns of traits that are characteristic of creative persons. (Guilford, 1950, p. 444)

Creative traits, by definition then, had to be considered to differ from "intelligence" traits in order to give them some potential for predicting achievement above and beyond IQ. Intelligence, of course, had been operationally defined through the IQ measurement long before work in creativity began. If researchers were to establish creativity as a trait, therefore, they faced the practical necessity of demonstrating substantial independence of creativity from IQ. This, in effect, is what the last twenty-five years of creativity measurement research has attempted to do, with only limited success (Wallach, 1971).

There were also pragmatic reasons for justifying the construction of creativity tests. Intelligence tests had proved valuable to society in many ways, including the more efficient deployment of manpower resources during both world wars, but the predictive value of IQ measures had been found to be poor in situations requiring production and evaluation of *new* ideas. In his 1950 address before the American Psychological Association, Guilford proposed that a trait approach to creativity could overcome this deficiency and thus could become a vital tool for the maintenance of America's scientific and technological superiority. From Guilford's perspective, it was more important to be able to *predict* creativity than to understand it. And, as it happened, many of the resources marshalled to support creativity research (a substantial portion of which went to Guilford himself) were poured into the development of tests to predict creative behavior in scientific laboratories and military settings (Wolfle, 1951). Practical as well as scientific considerations therefore influenced the desire to define and measure a trait or set of traits, different from intelligence, that would predict original and productive thought in technologically strategic settings.

Assumptions

A trait approach generally presumes that human beings come into the world with a set of potentials that will naturally express themselves except under the most dire conditions of deprivation. Everyone presumably comes equipped with some quantity of each of the essential human traits, and these quantities determine how well he will perform in many situations. Traits, from this point of view, are relatively immutable, stable and quantifiable, and if measured accurately, predict behavior in a wide variety of situations.[1]

A process emphasis, in contrast, focuses on the interaction between organism and environment—the ongoing, everchanging construction of behavior. Except in the obvious sense that each human being has certain inherent potentials, process psychology does not assume that the individual is a cluster of specific metric qualities which determine his future behavior more or less independent of environmental circumstances. Indeed, the very notion of traits seems to the process psychologist to be misleading, since behavior is always seen as a joint function of individual and situation; behavior itself is a sign of a process going on and not a function of a trait. In this respect, the process approach to human behavior concerns itself less with predicting who will achieve distinction than with understanding under what circumstances an individual (including exceptional individuals) expresses his or her potential. It is therefore not surprising to find that a trait treatment of creativity often gives little explicit consideration to factors affecting the likelihood that an individual's potential will be realized. This is the case because, in principle, the traits themselves provide the impetus to achieve their potential, making trivial issues such as the conditions under which one achieves full expression of potential.

[1] It should be noted that Guilford and others who have fostered traiit research have explicitly declined taking a stand on whether traits are "hereditary" or "environmental." I will show later how the logic of the trait-approach really leaves no choice in the matter.

In Guilford's classic paper, for example, only the most superficial treatment is given to intervention strategies or educational efforts to enhance creativity. With uncharacteristic brevity Guilford writes:

> . . . I will venture one or two opinions on the general problem of the development of creativity. For I believe that much can be done to encourage its development. This development might be in the nature of actual strengthening of the functions involved or it might mean the better utilization of what resources the individual possesses, or both. In any case, a knowledge of the functions is important. (Guilford, 1950, p. 448)

By "functions," of course, Guilford means traits. The role of environmental influence, then, is to either make better use of the "functions" or traits that a person displays, or to try to increase the functions themselves. A more active role for environment is allowed from a process perspective since there is assumed to be mutual regulation and construction of regularities in behavior between the individual and the conditions which prevail upon him.

By framing the problem of creativity primarily in trait terms, psychologists made both implicit and explicit decisions about what to look for and what to ignore when they began their creativity research. Unfortunately, some of these assumptions have been forgotten over the years. What began as a rather limited aim to produce some useful predictive measures has grown into a dominant "concept of creativity."

The general point to be made here is that the questions asked about a phenomenon, as Caplan and Nelson (1973) have argued, determine to a significant extent the range of answers that may be found. The trait approach to creativity was useful for the purposes for which it was developed, i.e., to guide the search for reliable measures of the traits of creative or potentially creative people. But in making this the goal of creativity research, certain other problems were ignored or equivocated. Still, trait approaches to creativity have made important contributions, and it is appropriate to summarize these contributions before going into the more process-based view in greater detail.

Creativity Trait Measures

A substantial body of data deriving from trait research now suggests that there is a realm of intellectual performance, testable by reliable means, that is independent of IQ and at least somewhat related to actual "real world" creative achievements (Wallach, 1971). The abilities in this realm are assessed by various measures, typically paper and pencil tests that deal with fluency in the production of ideas (cf. Crockenberg, 1972). Creativity measures thus contrast with IQ tests as well as with standard achievement tests, which aim to deal with abstract skills such as vocabulary, analogizing, using formal logic, manipulating spatial relations, or organizing parts into wholes.

   Like IQ tests, creativity measures provide tasks for the subject to perform, but usually there are no "right" answers. For example, in response to the question, "How many ways can you think of to use a brick?" a subject might respond, "to build a house," "to build a barn," "to use as a door stop," etc. The number of appropriate uses determines the estimate of "ideational fluency," the metric that contributes most significantly to creativity test scores. Other components typically include *unusualness* of responses (e.g., "A brick can be used to make the toilet use less water") and the number of different categories into which responses fall (e.g., Torrance, 1966).

   Critics have of course questioned the validity of creativity test instruments (cf. Crockenberg, 1972; Feldman, 1970, 1974; Nicholls, 1972; Wallach, 1968), but despite debate over how well creativity measures do their job, there is now little doubt that at least within the upper ranges of the IQ distribution (probably above 120 IQ) the relationship between creativity test scores and IQ is minimal (Wallach, 1971). More controversial than their independence from IQ, however, is the extent to which creativity measures actually predict achievement in nonacademic domains. Here, too, there is some supporting evidence for this correlation (see Wallch, 1971 for a good review; also Kogan, 1974), but this evidence is less compelling than that which tries to establish creativity measures as independent from IQ.

CREATIVITY AND EDUCATIONAL POLICY

Although the fruits of creativity test construction have been modest, the motives stimulating creativity research have influenced and, in turn, been influenced by educational reforms. The existence of a growing and vocal body of researchers committed to the development of new tests and creativity measures has given encouragement and support to educational innovation, with Guilford (1950) once again leading the way:

> Many of us teachers assert that it is our main objective to teach students how to think, and this means also to think constructively. Certainly, if we succeeded in this objective, there should be much evidence of creativeness in the end product. I am convinced that we do teach some students to think, but I sometimes marvel that we do as well as we do. In the first place, we have only vague ideas as to the nature of thinking. We have little knowledge of what specific steps should be taken in order to teach students to think. Our methods are shotgun methods, just as our intelligence tests have been shotgun tests. It is time that we discarded shotguns in favor of rifles. (Guilford, 1950, p. 448)

To the extent that schools have moved toward emphasizing the arts, critical thinking, hypothesis testing, "relevant" questions, and individualized instruction, the creativity test movement must be given some of the credit. Likewise, the extension of creativity test construction from adults to children of school age (Getzels & Jackson, 1962; Torrance, 1962; Wallach & Kogan, 1965) was stimulated by a desire to find ways to provide quality education for children who did not "fit" into the normal academic regime.

Creativity Training

While a variety of changes in educational practice have been influenced by creativity research, only one line of work bears directly on the educational process itself, and this line has been notably unsuccessful. It is useful to consider this work in some detail because it illustrates some of the problems into which the trait notion of creativity runs when attempts are made to extend it to the *process* of creative accomplishment, an aim implicit in Guilford's remarks just quoted. The work in question consists of attempts to increase creativity or creative ability by raising creativity test scores. (This rationale is directly analogous to one which led to the misleading conclusion that intervention programs which raise IQ scores produce changes in real world intelligence; see Kohlberg, 1968.) A number of programs intended to increase creative abilities have been undertaken (see Wallach, 1970, 1971 for reviews); the studies differ in the skills they train and in the techniques and procedures used to improve them, but *they all aim to influence creative ability itself.*

If creative abilities are presumed to be primarily *associative,* for example, then a program intended to increase the number, variety and unusualness of associations is stressed (see, for example, Reese & Parnes, 1970). If the number and variety of *categories* is taken as an index of creative potential, then a program intended to increase categorization skills follows. Likewise, various forms of problem solving and hypothesis generation have also been taught (e.g., Feldhusen, Treffinger & Bahlke, 1970; Olton & Crutchfield, 1969).

Although a number of these intervention programs have enhanced performance on various creativity tests, the programs can be shown to have been misguided in the belief that raising test scores improves creative ability itself, misguided by the very logic of the trait definition of creativity. Since a trait approach to creativity assumes that the traits to be measured will express themselves under most existing environmental conditions, it follows by definition that these traits should not be easily influenced by training (cf. Mischel, 1968, 1970). If they are easily influenced, they probably are not traits; if they are not influenced, they are traits because training does not affect them significantly. *Thus, the definition of traits precludes the possibility of change through intervention.*

Unless some revision of the trait view is permitted, these programs basically fail when they succeed and succeed when they fail. They fail in the former case because what they improve is performance, not the "underlying" ability. They succeed in the latter case because they support the notion that traits are not easily modified—but their "success," of course, comes at the price of no improvement in test scores.

The kind of revision of the trait approach to creativity that would be required for it to logically permit effective training studies has already been adopted in the trait approach to intelligence. Early education programs such as Head Start were rationalized in terms of the presumed effects they would have on IQ scores and, by implication, on "intelligence" itself. These programs were motivated by the belief that intelligence was not fixed at birth and could be potentially enriched or impoverished during the first four or five years of life by environmental conditions. The now common, misleading statement that intelligence is one-half determined during the first four years follows from this modification of the trait concept of intelligence (cf. Bloom, 1964; Hunt, 1964).

While there is now some basis for believing that IQ is at least somewhat modifiable during the first years (Scarr & Weinberg, 1976) it is only by unsupported analogy that the same argument can be made for creativity test performance. Indeed, to my knowledge no programs to improve creativity test performance have been attempted during the preschool years at all, so the analogy was at best a stretched and strained one, at worst simply irrelevant.[2]

Whether implausible or incredible, such a revision of the trait conception of creativity has also been implicit in the manner in which intervention programs have been rationalized. It is more likely that the fallacies in the trait researcher's assumptions would have become obvious to the proponents of intervention programs if the underlying assumptions of the modifiability of traits had been made more explicit. For example, the assumption that increasing acreativity test scores increases creativity itself rests on the mistaken belief that correlation implies causation, one of the most common errors made in such research. Wallach (1971) points out in this connection that although one variable may *predict* another, altering the former will not necessarily produce concomitant changes in the latter:

[2]The work of Jerome Singer (cf. Antrobus, 1970) is perhaps the closest to a training program at the preschool level. But Singer's work uses "creativity" tests as an indication that enhancing play and fantasy have significance beyond their own intrinsic values, i.e., that they affect creativity in some way.

That ideational productivity (i.e., creativity test performance) shows a moderate linkage with creative attainments does not offer a warrant for assuming that whatever enhances the former will, by virtue of that fact, also enhance the latter. (p. 21)

To actually enhance creativity, in other words, interventions must deal with creativity, not its correlates. Raising creativity test scores is no warrant to claim that "creativity" has been affected. Therefore, although training studies have generated considerable interest, they deservedly have had little impact.

Beyond IQ

A more positive, though indirect, influence of creativity research has been to help show educators that there is more to a child's intellect than IQ. Considering the pervasive influence of IQ tests on educational practice as well as on common knowledge and conventional wisdom about intelligence, convincing the public that IQ represents only part of the repertoire of human abilities has been no small achievement. Creativity research did not, of course, accomplish this change by itself (and it should also be noted that IQ remains in the minds of many, professional and nonprofessional alike, as the most powerful indicator of intellectual potential; cf. Brim et al., 1969), but interest in creativity helped to lessen the monopoly of IQ as an indicator of general ability.

A related shift in educational policy that is also partially attributable to the influence of creativity research is the growing tendency to rely less on test scores of any sort to determine admission to college and other special programs of study. Wallach and Wing (1969) have been perhaps the most influential among creativity researchers in fostering this trend. In their book *The Talented Student: A Validation of the Creativity-Intelligence Distinction,* Wallach and Wing showed that College Board (SAT) scores did not predict nonacademic accomplishments among newly admitted Duke University students. They urged admissions officers to consider evidence other than grades and test scores in admitting new students, and indeed, many universities have followed this lead. The argument in brief is that standardized IQ test scores predict only two aspects of achievement: the likelihood that a student will be able to do the work required by the college or special program for which he is being considered, and the grades he will receive. Since grades in college or professional school are said to have relatively little value for predicting success in a given field, it is therefore not unreasonable to select individuals at least partly on the basis of other, nonscholastic achievements. The result of such a policy is a more diverse student body, if not a uniformly excellent one, and a greater probability that the students will make worthwhile contributions in nonacademic domains. Although the Wallach and Wing research had many methodological flaws (cf. Feldman, 1970), these seem not to have stood in the way of its influencing policy.

Creativity tests have also been added to the armamentarium of the school psychologist with the rationale that some gifted students may be missed when screening only with traditional IQ tests (Bruininks & Feldman, 1970). What the schools then do with their newly discovered "extra talent," however, has not been as carefully planned. This is not surprising when considered from the perspective of the trait approach to creativity which generally assumes that a trait will express itself except under the most severe environmental deprivations. From this point of view, the responsibility of the educational system is not to influence traits but rather to *identify* them; a satisfactory education system is not necessarily one which adjusts to accommodate varying sets (or levels) of abilities and skills, but one which identifies existing talent in the population and expends its resources on encouraging the more gifted students to go forward, relegating the less talented to the lower ranks. Educational programs for "gifted" and "creative" students have therefore been typically limited to poorly defined "enrichment," which most commonly consist of offering greater quantities or variations of the standard school curriculum. The identification process by itself yields very little information about the nature of the abilities which might, in turn, suggest how curricula might be designed to effectively challenge the special abilities revealed by creativity or by other tests.[3]

In summary, most "creative abilities" research has emphasized: (a) measurement of capabilities that are believed to predict creativity, and (b) the selection of individuals with substantial "amounts" of these traits for special recognition. Very little information directing the organization of programs has followed from this work. While different settings may provide somewhat different programs for enhancing "creative potential," almost all seem to draw heavily on the regular school curriculum. To the extent that training programs to increase creativity have been undertaken, they have emphasized attempts to change underlying "abilities." In the case of open or informal schools, creativity measures seem to be used to buttress the policy decision to maintain a more informal program. While research guided by individual trait assumptions has succeeded in demonstrating the existence and importance of abilities other than IQ, it has been limited by its own assumptions to only recognizing a new set of traits. These assumptions make it difficult, if not

[3]The only major exception to this rather bleak picture is research examining the effects on creativity of open versus traditional classrooms (cf. Hadden & Lytton, 1968). As of this writing, relatively few studies have been done, and, as they depend on divergent thinking measures to assess creativity, they fall prey to many of the same fallacies as other intervention research.

impossible, to address the question of what to do to enhance their expression. In other words, the emphasis in all creativity trait research is on prediction and selection in preference to development and enhancement.

PERSONALITY TRAIT STUDIES

Another line of research based on a trait perspective has focused on the qualities of the creative personality as distinguished from creative conceptual abilities. The distinction between personality and ability is, of course, never a clear one, but the lines of investigation followed by those who profess interest in one versus the other have tended to be quite distinct. While Guilford had set the problem for the field in 1950 as the investigation of the overall creative personality, few have engaged in research designed to examine both the personal characteristics and the cognitive abilities that might be possessed by creative individuals. Guilford's own work has remained primarily in the area of conceptual abilities, while the work of other investigators has added to our knowledge of personal qualities or traits characteristic of creative individuals.

I will not attempt here to review the voluminous literature on the creative personality; in this section I will only deal with some of those studies which attempted to provide empirical measurement of various qualities of personality that might be related to creative productivity. I choose to focus the discussion on this empirical work primarily to draw attention to another problem that has plagued studies of creativity. I am referring specifically to what I believe is a conceptually limiting preoccupation with the importance of individual traits in determining whether or not creative work is likely to be done (Feldman, 1975). The trait approach has tended to deemphasize the subtle but critical role that various environmental conditions may play in the creative process, not the least of these, as we shall see, is the state of a body of knowledge itself.

To be more explicit, I would suggest that a very strong belief in individual responsibility has given an overriding vote in creativity research to the search for traits (cf. Sarason, 1978). The emphasis is reflected in the tendency to look almost exclusively for the personal qualities that distinguish individuals who have done creative work. This is not to say that the unique qualities of creative individuals are unimportant; it is simply to suggest that the preference for an individualistic explanation for creativity is one which, fitting well with prevailing cultural attitudes, may tend to blind us to other important factors. Consider the evidence.

Research effectively began with Frank Barron's finding in the early 1950s that art students described as "creative" by their professors tended to prefer objects, drawings, and block constructions of greater complexity of pattern than did students designated as relatively noncreative. This observation led Barron to do a series of studies exploring the possibility that creative individuals prefer the more complex and ambiguous than do noncreative persons. In studies spanning more than a decade, Barron (1955, 1968) demonstrated the general predictive validity of his preference measure with individuals from various professions and groups including artists, architects, physicists, and others. Generally speaking, it was true that individuals designated by superiors or peers as creative tended to prefer more complex arrays of stimuli than noncreative individuals. This led Barron to the conclusion that there exists a dimension of personality that runs along a continuum from complexity to simplicity, with more creative people falling at the "complex" end.

It should be evident that the intent of the research carried out by Barron and his coworkers was, as it was for Guilford, to identify and measure a quality of human behavior that would persist over time and predict differentially among individuals. Similar to the creative abilities work in this respect, the hope was to find stable, enduring, measurable qualities of the individual that would distinguish the more from the less creative. And within the limitations of the methodology used (from the previous discussion it should be evident that they are substantial), some reasonably reliable differences were found.

A related series of studies was carried out by Donald MacKinnon, a colleague of Barron at Berkeley. MacKinnon studied personality differences among groups of architects, physicists, mathematicians, officers in the military, etc. nominated as creative by their peers. MacKinnon used a battery of psychological instruments and did intensive interviews and assessments with subjects over a three-day period (in most instances). It was from this extensive set of observations that MacKinnon hoped to find how the creative individual differed from his peers.

As was the case with the creative abilities research, some modest additions to what we know about creativity have been made by this work. While the results have never been dramatic, over the years the MacKinnon group and others around the country have slowly built up reliable information about individuals who are said to be creative by someone presumably in a position to know. Without going into this literature in detail, a few representative findings give the flavor of this work, as summarized in this passage from a chapter I wrote on problem solving and creativity:

> As measured by psychological tests, . . . three groups of architects did differ in personality. The forty creative architects were more flexible and

open minded than the other groups. They also had a wider range of interests, had a greater preference for complexity, and were less interested in small details and in practical and concrete problems. They were described as more ambitious, dominant, and achievement-oriented, markedly more mature, emotionally and aesthetically sensitive, independent, individualistic, and enthusiastic. They seemed to accept themselves, to be more introspective, and to exhibit traits typically referred to as feminine. In social relations, they tended to be unconventional, rebellious, self-centered, and exhibitionistic. In fact the creative architects seemed to be relatively free from conventional restraints and inhibitions, unconcerned with the impression they made on others. And above a certain minimum (about 120) IQ did not bear any relationship to creativity. (Feldman, 1973b, p. 383)

I would like to mention once again why I think this line of research is important in the present context. This kind of personality research illustrates another aspect of the belief system underlying the trait approach to creativity. This aspect is perhaps best thought of as a preoccupation with qualities of the individual as the primary cause of creative productivity. To go a step further, the underlying assumption seems to be that those qualities that are the root causes of creativity are very general and do not depend on special talents. These qualities of the personality determine whether or not an individual is likely to make a substantial creative contribution; talents are taken more or less for granted as necessary but not sufficient.

For both the creative abilities and the creative personality trait research approaches the cause of creativity is located deep within the individual, in a relatively small set of very broad traits. The direction of cause is from inside out. If one has the qualities of a creative thinker and the personality of a creative person, then one will be creative. The specific domain of expression is a function of some more specific and less critical traits or talents that determine the medium through which the more general qualities of creativity will be expressed. I have tried to illustrate the sense of how this is supposed to work in Figure 4.1

THE PROCESS VIEW

A trait position concentrates on constructing accurate measures of traits and assumes that their expression will occur naturally; in contrast, the process position views the identification of traits as inadequate in the absence of specific programs that promote their expression and development. As Michael Wallach (1971) has written:

> If we want to learn about the enhancement of creativity, we had better consider training arrangements that make a person more competent at creative attainments themselves—such as writing novels well, excellence in acting, skill as a musician, or quality of art work produced. (p. 23)

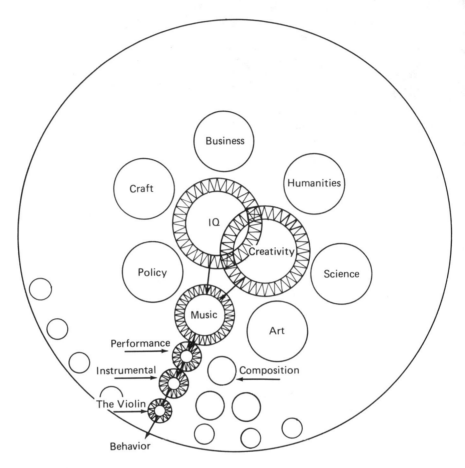

Figure 4.1 Cause and effect from the trait point of view. Illustration is of someone who becomes a violinist.

A second assumption of a process view, also implied in the above quote, is that it is a matter of crucial importance that the qualities to be fostered be enhanced through giving novices in a field the opportunity to develop their skills under the guidance of expert practitioners.

Obviously, discovery of talent is a crucial task, and a prerequisite to development. The problem has been, however, that the "traits" measured have been conceptualized as lying so deeply within the individual's personality, as being so much broader and more pervasive than any specific domain of performance, that specific programs for development of creativity would have to be very remote from the seat of the creative potential. Thus, the way in which traits are conceived tends to militate against both the enhancement of more field-specific abilities and the

100

careful consideration of relationships between domains of performance and individual predispositions, the fine tuning of individual to environment.

To move the notion of creativity more into the domain within which it is practiced, we must shift our vantage point from the qualities of the person producing creative works to the creative work itself—the product. Following this, we will return to a consideration of creative processes.

Identifying Creativity by the Product Rather Than the Person

It is true of course that creative people are not creative at all times, that some products of even distinguished individuals are not at all remarkable. Indeed, applying the most stringent criteria, it is rare for an individual to make truly lasting contributions more than a few times during a lifetime.

A very different way of thinking about creativity is to focus on creative works themselves rather than on the individuals who produced them. By attempting to identify and categorize creative products, the task for research is to establish what makes a creative product differ from a noncreative one. Taking the product as a point of departure leads to the possibility of giving differential weight to the quality of creative works, providing some way of quantifying the "goodness" of a work that has been produced. This has not been a very popular pastime of creativity researchers, but substantial progress toward establishing criteria for the evaluation of creative products has been achieved by Philip Jackson and Samuel Messick (1965). I will describe this work in some detail because it illustrates two points that follow from the previous discussion, but that are not obvious. First, the Jackson–Messick work shows that new light can be shed on creativity when the preoccupation with traits is transcended—in this case, when the focal point is moved from person to product. Second, the evaluation of creative products leads to the realization that the specific domain in which creative work is produced must be mastered before creative processes can be understood. Consider the criteria proposed by Jackson and Messick for determining the quality of a creative product.

The four criteria by which creative products are judged, according to Jackson and Messick, are *unusualness, appropriateness, transformational power* and *condensation of meaning.* Jackson and Messick call these criteria *response properties* because they are presumed to produce aesthetic responses of various kinds in a viewer or appreciator of a creative work (see Table 4.1).

Table 4.1*

Response Properties	Judgmental Standards	Aesthetic Responses
unusualness	norms	surprise
appropriateness	context	satisfaction
transformation	constraints	stimulation
condensation	summary power	savoring

*P. Jackson & S. Messick, The Person, the Product, and the Response: Conceptual Problems in the Assessment of Creativity. In M. Bloomberg (Ed.) *Creativity*. New Haven: College and University Press, 1973, Table 2. Originally appeared in: *Journal of Personality*, 1965, *33*, 309-329.

The response property of unusualness may be most readily grasped in a quantitative sense; to be judged creative a product must be highly original, i.e., it must occur only rarely. This criterion is utilized to some degree in current creativity tests (e.g. Torrance, 1966), as is the appropriateness property next to be described. The response in the viewer that unusualness is supposed to produce is that of surprise.

Appropriateness refers to the fit of a solution to the problem which stimulated it; an appropriate solution may stimulate a range of reactions in a viewer from "about right" to "an astonishingly perfect fit!" The notion of a "shock of recognition" often is invoked to give a sense of what the reaction is like when an appropriate solution has been grasped, almost as if one had seen the product somewhere before but in fact never had. As Bruner (1962) has remarked, what makes something obvious in this way is that at last one understands it.

The two remaining criteria, transformational power and condensation of meaning, are more difficult to describe. By transformational power Jackson and Messick refer to the extent to which a solution *breaks free* from the constraints of the original problem, departing from it in a manner which stimulates further thought and reflection. In its most powerful form, a transformation leaves a problem forever changed and a new set of problems is stimulated by the appearance of the product. The Copernican revolution and the theory of evolution are examples of powerful transformational solutions to problems which posed severe constraints.

Finally, the property of condensation refers to the interplay between complexity and simplicity found in the most extraordinary creative works. Einstein's formula $E = mc^2$ and the deceptively simple paintings of Albers are examples of extreme condensations of meaning. While the aesthetic response to transformational power is said to be stimulation and wonder, the effect of condensation of meaning is to produce *savoring*, because the work has summary power that allows extended contemplation. The meaning held, for example, in the simple equation stating the relationship between energy and mass is so great as to be worthy of a lifetime's contemplation.

Unfortunately, little progress has been made in operationalizing these response properties in creativity research. Only one exploratory study has been completed to date, this by the author and his associates (Feldman, Marrinan & Hartfeldt, 1972); it merits a brief summary at this point.

In the Feldman et al. study, Torrance "creativity test" protocols were reanalyzed on the basis of three of the four response properties suggested by Jackson and Messick. The study used only the first three of the criteria since, in practice, the task in Torrance's test does not lead to condensation of meaning, at least not in the sample of high school students tested. Two judges were trained to estimate their aesthetic responses to the test answers, using their reactions to unusualness, appropriateness and transformational power as the scoring criteria. The hypothesis of the study was that the individuals judged most "creative" on the basis of the Jackson and Messick criteria would not be the highest scorers based on Torrance's (1966) standard creativity test procedure.

When asked to choose the six most powerful transformations among the Torrance protocols (a typical item is "how many uses can you think of for a tin can?"), the two judges agreed perfectly on their choices. The individuals who produced these six most powerful reponses ranked 2, 8, 11, 57 and 79 out of 87 subjects in terms of their creativity test scores as calculated by Torrance's procedures. (Two of the six most powerful answers were produced by the subject ranked 57th.) Thus, while there was some tendency for subjects who scored well on the Torrance test to produce powerful transformational responses, three of the six most powerful responses were produced by middle- and low-ranking subjects (see Table 4.2). Thus, some of the most "creative" answers were produced by low scorers on the Torrance test.

While the Feldman et al. study was a small pilot effort, it did suggest that empirical testing of the aesthetic response properties proposed by Jackson and Messick is at least feasible. *But the most important lesson learned from the study was that it was not possible to judge the quality of the protocols without first becoming "experts" in creativity test protocol scoring.* This conclusion seems obvious in retrospect, but it was not apparent in prospect. To put it more broadly, the criteria for evaluation of creative works are inextricably entwined with the field of effort within which the work is produced. Hypothetically, Jackson and Messick's criteria can be applied to any domain. But practically, each domain utilizes the criteria uniquely, and anyone proposing to apply the criteria must have reached a degree of mastery of the domain in question.

Table 4.2

Torrance Test Scores and Rank of Subjects Judged
to Have Produced the Six Most Powerful Transformations

Subject	Sex	Torrance Total Score	Torrance Flexibility Score	Rank (out of 87)	Activity Number*	Transformation
A	F	296	74	2	7	"Prejudices concerning faces would disappear, but new ones would develop concerning feet."
B	M	229	59	8	6	"Why not make a tin can that destroys itself after being used so as not to litter highways."
C	M	194	36	11	5	"Capture good oxygen from polluted air."
D**	M	108	27	57	7, 7	"Babies would never learn how to walk because crawling would be better." "The midgets would have the best deal."
E	F	74	23	74	7	"Murders could not be witnessed and therefore not tried."

*ACTIVITY

#5 *Unusual uses* of tin cans

#6 *Unusual questions* about tin cans

#7 *Just suppose* a great fog were to fall over the earth and all we could see of people would be their feet. What would happen? How would this change life on earth?

**This subject had two of the six transformations judged to be most powerful.

This wisdom gained from hindsight is helpful in furthering our discussion of creative processes; the same generalizations seem to be equally true of creative *processes* as of creative products. The creative processes that I will discuss are also intended to be universally applicable, but they make no practical sense isolated from the field in which work is produced. This should be kept in mind as we proceed. Since I have few specific examples to cite, the dangers are substantial of seeing the processes of creativity as existing independent from a domain; they do not. Indeed, one of the aims of the process approach to creativity taken here is to explicitly question the premise of trait theory that creativity is a deep, pervasive, and stable entity existing independent from other more specific aspects of the individual.

CREATIVITY AND DEVELOPMENT: AN ANALOGY

The crux of my view of creative process is an analogy, or at least a partial analogy. Simply stated, the analogy rests on the belief that Piagetian stage-to-stage advances and creative accomplishments share certain common qualities. Recall that the primary aim of the trait approach was to look for differences, to make distinctions. Without denigrating the usefulness of this kind of activity, it does tend to draw attention away from *continuities,* continuities that may be as revealing as differences.[4] As the reader will see, the analogy to be drawn directs attention to possible new relationships and also makes distinctions heretofore blocked from view. There are two main features of the analogy. One is that the *experience* of achieving a qualitative advance is similar in both general intellectual development and in creative works. The second is that the *disequilibration* process suggested by Piaget occurs in certain fundamentally similar ways in processes reflective of both kinds of advances.

The Experience of Creativity

The crucial assumption of Piaget's stage theory of intellectual development is that new systems of operations, or rules for thinking, are constructed by the child and that these rules reorganize and expand existing modes of thought (Van den Daele, 1974). Piaget (1971) makes no pretense at being able to explain how these constructions occur and, as mentioned earlier, calls this problem "the great mystery of the stages." Although Piaget does not consider creativity per se he does label

[4]One of the most common distinctions made between analytic thinking as required on IQ tests and creative thought is the difference between making distinctions versus making analogies (Bruner, 1962; Guilford, 1950), so it is not surprising that my thinking would take this turn.

newly completed thought operations as "novelties" or "creations" (Piaget, 1971). It is clear from the contexts in which the terms are used, however, that Piaget means by creations the universally acquired organizations of the cognitive apparatus that all children are believed to achieve; these novelties are thus creative only in the sense that the child has achieved a mental reorganization for the first time, going beyond his own limitations.

Piaget leaves little doubt that the initial achievement of a new set of rules of thought—no matter how common a set—can be a profound experience. Two instances of a sudden transition from one stage of reasoning to another illustrate Piaget's observation that there may occur a sudden insight that accompanies the shift in perspective, followed by a sense of having just discovered something incredibly *necessary* and *obvious*. Piaget (1971) describes the occasions in this way:

> . . . The striking thing here is that the child reaches this feeling of necessity as soon as he has understood the phenomenon in question. One can sometimes witness the precise moment when he discovers this necessity. At the beginning of this reasoning he is not at all sure of what he is stating. Then suddenly he says "But it's obvious." In another experiment where Bärbel Inhelder was questioning a child on a problem which is not as in the above situation that of seriation but of recurrent reasoning, but which also involves the feeling of necessity, the child was at first very uncertain. Then suddenly he said, "Once one knows, one knows forever and ever." In other words, at one point the child automatically acquires this feeling of necessity. (p. 5)

This coincidence—seeing a child solve a problem in a profoundly new way at just the time he or she happened to be in the experimental situation—gave Piaget the opportunity to observe a reorganization in the making. Despite the near universality of these particular achievements, every child who first conserves number, seriates for size, classifies according to a higher order category, etc. finds that he has acquired a deeply significant shift in capability. This jump forward (not necessarily temporally rapid) occurs following a period of sustained effort, resolves a whole set of related problems, and opens up new realms of experience (Kohnstamm, 1970).

Creative insights have been described in similar ways, although the terminology used is somewhat different (e.g., Ghiselin, 1952; Wallas, 1926). Jerome Bruner (1962) for example defines creativity as the occurrence of "effective surprise" in an individual who has produced a new work and/or who comprehends and appreciates that work for the first time. Effective surprise is to experience "the unexpected that strikes one with wonder and astonishment." Such experiences, Bruner continues, "have the quality of obviousness about them when they occur, producing a shock of recognition following which there is no longer astonishment" (p. 18). According to Bruner, effective surprise characterizes insights and achievements in all domains and at all levels of human endeavor; it is, as he puts it, the "hallmark of creativity."

The analogy between universal intellectual achievements and creative ones suggested by the preceding paragraphs has already appeared in the literature of educational thought in at least one place. A paper called "The Having of Wonderful Ideas" by Eleanor Duckworth (1972) presents an argument for the relationship of Piaget-like shifts in logical development to the entire spectrum of intellectual achievements, including creative ones. Duckworth draws the analogy most broadly:

> The wonderful ideas I am referring to need not necessarily look wonderful to the outside world. I think there is no difference in kind between wonderful ideas which many other people have already had, and wonderful ideas which nobody has happened upon before. That is, the nature of creative intellectual acts remains the same, whether in an infant who for the first time makes the connection between seeing things and reaching for them . . . or an astronomer who develops a new theory of the creation of the universe. In each case, it is a matter of making new connections between things already mastered. (p. 231)

Duckworth's "wonderful ideas" presumably come about through reorderings of previously unrelated elements. Of this process Henri Poincaré wrote that fruitful combinings "reveal to us unsuspected kinship between . . . facts, long known, but wrongly believed to be strangers to one another" (in Bruner, 1962, p. 19). It is as if one had "known" how the facts should cohere but simply had not perceived the obvious. The initial integration of parts into a whole may bring astonishment and wonder, accompanied by the sense that the whole has achieved its necessary form. Once the solution is achieved, the result may seem so obvious as to be laughable—after the fact.

Bruner also describes an aspect of the experience of creation that he calls "the freedom to be dominated by the object." Once a task is begun or a problem is perceived, a point comes when it begins to demand its own completion. The precise form of the end product is not clear, but its seemingly autonomous need to reach completeness is very powerful as a motivating force.

A final and related attribute common to Piagetian advance and creative accomplishment is the *irreversibility* of the change in perspective that the new achievement brings. By irreversible I do not mean that earlier forms of knowing are cast aside altogether, but only that the new perspective is always available (if not always chosen) for dealing with a class of problems. Once achieved, there is little likelihood that the individual will return to a prior state of organization of thought. As

Inhelder's young subject exclaimed, "Once one knows, one knows forever and ever."

This description of aspects of creative insight mirrors that of the initial completion of an "equilibrated structure," such as in Piaget's conservation and seriation examples cited earlier. A newly equilibrated Piagetian structure reorganizes previously unrelated elements according to a new set of rules. The reorganized whole functions in ways quite different from that which it replaces; each successive equilibrated structure is more stable, inclusive, and encompasses more possibilities than the previous one (Flavell, 1963, 1971). Bruner's phrase "the reordering of experience" is a most apt description of Piagetian stage advance, although it was written to describe creativity.

In summarizing, there are four attributes that creative accomplishments of all varieties, including Piagetian universal achievements, seem to share in common. They are:

1. The initial consolidation of a newly reorganized structure or way of dealing with problematic situations is often accompanied by astonishment or surprise.
2. This solution, once achieved, often seems obvious, and one finds it hard to believe that it was possible to ever have thought differently.
3. As one moves toward a solution there is often a strong—but difficult to describe—sense that the solution is "pulling" one toward it. This helps account for the fact that one often "recognizes" the solution when one achieves it, almost as if one had known it all along but had not quite been able to express it. Picasso has called this process "successive crystallizations of the dream," where the "dream" or solution itself never changes fundamentally but its manifestations on canvas become closer and closer approximations (Ghiselin, 1952, p. 27).
4. There is, finally, the irreversibility of a solution once it is achieved. While other modes of dealing with a problem do not necessarily cease to exist, the new solution expands for all time the available means to organize experience. The solution will be taken as superior and applied to whole classes of relevant (and often irrelevant) problems.

Obviously, the four attributes described in this section as common to the achievement of creative products in all forms, including Piagetian stagelike advance, are not independent. Taken together, however, they do convey the sense of analogy that I have tried to draw revealing continuities among the experiences of qualitative advance—whether they happen to be universal or unique.

CREATIVE PROCESSES AND THE EQUILIBRATION MODEL

We have discussed the criteria by which a creative work may be judged, and we have discussed the experiences that accompany a creative advance. Considering these matters sheds some light on the nature of the creative process. It is important to keep in mind, however, that the analogy drawn between Piaget's explanation of stage-to-stage advance and creative insights is based primarily on those aspects of Piagetian theory which deal with *process*; these aspects are usually referred to as the "equilibration model." The equilibration model is Piaget's attempt to describe in process terms the transition between stages of cognitive development. It should be mentioned that the equilibration model, while it is central to the present discussion, has not been so central to the work of Piaget over the past thirty years or so; that is, he has spent relatively little time elaborating upon it until quite recently (e.g., Piaget, 1975, 1977).

It is not my intention to go into great detail in describing the equilibration process; this has already been done in Chapter 3. But given the fact that the equilibration model is so central to the formulation presented here, I will briefly outline the features that pertain most directly to the problem at hand.

Each individual child (or adult) deals with the world in terms of a set of rules which are available to him. These rules are organized into constellations which make up the child's set of "schemes," or later, "operations," all of which might be taken as the frame of reference that guides the child in the processing of information. For Piaget, there are four (in some accounts only three) such general frames of reference that succeed one another from the birth of the child through adolescence. It is the equilibration process that is postulated to account for the fact that new constellations of rules are constructed, and that older ones are allowed to lapse into disuse. The manner in which these world views are constructed is pretty much as follows.

At any given point in time a child is capable of perceiving a certain range of problems that might occur within his purview. Some things that occur are simply not perceived; other things are perceived differently by individuals at different developmental levels. In the conservation of mass, for example, a very young child will simply not see a situation as problematic when a ball of clay is rolled into a long thin rod, back into a ball, and back into a long thin rod said to have changed its mass. The child will quite contentedly report that the amount of the clay changes with its form.

It may not even disturb the child to have a peer sit next to him and give blatantly different responses to the same question. In one of our own experiments with map drawing (Snyder & Feldman, 1977), two fifth graders sitting beside one another were drawing buildings from different perspectives. One student, who was drawing his buildings from a more or less 45° angle, complete with windows and chimneys, observed his neighbor drawing more abstract tops of buildings from a 90°

perspective. Neither child showed any sign of distress that the other had chosen a different way of dealing with the task; the discrepancy was not problematic to them, even though the 90° perspective is a more evolved, later developing system.

The critical point is that to be perceived a problem must fall between what the individual knows and what he feels capable of dealing with. If the discrepancy is too large, the child (or scientist) simply does not perceive it as problematic. If the discrepancy is too small, the child will "assimilate" the information to his already existing modes of dealing with the world. In other words, our cognitive apparatus seems to have a basically conservative initial tendency. If possible, the situation will be recognized as analogous to and applicable to another situation for which an already existing solution is available. It is only when the situation is perceived as unassimilable, yet soluble, that the conditions for change are present.

If the child is sufficiently upset by a perceived discrepancy and is not totally overwhelmed by it, there is an increased probability that the child will attempt to "accommodate" his way of looking at the world to the demands of the new situation. Thus, there seems to be an optimal discrepancy between where a child is developmentally and where the most promising problems lie in terms of stimulating genuine change (Kagan, 1971; Langer, 1969).

Alternatively, a situation perceived to be problematic may be too much of a threat to the existing hard-won view possessed by the child or adult. If the change is seen as too threatening, the child will be confused, disorganized, and anxious, and the likelihood of constructive change is not great. Once the disorganization and confusion has been reduced to a tolerable and then stimulating level, a more optimal state of "disequilibrium" can be achieved, and progressive change may take place. Following our analogy, a premise of the process view of creativity is that the same conditions that describe the equilibration process for general cognitive developmental advance pertain to unique advances as well. The distance between the two ends of the hypothetical continuum of advances is very great in terms of rarity, dependence on special environmental conditions ("cyrstallizing conditions"), and impact on other individuals, but not great in terms of the processes of transition that bring the advances about.

There are differences, of course, in the nature of the problem solved in each case, especially in the broader implications of a product or solution. Generally, it seems reasonable to assume that the more universal, broader, more fundamental shifts in point of view described by Piaget would pertain to and influence virtually everything experienced by the individual. Depending on the nature of the field in which unique work is done, the implications of an advance may or may not be so profound. Still, and in contrast, the impact of a developmental advance that is achieved by everyone has little effect on a domain of knowledge, despite its profound effect on the child. A unique advance may alter for all time a field of study or a way of thought.

Crystallizing Conditions

An aspect of the equilibration process that also merits brief mention here pertains to the conditions under which developmental advances take place. Since we assume that (by definition) the advances in thought described by Piaget occur universally, it follows that the environmental conditions requisite for these achievements also occur universally.

It should be obvious that one of the ways in which Piagetian and non-Piagetian advances differ is in the specific crystallizing conditions under which they occur (Feldman, 1973a). At the least, we know that the conditions for the former are more pervasive, common and effective than the conditions for all others. The nature of the various kinds of nonuniversal environmental conditions has been taken up in Chapter 1; suffice it to say that all forms of advance are presumed to be achieved through some form of equilibration process. The circumstances which give rise to these processes may differ greatly, however.

UNIVERSAL AND UNIQUE: TWO POINTS ON A CONTINUUM

I have argued that the child who has initially achieved a Piagetian stage advance has, in some ways, had a similar experience to the individual who has found a totally new way to solve a problem at the frontier of a field. Everyone eventually climbs at least most of the Piagetian peaks, while few individuals create totally new and powerful landscapes. The child has changed his hard-won style of thought while the "creative" individual may have provided a solution with the power to change an entire field.

As already noted, the achievement of one of the universal advances or one of the steps in a sequence of such advances can be as profoundly moving as the achievement of a more lofty insight. The fact that universal intellectual advances are achieved by all individuals makes them no less significant to a particular individual at a particular point in his development. Acquiring more powerful rules and principles to organize experience are the inheritance of any human being in any human culture, but it is an inheritance that must be earned. Achievement of a universal advance is thus "creative" in the sense that it could not have been totally taught, that it has been constructed by the individual in response to a perceived problem needing solution, and that its achievement is often greeted with great satisfaction and delight. It is *not* creative, however, in terms of the impact it has on others, on a field of knowledge and action, or on a technology of communication, expression or practice (Salomon, 1974).

While the achievement of an advance may be subjectively much the same regardless of the particular level of accomplishment or field in which it occurs, the evaluation of that achievement by others varies greatly. Adults react with amused and knowing circumspection when they observe a child's realization that the transformation of clay into a ball and back into a long roll does not change the mass of clay. To the child this awareness may be a wondrous achievement, and so it is, but it is an achievement as common as walking.

How Picasso Paints a Picture: The Process View Applied

To illustrate how the notion of the creative process that I have described may operate within a discipline, I have chosen to consider in brief the manner in which Pablo Picasso went about producing a painting. The following is a passage taken from an interview in which Picasso reflects on his own creative processes:

> It would be very interesting to record photographically, not the stages of a painting, but its metamorphoses. One would see perhaps by what course a mind finds its way toward the crystallization of its dream. But what is really very curious is to see that the picture does not change basically, that the initial vision remains almost intact in spite of appearances ... I perceive, when this work is photographed, that what I have introduced to correct my first vision has disappeared, and that after all the photographic image corresponds to my first vision, before the occurrence of the transformations brought about by my will. (Ghiselin, 1952, p. 56)

Picasso seems to be saying that he has a guiding image or vision in mind before he picks up paint and brush, before a single daub is placed on the canvas. Over the course of time what is put to canvas is intended somehow to match the template he had produced prior to beginning the painting. The original vision, according to Picasso, never really changes, but some of the transformations or, as he puts it, the "metamorphoses" of the painting represent closer and closer approximations to the original idea. The intention or "will" to render onto canvas that which is in the mind apparently does not succeed until the last try, at least for Picasso. The early products are in fact distortions of the vision; the will to produce that vision is able to achieve its purpose only by successive approximations, only by "stripping away" the irrelevant transformations.

Thus, Picasso completes a series of renderings which he tests against the image that guided their production. There is from the outset a sense (although an incomplete one, as we will see) of what the end result should look like. Presumably, the product eventually corresponds closely enough to the vision or template such that Picasso would say "Enough!"

This process, while it is not described in the rich detail it deserves,[5] seems straightforward enough in outline. The artist has an intention, which Picasso calls a vision, an aim to produce on a two-dimensional surface the image that he has somehow conjured up. He selects from the materials that are known to him those which he guesses are most likely to permit his intention to be carried out. He also selects from his tools and techniques those that appear most promising for transforming the materials into an organized whole. Having made these selections the artist then puts his first approximation into the concrete, real world of externally perceivable entities, for himself (and perhaps for others) to view.

At this point Picasso, whether explicitly or implicitly, consciously or unconsciously, decides if his tools and techniques have allowed him to produce a work close enough to the original intention or vision to be satisfactory. As Picasso says, generally these earlier attempts tend to distort rather than express the original image or vision. The painting is finished when it corresponds closely enough to the original intention for him to be satisfied. Perhaps a photograph of a painting permits the artist to finally see the painting as completed, whereas the painting itself may still reveal too much of its history. This point remains unclear, but from Picasso's report it does seem that a dynamic, ongoing process of comparison with an internal criterion continues until he is satisfied with the match of painting to "dream."

Picasso asserts that the painting as completed is an accurate expression of the original intention, that it corresponds to and expresses the image in a way that can be shared with others, and that it is satisfying to the person who produced it. While it may be going too far to say so, the motivation to produce the painting seems to be primarily a function of the desire to make explicit, or to express through a medium, a likeness of the imagined vision. Another source of motivation, obviously related, is the wish to communicate that vision to other individuals whose experi-

---

[5]See R. Arnheim's (1962) *The genesis of a painting: Picasso's Guernica* for a more detailed analysis of the development of Picasso's great mural.

ence permits them to share it with the painter. Thus, only the artist himself knows when the painting is complete.[6]

While this is probably an accurate enough outline of how Picasso guided the production of a work of art, there are a number of ambiguities that demand attention. One of these is the question of where the vision or image comes from in the first place. The second concerns the extent to which, if at all, that vision changes as a function of the attempts to express it through the particular form that intermediate products might take, or through other transformations that may occur between the original apprehension of the product and the decision, often much later, that the artist has done enough. Finally, there is the question of what happens when all of the materials, all of the tools, all of the techniques, and all of the wisdom and intuition that the artist has at his disposal are not capable of expressing the artist's vision. What happens then?

Each of these questions merits full and thorough consideration, but we will permit ourselves to touch upon only a few points.

From Where? To say that we do not know where an intention or image or vision comes from is to understate the case in the extreme. What we can say is that a vision depends upon the availability of at least somewhat satisfactory techniques to render it through a medium of expression. This is not to say that all people, including very young children, only have images when they are stimulated by a particular technique or method of expression. An image which a person uses to communicate with himself requires no externalizing medium, but an image which is to be communicated to others must somehow be expressed (Tyler, 1978). Incomplete images, or images which are not fully adequate to express the intention of the individual, may be refined through the use of a feedback process between mind and medium. This is in fact what I believe actually occurred in Picasso's description of "the manner in

[6]The viewer of the work perhaps experiences both the intention and its expression simultaneously, although in another part of the quoted interview Picasso suggests that each person experiences a painting in a unique way. Both could be true. Still, the most powerful works of art may be said to produce responses in viewers which the viewers did not know they had, to stimulate visions that were not spontaneously produced, to create intentions that are carried out and satisfied through appreciation of the work. Thus, the experience of the producer of a work is in some ways similar to, but in some ways very different from that of the appreciator of the work. Once a vision is present, an intention is perceived, the artist and the appreciator of art engage in many of the same activities. The artist produces an approximation on his canvas, and judges its adequacy to express or represent that vision. The appreciator or viewer of art judges the extent to which a product stimulates a response that the viewer did not know was there, creates intentions that were either disorganized or directionless, but obviously cannot judge the product in relation to a vision which preceded it (cf. Jackson & Messick, 1965; Bruner, 1962).

which the mind finds its way toward the crystallization of its dream." If an intention or vision were somehow complete and satisfactory there would be little need to express it through a medium, nor would there be a need to transform and reorganize materials until they take on a satisfying form.

My contention is that the original vision, although perhaps anticipated in outline, is lacking in crucial detail, and that in fact only its barest form is perceived at the outset.[7] The process that the artist goes through is one of consolidation or even *construction* of what is initially only a very sketchy notion.

In spite of Picasso's claim that a finished painting reflects the original vision, I think this is unlikely to be altogether true. What seems more likely is that Picasso had a general idea or intuition about what he would like to express through his medium. The medium itself was used to give further meaning to the intuition. What was produced on canvas became part of the vision, changing and informing it. Thus a vision, in the sense that we use the term, guides the use of materials, tools, and techniques; it permits the acceptance of some, the rejection of others, decisions about whether one is getting closer to or farther away from the original intention. But the vision itself changes subtly with each new attempt to express it.

Finally, product and vision become almost indistinguishable, and it is at this point that the vision has approximated the product and the product has approximated the vision. It is the individual compromising with himself. The medium is used to complete an incomplete intention, the expression of that intention is made possible through attempts to use a medium to represent it. Thus, while we cannot say precisely where visions or images come from, we can say that those visions are either incomplete, in which case they must be completed through the use of a medium of expression, or they are sufficient for the purposes of "internal" communication and need not be expressed through a medium of communication.[8]

Technique. The second issue concerns the particular set of techniques that are used by the artist. It should be obvious that disciplines

---

[7]This contention can be recognized as related to the "gestalt" view in psychology (cf. Arnheim, 1954).

[8]Einstein, when asked to describe how he thought about problems in physics, was unable to put into words the "internal language" he used: "the words or the language, as they are written or spoken, do not seem to play any role in my mechanism of thought. The physical entities which seem to serve as elements in thought are certain signs and more or less clear images which can be 'voluntarily' reproduced and combined . . . the above mentioned elements are, in my case, of visual and some of muscular type. Conventional words or other signs have to be sought for laboriously only in a secondary stage . . . (Ghiselin, 1952, p. 43).

have evolved to provide the means to express intentions and communicate "visions." The process through which one acquires the tools, techniques and wisdom of a discipline have not received serious attention in the psychological research literature, but it should be clear that creative work cannot be done except through the use of a medium of expression and communication. And these media cannot be acquired without hard, dedicated and persistent work. The act of painting allowed Picasso to feel the satisfaction of being able to complete a work. Other disciplines allow similar feelings in other ways.[9]

Visions, images and intentions seem to be produced from the whole range of experiences of an individual, but also to be constrained and limited by the particular media through which they are expressed. Einstein's intentions, however aesthetic, were probably best expressed through the discipline he had acquired. Similarly, Picasso's visions, however cosmic or mathematical, were probably those which could be best expressed through the medium of painting. Thus, it seems reasonable to conclude that the selection of a discipline is crucial both in terms of the kinds of images that one will be able to produce as well as the techniques available to represent (and construct) them.

Finally, we might ask what happens when a practitioner of a discipline, someone who wishes to express a "dream," has exhausted all the possibilities that his discipline offers and finds that the "original vision" (as Picasso put it) is still not captured in the product. When an individual reaches the limits of his craft, when all of the tools, techniques, materials and intuitions have been exhausted and the intentions of the worker still have not been satisfactorily expressed, then the conditions exist that seem to be requisite to the invention of a new technique for the expression of meaning. In other words, as long as an individual is able to express himself through the available forms in a medium there is little likelihood that new forms will be created.

Therefore, creative work of a more powerful sort probably comes about when a practitioner has reached the limits of his discipline. He must find a way to express an intention that guides him toward new combinations, different realms of experience, divergent domains, and other more radical searches for a way to fulfill the need for more complete representation of the vision that guided the whole process (Gruber & Barrett, 1974).

Mastery of a discipline or domain, of a way of dealing with certain problems, opens up at each level new problems to be solved, new experiences to assimilate, new techniques to master. This is as true for those

[9]In contrast to Picasso's feeling of satisfaction, Brewster Ghiselin (1952, p. 13) quotes young Van Gogh in a letter to· his brother: "I am a prisoner in an I-don't-know-what-for horrible, horrible, utterly horrible cage . . . . Something is alive in me: what can it be!"

media through which we are all able to express ourselves tolerably well, such as language or arithmetic, as it is for media through which very few of us express ourselves, such as poetry or chess. When the level of mastery of a discipline, medium, or body of knowledge and skill reaches the point where a problem is perceived which is unprecedented and unique, there is nowhere to go but to new combinations—other media, other realms of experience—for leverage in solving it.

Although the specific elements used to solve the problem may come from various sources, there is enough of a sense of what it will be like when it is completed for the worker to be able to select and judge the appropriateness of each contending solution. Thus, the "shock of recognition" that is so often believed to follow a remarkable solution suggests that guided search in a well-mastered context makes the elimination of alternatives possible, the identification of a solution sure-footed, and the "recognition" a realization that a satisfying construction is at last complete.

A Developmental Analysis of the Thinking of Charles Darwin

The only published example I know of this kind of process approach to creative thinking is found in a book about Charles Darwin by Howard E. Gruber and Paul H. Barrett (1974). In this work Gruber traces the transformations in Darwin's system of thinking about evolution during the years 1837 to 1839 and shows that Darwin struggled with and essentially achieved the outline of the theory of evolution many years before it was eventually published in 1859. It would be impossible to capture in a summary the subtleties and complexities of Gruber's analysis, but a brief account of his discussion may enrich the view of creativity as process that is put forward here.

Gruber, too, has been influenced by Piaget, and he explicitly explores the relation between Piagetian universal thought structures and Darwin's highly unique ones. In a review of the Gruber–Barrett work (Feldman, 1975) I pointed out (as I have done in this chapter) that the analogy between Piagetian and creative thought advances is not an obvious one, yet Gruber makes a compelling case that Darwin's thought structures were transformed through a Piaget-like transition process. In particular, Gruber shows how various parts of the theory were present at more than one point in Darwin's formulations, only to drop out and later be resurrected when his overall organization of the field had advanced to the point where the old element could be more meaningfully integrated.

In some respects Gruber's attempt to trace the transformations in Darwin's thinking about evolution resembles our own attempt to analyze the elements of the domain of map drawing (see Chapter 3). It is of course true that the field of evolutionary biology is much broader and more complex than map drawing. It is also true that we were organizing the existing domain of map drawing into developmental levels and discrete elements for a purpose different from Gruber's. Our purpose, it will be recalled, was to use a relatively well-defined problem as a basis for building a model of transition processes, i.e., to glimpse the set of movements that make up a developmental transition. Gruber's purpose in *Darwin on Man* was in this respect more akin to that of Chapter 2. Evolutionary theory could be seen as a major reorganization in a field of knowledge; Darwin's thinking, background and experience were the set of conditions giving rise to his novel interpretation of change in speciation. Still, the similarities between Gruber's approach to creativity and the approach proposed in this chapter are quite striking, as this passage illustrates:

> We know very little as yet of the process by which a new idea is produced. Let us suppose that each new variant is not an isolated idea but a change in the properties of some larger mental structure of which it is a part. Let us suppose, furthermore, that those parts of a system of ideas that are free to vary at any given moment are variable only within certain limits. This would be analogous to what we might say of any other part of a living system—that it is variable in its functioning, but within limits that depend on its place in the system as a whole.
>
> There are many things we do not know. How are individual ideas produced? Are new ideas common or rare? Are they recurrent or unique? In spite of all this ignorance, there are a few definite things we can say.
>
> A new idea can be recurrently new in one brain in the special sense that the first time it occurred it was not incorporated in a stable structure and therefore on a later occasion it *feels* new; or in the sense that its recurrence marks the transformation of some larger system, which did not occur the first time. The recurrence of the same novelty in the realm of ideas would be analogous to the repeated occurrence of the same mutation in the field of genetics . . . (Gruber & Barrett, 1974, p. 248–249).

The resonance of Gruber's analysis with our Chapters 2 and 3, as well as with this chapter, should be apparent. In particular, highlighting Darwin's overall purpose i.e., to formulate a better theory of evolution, is concordant with our notion of moving through the levels of a field until one reaches the limits of what that field can assimilate. For Darwin, of course, it was necessary to transform the field in order for it to accommodate the facts of nature as he perceived them: enormous variability among and within species, natural environmental forces influencing extinction and survival, qualities that remained stable despite changing conditions, chance, etc.

Gruber's treatment of novelty in Darwin's thinking as forming the "leading edge" of a configuration or system of ideas, too new to be useful until the overall system had ripened, bears close resemblance to our treatment of the role of novel elements in the transition process in map drawing. For Darwin, the concept of natural selection as a positive evolutionary force was a novelty which first occurred before he was able to use it, and again later, when he could appreciate its importance, and he seized it as a "missing element" in his theory (cf. Gruber & Barrett, 1974, pp. 103–106).

Map drawing and evolutionary biology are very different domains, to be sure. Darwin and the average ten-year-old are also very different in the systems of thought and the stores of knowledge available to them; they are pursuing different goals as well. The ten-year-old has begun to construct a hypothetico-deductive frame of reference within which to interpret aspects of the world that he or she has begun to perceive; Darwin organized his life around the goal of achieving a more powerful theory of evolution. Yet the achievements of both kinds of pioneer are in the family of developmental endeavors, sharing many of the same fundamental transition processes even as they reflect vastly different accomplishments. To spell out in detail the similarities and differences between the development of map drawing and of Darwin's work would require a chapter of its own where we could explore how this kind of case study approach illuminates the general process of creative thinking.

Missing from Gruber's account, of course, are the conceptual links between universal and unique (see Chapter 1) that make clearer the unique qualities of Darwin's thinking and the differences between thinking at the frontiers of a field and thinking at other levels and in other regions of developmental advance. Still, the Darwin analysis is a striking example of the value of a developmental process frame of reference for the understanding of creative thinking. By drawing attention to the developmental features of Darwin's thinking, Gruber has made a contribution to the understanding of all creative processes; it is this frame of reference that gives Gruber's work its power and its generality beyond the specific case. Obviously I hope that the extensions of developmental theory proposed elsewhere in this book and drawn upon in this chapter will enhance the viability of a process approach to the study of creativity.

5

eaRly proòigious achievement, òevelopmental theoRy anò eòucation

Fred Barlow, the author of a semipopular book on child prodigies published in 1952, wrote: "From time immemorial, unusual specimens of humanity have attracted and amazed the wise men of the ages, but it is only during the last century or so that the study of mental prodigies has been conducted on a scientific basis" (Barlow, 1952). Barlow proceeds to present a fascinating array of anecdotes about prodigies, both legendary and obscure, of which the following is a typical example:

> Christian Fredrich Heinecken, a German, who was known as the Infant of Lubeck from the place he was born in 1721, is said to have talked wihin a few hours after his birth. Besides his remarkable faculty for numbers, he is said to have known, at the age of one year, all the principal events related in the Pentateuch; at two was well acquainted with the historical events of the Bible, and at three had a knowledge of universal history and geography, Latin and French. People came from all parts to see him, and the King of Denmark had him brought to Copenhagen in 1724, in order to assure himself of the truth of what he had heard regarding him. But shortly after this, little Heinecken was taken ill and predicted his own death, which took place in 1725, at the tender age of four. (pp. 135–136)

To the extent that scientific inquiry is represented in this passage and in the interpretations that follow it, it is in the form of opinions of various authorities about the nature of prodigiousness in children. Not surprisingly, given that Freudian and Darwinian interpretations of human behavior were both commonly invoked at that time, Barlow's "scientific" explanations tended to categorize prodigiousness as either unconscious

121

or inherited. Without denigrating the place of unconscious thought or the role of heredity in mental ability, however, the phenomenon of the prodigy is certainly not adequately explained by these factors any more than are the origins of psychosis, or for that matter, genius. With all due respect to Barlow's efforts, the fact is that child prodigies, while they have probably fascinated wise (and less than wise) men for ages, to this day have rarely been studied scientifically; indeed, they have rarely been studied at all.

For most of recorded history it was generally accepted that some things were inexplicable. To attempt to explain earthquakes or leprosy or madness was to tempt fate. For reasons neither clear nor obvious, prodigiousness in children seems to have been one phenomenon which has remained unexplained for as long as any in human history. One hint about why there has been such longstanding reluctance to take on the prodigy as a scientific problem may be contained in the meaning of the word itself.

The world "prodigy" has a long history. The present word has its origins in the Latin *prodigium,* which means literally "to say before" (*Webster's Third New International Dictionary,* 1961). From its early meanings as "something out of the usual course of nature (as an eclipse or meteor) that is a portent, omen or sign," and ". . . one that is abnormal or monstrous," the word prodigy referred to anything extraordinary or inexplicable for centuries. As scientific explanations for human behavior became more accepted, the term came to refer to "one that excites admiration or wonder" or "an extraordinary, marvelous or unusual accomplishment, deed, or instance."

In the last fifty years, the meaning of the word prodigy has come to reflect the impact of psychometric views of giftedness; prodigy today means "a highly gifted or academically talented child" (*Webster's,* 1961). I have discussed elsewhere the changing meaning of the word prodigy and of other terms associated with giftedness in children such as "precociousness" and "genius" (Feldman, 1979a). Briefly, the effect of the gifted child movement, which was founded by psychometricians in the 1930s, was to make IQ the metric by which various degrees of giftedness, including prodigiousness, were to be measured. Since by this definition a prodigy is simply a somewhat more extremely gifted child, i.e., a child with a higher IQ score, then both giftedness and prodigiousness are explained by their common association with IQ. It also followed from the IQ definition of giftedness that it was unnecessary to study truly extreme cases of ability because such children were not different in kind, only in degree, from their more modestly gifted peers. This seems to be one of the reasons that no systematic empirical studies of child prodigies have been carried out in this country.

It is true that these most recent changes in meaning reflect a further demystificiation of the phenomenon of the prodigy, and that such a process perhaps necessarily precedes systematic scientific inquiry.[1] But a byproduct of this process has been to ignore the unique qualities of the prodigy by equating him with the academically talented child. As we shall see, the available evidence indicates that prodigies do indeed score well on standard intelligence tests, but not higher than other children identified as gifted. An explanation for the *extraordinary* performance of a prodigy must go beyond the presence of a high IQ. So far as is known, prodigies have IQ scores no higher than thousands of other children who do very well in school but who show no signs of such extraordinary performance in a field that is usually only the ken of adults. It is this truly extraordinary performance that is the hallmark of the prodigy and that begs for an explanation.

In the decades since World War II, the credibility of the IQ notion of intelligence has come under intense scrutiny. It is safe to say at this point in time that, while not without its supporters, the viability of IQ as an indicator of basic intelligence is at a fifty-year low (Elkind, 1967; *Harvard Educational Review*, 1969, Nos. 1, 2, 3; Resnick, 1976). Regardless of the other effects of the declining confidence in the meaning of IQ scores, it is probably good news for the study of prodigies since the emphasis on IQ seems to have inhibited inquiry into the nature of prodigiousness in children.

The waning of the psychometric view allows us to reconsider the prodigy as a unique expression of human capability and to restore some of the ancient meaning of the term. Implied by this turn of events is the belief that prodigiousness is again worthy of study in its own right. It also raises the question of what frame of reference shall guide us. The premise I wish to pursue in this chapter is that the same frame of reference which seems to be replacing IQ as a way to think about intelligence will also prove to be a worthy guide to understanding prodigiousness in children. Cognitive-developmental theory as exemplified in the work of Jean Piaget and his followers has had increasing impact on the field of intellectual development (e.g. Brearly, 1970; Elkind, 1976; Furth, 1970; Schwebel & Raph, 1973); a Piaget-based conception of intellectual development also guides our consideration of the nature of the child prodigy. However, in this chapter my aim is more ambitious: I hope to show that cognitive-developmental theory will itself be enriched and transformed as it attempts to encompass the prodigy. Perhaps most important

[1]Scientific research on prodigies is not wholly nonexistent. While there have been no major works done by American investigators, two books on the subject by European psychologists have appeared: cf. Revesz, G. *The psychology of a musical prodigy.* Freeport, N.Y.; Books for Libraries Press, 1970, orig. Harcourt, Brace, 1925; Baumgarten, F. *Wunderkinder psychologische untersuchungen.* Leipzig: Johan Ambrosius Barth, 1930, translated by Susan Phillips, Department of German, Tufts University, 1976.

for the purposes of the present chapter, I will try to show that the kinds of changes required to make developmental theory more relevant to child prodigies will also enhance the theory's potential to inform and guide the practice of education.

DEVELOPMENTAL THEORY AND PRODIGIES

Cognitive-developmental theory is, of course, identified with the work of Piaget and his collaborators at the University of Geneva and elsewhere around the world. The cognitive-developmental point of view has been elaborated and extended by investigators both within and without the Piagetian camp (for example, Langer, 1969, 1974; Turiel, 1966, 1969, 1974; Inhelder et al. 1974; Kohlberg & Mayer, 1972), but prodigies have not been included in these elaborations. The basic tenets of the theoretical point of view have been presented elsewhere and need not be elaborated here (cf. Cowan, 1978; Flavell, 1963; Furth, 1969; Kohlberg, 1966, 1969; Inhelder & Chipman, 1976). For the present discussion, we will reexamine the major assumptions of cognitive-developmental theory to see how well they might apply to the phenomenon of prodigiousness in children (see also Chapter 1). Recall that these assumptions are ones of the universality of cognitive advance, the spontaneousness with which stage-by-stage progression is achieved, and the constructive nature of the progression itself.

Universality and Sequentiality

Obviously the prodigy is an extremely unusual phenomenon, and would seem to reflect anything but universal achievements. But in another sense there are aspects to the prodigy's experience which can be properly considered universal. In other words, while it may well be impossible to explain the unique characteristics of a prodigy in terms of universally achieved cognitive advances, it may nonetheless be instructive to consider the extent to which a prodigy shares such universal cognitive-developmental experiences with others.

According to theory, prodigies will go through the same set of stages in the same sequence as other children around the world, but they can be expected to move through these stages at a more rapid rate (Piaget, 1973). Piaget writes:

> These same stages were found everywhere. But on average no earlier understanding was found with the children of Geneva, even those of a distinguished rank, as we shall soon see. In other words, there is a minimum age for understanding these concepts except, of course, for certain selected social groups, such as children of the talented. (p. 7)

In fact, by its very nature, the universality assumption demands that all children who are not organically damaged should exhibit the same basic pattern of development. Thus, according to theory, prodigies would not be exceptions to either the universality or sequentiality assumptions. Prodigies may show evidence of having achieved later stages of intellectual development at an earlier age than other children, enabling them to use their higher-level capabilities to master a complex field. Their path to more advanced levels in thinking, however, should be the same as that of other children, passing by the same landmarks in the same order. The only difference is that the typical child is taking a stroll, while the prodigy may be sprinting for all he or she is worth.

Spontaneousness

Although cognitive-developmental theorists have not directly addressed the issue of whether prodigies display the same spontaneousness in their cognitive advances as do "typical" children, it is reasonable to expect that the achievements of prodigies would be considered by these theorists to emerge spontaneously in much the same way that other, more common developmental milestones are achieved.

There are really two issues here: one concerns the emergence of those universal domains of thought where there is no reason to expect prodigies to develop in different ways from other children. Prodigies would be expected to advance through these stages spontaneously, as do all other children. The second issue is more problematic and relates to the special achievements of prodigies. Are these achievements also the product of spontaneous forces? Certainly the folklore surrounding child prodigies suggests that their mastery of various domains is not dependent upon instruction or special conditions in their environments. As we shall see, folklore is misleading in this respect; while prodigies frequently show spontaneous interest in and progress with little instruction through the early levels of their fields, intense, systematic, prolonged instruction is invariably the rule.

Construction of Stages: Hierarchical Integration

The fourth assumption of developmental theory is that later stages are constructed out of earlier ones. This is known as hierarchical integration. When applied to child prodigies, this notion would imply that prodigies achieve succeeding developmental stages through a set of transition processes that are the same as those of other children. Again, insofar as the general stages of development are concerned, there is no reason to expect a child prodigy to move from stage to stage in a way fundamentally different from other children.

Cognitive-developmental theorists have generally not considered transition processes in domains other than the broad developmental stages (except in moral judgment and reasoning; cf. Kohlberg, 1971; Turiel, 1974), and hence the question of how individuals advance in more specific fields of endeavor cannot be answered in any great detail. It seems parsimonious, however, to expect that prodigies would use the same processes of transition as other children both in general developmental transitions and in the more specific ones associated with progress in their own special fields.

It is important to keep in mind here the distinction between the more general developmental progress associated with current cognitive-developmental theory and those more specific achievements characteristic of the prodigy. Developmental theory has emphasized the former and ignored the latter. In developmental theory the emphasis is upon universal sequences of logical abilities, not upon more specific manifestations of ability as seen in a particular nonuniversal domain such as mathematics or drawing or dance. The more general stages of development are typically viewed as providing the underlying capacity needed to achieve mastery in any specific field. Therefore, from a developmental perspective, the most straightforward interpretation of the achievements of a child prodigy would be that they represent an unusual application of more advanced stages of thought to a specific field or domain.

This interpretation of the prodigy as a child who can reason about some domain at an unusually high level raises a question of *synchrony* in development. Piaget's theory stipulates that advances in the underlying logical system must precede progress in specific domains. Kohlberg, for example, argues that the Piagetian stage of concrete operations is a necessary prerequisite to the more advanced levels of moral judgment and reasoning (Kohlberg, 1969). Thus developmental theorists would assert that general developmental progress should precede specific mastery. Furthermore, it is argued that a general transformation of the logical system takes place more or less across the board, i.e. synchronously. Piaget calls this notion of general movement forward "structures d'ensemble," i.e. structures of the whole. By this term Piaget suggests that once the capacity to reason at a more advanced level is achieved, it is achieved for all problems.

All developmentalists, including Piaget, agree that the use of any stage of reasoning—concrete operations for example—becomes more widespread with age. According to Piaget and his coworkers there is also an orderly sequence to the kinds of problems to which the new logical structures are applied. Piaget uses the term décalage to describe the delay in the application of structures to new problems. The cause of décalage is the "resistance" of various problems to the application of the logical structures (Piaget, 1971). Some problems are more amenable to solutions using the new structure while others are not. For example, it is easier to apply the operation of categorizing to a bunch of red and blue

flowers sitting in a vase than it is to apply the same categorizing operation to two flocks of birds in flight. The flowers sit sedately and allow
themselves to be put into piles based on their differing colors, while the
birds move about in space and "resist" the operation of counting (Piaget,
1971). It is not the availability of the categorization scheme but rather
the difficulty in applying it that accounts for the delay in using the
scheme in the latter case. According to Piaget, the apparent asynchrony
in the achievement of concrete operations, as illustrated in the categorization example above, is actually a delay only in the application of these
operations to specific problems. As we shall see, however, the very existence of prodigies poses problems for this notion of synchronous development.

The four assumptions of cognitive-developmental theory ostensi-
bly hold for all children, even prodigious ones. The study of child prodigies then can begin by using developmental theory to examine those
ways in which prodigies are the same as or different from other people.
Is a prodigy simply a preripened adult, as the ancient meaning of the
term suggests, or is it that the prodigy has a different (i.e. faster) internal
clock but is otherwise similar to the rest of humanity? Is the form and
pattern of development in a prodigy different in nature or merely different in speed? Is the prodigy "taught by nature" or pushed to excellence by ambitious parents or teachers? Developmental theory sharpens
these questions and puts them in a form where evidence bearing upon
them might be gathered. This sharpening and focusing may not in itself
put the study of prodigies squarely "on a scientific basis," but it should at
least pose questions which are answerable through the collection and
interpretation of data.

AVAILABLE EVIDENCE

Having considered issues about child prodigies that are sharpened by
cognitive-developmental theory, we may turn to the literature for evidence about prodigious achievement. Here we run into a virtual brick
wall. Only the scantest of evidence exists. As mentioned earlier, there
have been no systematic studies of child prodigies reported in the
American psychological literature.[2] Only two major works exist in the

[2]Kathleen Montour recently published a paper about one of the most noteworthy
prodigies born in this country, William James Sidis. Montour's case study provides fascinating anecdotes about Sidis's life and interesting interpretations as to the cause of his demise.
As such, it probably falls more into the realm of biography or psychohistory than
psychological research. This, of course, is a matter of opinion, and some may see Montour's piece as an exception to my contention that studies of child prodigies have not
appeared in the American literature. (see Kathleen Montour, "William James Sidis, the
broken twig," *American Psychology,* 1977, *32,* 265–279.)

literature that may fairly be called psychological research (Revesz, 1925; Baumgarten, 1930).

Both of these works are case studies; little empirical precedent existed for either (although the Revesz work was cited by Baumgarten). The investigators used a combination of interviews, observations of children both in and out of performing situations, formal assessments using the available techniques of the day, and anecdotes from families, teachers and acquaintances to gather information about the children they studied.

Revesz's book is about a single musical prodigy, Erwin Nyiregyhazi, while Baumgarten studied nine children whose achievements had brought most of them to public attention before the age of twelve. These children included "two piano virtuosi, two violinists, one orchestra leader, one girl artist, one geographer and one boy chess wonder." Although the amount of information about each of the cases in the Baumgarten book is much less than the single case studied by Revesz, there are certain methodological similiarites between the approaches taken by the two investigators.

The only other empirical study of prodigies of which I am aware is one that I have undertaken over the past few years. My study is similar to those of Revesz and Baumgarten in that it uses a case study approach, but my methods have differed somewhat from theirs. To the extent that I have used formal assessment procedures, I have done so with developmental rather than psychometric measures. I have not, for example, done any IQ testing with my subjects. Both Revesz and Baumgarten used various measures of the sort which were later to become parts of IQ tests, although neither researcher could actually compute IQ's for the prodigies. In addition, I have tended to concentrate on examining the process of educating these children in their specialities, observing closely the ways in which their teachers instruct and guide them to more advanced levels of achievement.

My study has included as many as six children over the three years I have been actively engaged in this research, but I only have developmental data on three of my subjects: two eight-year-old chess players and a ten-year-old composer. In addition I have observed and interviewed a six-year-old writer, a two-and-a-half-year-old child with exceptional abilities in mathematics and language, and a six-year-old natural science prodigy. I have also made less formal observations of several other children who are under the age of ten and who show remarkable precocity.

Given the paucity of current knowledge, then, whatever conclusions we might draw about the nature of cognitive development in prodigies will have to be provisional and tentative ones. In this respect my interpretations of prodigious achievement should be taken as best guesses and suggestions rather than as firm conclusions based on extensive observations of a large number of prodigious children. I do have strong impressions built up over the years I have been doing this research, but as has already become clear, I also have a theoretical position which may tend to select certain aspects of the prodigies' behavior and to ignore others. The following is a brief review of the evidence that has been collected to date about children who show early prodigious achievement.

The Early Cases

Erwin Nyiregyhazi. Much of Revesz's study is concerned with comparing young Erwin's musical ability with that of other legendary prodigies of the past and of the great musicians of the day. While his earliest achievements were recounted by his parents and are therefore not altogether reliable, a picture nonetheless emerges of a very talented young child indeed. By the end of his third year, according to parents and "friends," Erwin had demonstrated perfect pitch and could reproduce any melody wtih great ease and precision. He began to play the piano at four and composed "little melodies," and in his fifth year his music-oriented family finally provided the youngster with formal lessons. From ages six to twelve Erwin achieved a certain notoriety, playing before the English Royal Family (he was Hungarian) and numerous other audiences in Budapest and Vienna. In 1918 the fifteen-year-old Nyiregyhazi came to the U.S. to pursue his burgeoning career.[3]

Revesz devotes much of his discussion of Erwin's prodigiousness to the child's acoustic and musical faculties, sight-reading abilities, musical memory, response to musical training, improvisation and modulation, and of course to Erwin's compositions themselves. In all categories, Erwin's ability seemed to match or exceed that of any known child musician alive or dead, at least insofar as could be ascertained through Revesz's testing. It seems a safe generalization to say that in all aspects of music, including the creative aspect, Erwin Nyiregyhazi could hardly have been a more remarkable prodigy.

In other areas of development Erwin was precocious but not to the same degree as in his music. In general intelligence, as measured by the best available psychometric test, the child was "above normal." The IQ

---

[3]Strangely, he arrived in the United States only to drop out of sight a few brief years thereafter. One is moved to ask why a child of such incredible early achievement and promise should have stopped performing; unfortunately, there do not seem to be any ready answers to this question (he continued composing, although he did not publish his works for nearly five decades). Nyiregyhazi has recently resurfaced, and while he has released recordings, he will still not perform in public; see *Saturday Review*, April 15, 1978.

metric was not used then, but it is reasonable to guess that Erwin would have scored above 140 IQ (see below).

Revesz found, though, that the mental test was inadequate for assessing the true nature of Erwin's capabilities, and went to some lengths to illustrate why this was so:

> He analyzed his own inner life in the manner of a trained psychologist, he talked about his observations on himself clearly and consistently, and that which will appear still more marvelous to many people—he expressed himself with great caution and remarkably pregnant phraseology. He often asked me whether what he was about to tell me would get "into the book," for in this case, he said, "I want to express myself correctly, and you must pay great attention to me; for a single wrongly-chosen word may alter the meaning of the whole thing." (p. 42)

The most remarkable anecdotes reported by Revesz are those which deal with Erwin's own compositions or the compositions of others. Of his own work, Erwin is recorded as noting:

> In composing, one wants the heart and the head; the heart alone or the head alone is not sufficient, for the heart may turn away a man from what is genuine music, and the head alone does not produce an expression of emotion, but merely scientific music, which may be interesting, but is not always beautiful. (p. 45)

Unfortunately, Revesz does not give us the age at which Erwin made these remarks, but they would be remarkable for any child, to be sure.

We may ask whether Erwin was a small adult in all aspects of his personal and intellectual life or whether he was a child with remarkable musical ability. Revesz tries to show that Erwin was not precocious in the sense of being predeveloped or preripened, but rather that he was a child in every sense of the word save the fact that his capabilities in music were extraordinary: "Erwin was a child in the full sense of the word: a clever, gay, friendly, charming boy" (p. 57) and "a . . . thorough observation of the trend of his mind and soul showed, however, that his activities, if they were in any way more developed than those of his contemporaries, were so only insofar as they were connected with his artistic activity" (p. 58). Thus, Revesz interprets Nyiregyhazi's musical prodigiousness as existing apart from his general development as a child, not markedly altering the other qualities that one expects to find in children of Erwin's age.

Wunderkinder

Baumgarten's research efforts were motivated by a desire to lessen what she perceived as a preoccupation with the achievements of child prodigies at the expense of attempting to understand the whole personalities of such children. In particular, she was interested in whether or not the precocious ability a child exhibited in one particular area was paralleled by capabilities in other areas. This question is similar to the question Revesz tried to answer for Nyiregyhazi; however, Baumgarten's interests extended further to include the children's attitudes toward their achievements, environment, family, etc. Baumgarten wanted to know if the child prodigy differs from other children in several different respects, including daily living.

Baumgarten's reports are briefer and more cryptic than Revesz's single case study, and her tests and assessments more general. She did not attempt to test the child's capability in her or his special field as Revesz had done with Nyiregyhazi. Instead, Baumgarten used a varying set of both standard and *ad hoc* measures to assess the abilities of her young subjects. Frequently travelling to the locations of concerts and performances around Europe to meet these children, Baumgarten's methods were necessarily adapted to the various interviewing situations. This, of course, makes it difficult to compare the cases with each other, but there is enough similarity in approach, method, and interpretation to draw some tentative generalizations.

The question of whether the prodigies Baumgarten studied are better considered children with great ability or small adults is easy to answer. Only in situations where a child was called upon to perform or behave like an adult would one get the impression that one was dealing with a small adult. Otherwise (and for the most part) the subjects in Baumgarten's study displayed the usual array of behaviors characteristic of children their age. Baumgarten writes, for example: "It is noticed with pleasure that these children are not what one would call precocious; on the contrary it is often their childlike naivete which is noticeable" and: "Generally the majority of these children appear to be an unusual mixture of child and adult. This mixture has a certain charm."

From these comments and from the descriptions of the children themselves, it is clear that these children were not human begins who were in any sense "monstrous." They were, rather, children who had been influenced by the talents they possessed, by the environment in which they found themselves, and by the responses of others to their gifts. Their presence was neither awesome nor fearsome. The children were different in some ways from others, to be sure, and these differences were not limited to their extraordinary gifts. For one thing, they had a great sense of responsibility to use their gifts for the benefit of their families. As a group they were (according to Baumgarten's summary) ambitious, pragmatic, wary of those who would do harm to them or their careers, passionate about their special fields, and generally unafraid of performing in public.

Each child also displayed a distinctive and unique set of personal qualities that distinguished her or him from others. Baumgarten believed that the actual gifts of her subjects were not all that rare but that they happened to be recognized and nurtured more in some environments and families than in others. The children themselves, however, were quite certainly unusual, and like Revesz, Baumgarten set out to try to determine the relation between the prodigies' specific talents and their more general intellectual functioning. The evidence presented in *Wunderkinder* speaks directly to the issue of IQ and prodigiousness. With but one exception (a child who spoke only Yiddish and whose family was very poor) the children performed well on a battery of standard intelligence test items. Although difficult to estimate in today's IQ terms, a rough guess at the range of scores would be from 120 to at least 160. The one exception was the child mentioned above, who was severely disadvantaged in the testing situation by linguistic and cultural factors. It is reasonable to conclude that this group of children exhibited remarkable capabilities in terms of their general intellectual performance. Yet it must also be stressed that thousands of children score in the IQ range 120–160, and very few of them achieve the success and notoriety of the subjects in Baumgarten's study. Indeed, the monumental 60-year-study by Terman and his associates has shown that few of the 1000 young children who scored above 140 IQ on the Stanford–Binet test have achieved truly great eminence in their lifetimes (cf. Vols. I–V, *Genetic Studies of Genius*; also Feldman, 1979b; Sears, 1977). Thus, while Baumgarten's prodigies were generally quite bright in the usual sense of the word, their general intellectual level cannot explain why they were so outstanding in their particular fields.

Fortunately Baumgarten recognized that the children's overall intellectual competence could not adequately account for their special talents. Not content to reach a judgment about the general level of ability of each child, Baumgarten searched her data for clues about areas of especially good performance; she even tried to see patterns or combinations of abilities that distinguished the group as a whole or any one of the children individually. It must be stressed once again that Baumgarten's methods and thus her data are very fragmentary, but some interesting leads emerged, particularly in the combinations of abilities that individual children seemed to display.

As example or two will communicate the flavor of Baumgarten's results. Some of her findings are counterintuitive, such as the following:

> It has been recorded that many a prodigy could not solve the tasks that a normal child solves without difficulty, and then on the other hand the most difficult tasks provide absolutely no difficulty at all. We saw how the violinists and pianists demonstrated bad hand coordination in bending wire, in drawing and folding and cutting, etc.: although in one case a girl violinist demonstrated good technical qualities and a gift for drawing.

We also learn that a six-year-old boy who was extraordinarily good at map drawing had difficulty making a circle out of two or three sections, a pentagon from two sections, or a rectangle from three sections. Yet he solved Porteus maze problems, finding correct routes through mazes up to and including those appropriate for fourteen-year-olds. This same child was able to draw a reasonable geographic map of a route the family had driven from Bern in Switzerland to Italy and also the trip back by a different route!

Other combinations of abilities seem to make more intuitive sense. A chess prodigy had a good memory for numbers and was adept at abstract tasks like answering hypothetical questions such as are posed in the Talmud. It is clear that no single pattern of specific abilities characterizes the group as a whole, yet Baumgarten found certain distinctive combinations of abilities in each of the children, combinations which could plausibly be linked to the fields in which the prodigies performed. There are, of course, real problems in trying to make sense of the Baumgarten data: in most instances only one prodigy was tested in each field, making it hard to tell if a combination of abilities was idiosyncratic or common to a field. The tests used were often outrageously labeled. For example, choosing the "prettier," i.e. more Anglo-Saxon, of two line drawings of female faces is called "aesthetic sensibility" (this item is still included in the Stanford–Binet). Despite these limitations it seems reasonable to conclude that "general ability" was quite high in these children, and that specific combinations of abilities could be identified which provide a suggestive though clearly incomplete explanation for their early achievements. Perhaps, as Baumgarten believed, it is necessary to cast a wider net than the testing of intellectual abilities to explain the prodigy's remarkable achievements, examining factors of inheritance, temperament, family, education, environment and culture.

While my own work with prodigies has not considered all of these issues in detail, I have tried to broaden my approach to include aspects of the phenomenon of prodigiousness in children not present in these earlier accounts. Furthermore, I have found it necessary to consider what changes in theory would be necessary to account for prodigiousness in children in the light of the available evidence.

The Current Study of Prodigies

Two Young Chess Players: A Study in Contrasts. During the Fall of 1975 I began to study, on an informal basis, two young chess players from the New York metropolitan area. Both were eight-year-olds at the time. Each was ranked in the top twenty chess players under age thirteen by the national system based on tournament play. Although approximately of equal overall strength as chess players, the two young boys were markedly different in almost every other quality I could detect. I have observed both children in lessons with their Chess Master teachers, at tournaments, in social situations with other members of their families and other chess players, and have also spent some time talking with them individually. The observations took place over approximately a two-year period and were largely unstructured. Tape recordings and transcripts were made of some of these sessions. The question guiding my work with these children, as well as with others I have observed, is the extent to which they exhibit combinations of childlike and adult qualities, particularly in their thinking.

Child A is rather small for his age, a thin, intense and quiet child. Outside of the chess club, where I watched him play and where he takes his chess lessons, there is nothing that would strike an observer as unusual or extraordinary about this child. His behavior is typical for his age, although he would certainly not appear as gregarious as other children, at least in those settings where I have had the opportunity to observe him. Child A usually arrived for lessons or meetings or tournaments with his father; an obvious warm and affectionate relationship exists between father and son. The father spends much of his weekend time arranging, transporting, waiting, assisting and encouraging his young chess player son. This is not done, so far as I can tell, because the father has ambitions for his child. It rather seems that this father is simply trying to help his son do something which is obviously important to the boy.

It is at the chess board that my subject shows his most distinctive characteristics. I have rarely seen a more intense, tenacious, nondistractable child of this age. At a tournament I watched this boy spend almost eight straight hours at a chess board with only a brief break for lunch (of which he ate very little). Watching this child play in a tournament is a study in concentrated energy. His entire collection of intellectual and emotional resources seems focused on those 64 squares in front of him. He rarely gets up to leave his board during play, preferring to exert his will over the pieces in front of him and, ultimately, over his opponent. He frequently plays against individuals three times his age or more, but this seems to make little difference.

The only occasion when I saw direct evidence of my subject's youthfulness was at a prestigious tournament in New York which happened to be taking place at the chess club where he was scheduled to have a lesson. As some of the better known chess players arrived, my young subject showed his enthusiasm and excitement as he met his heroes. He arranged for a quick "pick-up" game with one of the participants before the tournament began, losing the game to the Grand Master only after 25 moves. This was a performance considered quite remarkable for a player of his age and rating. He beamed with childish pride and excitement as he made his way among the room full of adults.

The other chess player I have studied seems, in contrast, to play for the sheer joy of the game, and although he works hard at it, seems much less invested in chess and much less intense and focused in his approach to the game. Whereas Child A rarely moves during a game, Child B is up and down like a yc-yo at almost every exchange of moves. He also seems to have a more "philosophical" attitude toward winning and losing—he is relatively little disturbed when he loses and less triumphant when he wins.

For this child, chess is only one of several interests; sports also play a large part in his life. If baseball season comes along, chess is put aside for a time. Child B's father has expressed ambivalence about his child playing chess, since he sees many other possible fields in which his son might excel, including baseball. Nonetheless, Child B's father also puts an enormous amount of his own time and energy into his son's chess career. In contrast to Child A's father, whose primary purpose seems to be to respond to his son's interest in the game, Child B's father pursues the additional goal of success, notoriety, and publicity for his son's accomplishments. The child himself seems remarkably unaffected by the considerable attention lavished on him or by the remarkable fact of his own achievements. Child B seems to take the whole chess experience with healthy good humor. This is not to say that he does not enjoy his role as a chess prodigy, nor that he does not put tremendous effort into his game, only that he does not seem overly affected by attention or success. This is the case, actually, with both young chess players who, by the way, know each other and have played each other from time to time in tournaments. They are taught by different teachers, however.

These teachers, like their students, present a study in contrasting styles, although some aspects of their methods of teaching chess have proved to be quite similar. Child A's teacher is a young Master, a former chess Olympian, who placed his young student on a rigorous regimen of chess discipline. The other, an almost legendary teacher of great chess players, teaches in a more relaxed, less demanding way. Good-humored banter and friendly sarcasm between teacher and student are frequent for this pair. Obviously very attached to one another, teacher and student thoroughly enjoy themselves at each lesson. Thus, on the surface, the two teachers' styles seem to complement the styles of their students. It is possible, of course, that the teachers were chosen for these qualities, or that they adopted a style appropriate for each student. There is no evidence, however, that either of these teachers was selected for these reasons, and from watching them with other students, their styles seem to remain relatively consistent across students.

Despite the surface differences there are also some striking similarities in the actual substance of their lessons. Both teachers, the young disciplinarian and the patriarch of chess, constructed a "curriculum" consisting primarily of games of the great masters of the past. Each chose a former world champion whose style of play most resembled his student's and used this champion's games as a base on which to build a curriculum. Also, each teacher seems to lead or guide his student through the great transformations in the game of chess over the past century or so. Finally, each teacher goes over, move by move, recent games that his student has played in tournaments and important games in other recent tournaments. Teacher B also tends to provide his student with much literature and folklore about chess, whereas Teacher A concentrates on homework problems, specialized lessons on openings and endgames, and building specific skills through drill and practice.

Overall, my impression of these two eight-year-old chess players is that, except for in a chess club, one would be hard pressed to find qualities about them that set them apart from other eight-year-olds. Different from each other to be sure, both seem in their individual ways to be healthy, well-adjusted, happy youngsters who happen to have an extraordinary talent. If there is any quality about them that is distinctive, it is perhaps their ability to be at ease with adults, at least in chess-related situations. Certainly both boys are bright and would almost certainly be labeled academically "gifted." But what is most remarkable about these youngsters is not that they are intellectually talented in general, but that they seem so much like typical children their age in every way except chess.

As typical as both boys seemed to be as eight-year-olds, they were truly exceptional chess players for their ages. As was true for the prodigies in Baumgarten's study and to some extent for Nyiregyhazi as well, perhaps the most striking pattern that emerges in these two boys is that combination of childlike qualities and adult capabilities.

A Young Composer and Violinist. In the summer of 1976 I began the first of many visits with Child C, a nine-year-old composer and violinist. I arranged to see this child through his composition teacher, who is a composer of some standing living in Boston. The child is driven by his mother to Boston for these lessons each week from a small city in another state more than two hours away. Sometimes a younger sibling (aged four at the time) accompanies them. In the two years that I observed this child I have only met the father once, at a concert near the family's home city, while my assistant met him on a visit to the family home to administer a set of developmental measures (to be discussed later).

I was told by his composition teacher that Child C was the most extraordinarily promising student this teacher had ever taught or known. "He's too good to be true" the teacher said in an early interview. Serious, adultlike, intellectually advanced, highly motivated and competitive, this student has been composing since he was six, sometimes writing works he could not play himself because of limitations in his own reach and finger span. Possessed of near-perfect pitch, Child C's skills were being honed by a bevy of five or more teachers at three or more locations around the city of Boston. Besides the theory and composition classes I attended most frequently, Child C attended violin, solfege, chamber music, and piano lessons, as well as a monthly master class for the violin. All of these classes took place on the same day (with the exception of the monthly violin master class).

Several years later, when not yet twelve, Child C won a competition to play a solo violin piece with an orchestra near his home city. He was officially too young for the contest, but had been permitted to enter when his teachers intervened. As far as I could tell, Child C showed no apprehension before, during or after the performance. He seemed to have the flair of a solo performer and loved to perform in front of an audience. He also seemed to have a noble presence, accepting congratulations and basking in the attention, yet not being surprised or overwhelmed by it.

More remarkable still was a performance I attended at a local civic organization in his home city. The accompanist for the performance had refused to play the day before the scheduled event. After a day described by his mother as "the worst day of my life," and after a last minute replacement had been driven in from Boston, I watched the boy take the stage with poise and confidence and then give the finest performance of his young career, as judged by his composition teacher. This teacher is quite opposed to the child's performance career but still had to grudgingly acknowledge how good the performance had been.

During the first year I observed Child C the tension between the two careers of performer and composer reached a climax. This tension now seems to have been resolved, more or less, and the child is pursuing a career as a solo violinist. He is entering competitions, studying with prominent master violinists and is otherwise being groomed for the soloist role.

It should be noted perhaps that Child C, along with the two young chess players, attends public school and does very well at his studies, although perhaps not brilliantly. Neither athletic nor particularly socially outgoing, Child C seems to have more difficulty getting along with classmates and neighborhood children than do the chess players. Yet, the overall impression is one of a happy, well-adjusted and often charming young man. Perhaps because he was two years older than the chess players, and perhaps because it is just the way he is, Child C seems less a mixture of child and adult than my other subjects. Only when at home did his childlike qualities surface. My asisstant describes an episode in which Child C arrived home from school with a bruised knee, and, for all his prodigiousness, behaved like any other ten-year-old when his mother asked what had happened: with a mixture of indifference and embarrassment, matter-of-factness and acceptance of concern were evident in the young boy's behavior.

A Scientist, a Writer, and a Very Remarkable Three-Year-Old. The three children described above were my original three subjects. As part of the study they were given a battery of developmental measures to be described in the next section. In addition, I have had the opportunity more recently to observe several other remarkable young children, of whom the three to be described briefly in this section are perhaps the most noteworthy.

Two of the children were six years of age when I first met them, and the third was two-and-a-half. All are boys. Child D, an impish looking six-year-old, was referred to me by a colleague who studies mathematical talent in children. Certainly Child D *is* talented in mathematics; he is tutored by a mathematician weekly, but his passion seems to be natural science. I was told by his parents that he reads college level physics textbooks, that he has read more than 100 of Isaac Asimov's books (including both science fiction and science), and that he has a passion for the Smithsonian Institution. In my meetings with Child D, I have been impressed with his enormous, almost encyclopedic store of facts which he interjects appropriately in arguments (into which he ingenuously lures unsuspecting psychologists). In particular, his grasp of geography and the spatial qualities of the universe is incredible. It is as if he shared the typical fascination of six-year-olds with the planets, but took it to a level of comprehension beyond that of most adults.

With bright blue inquisitive eyes, an athletic body, an engaging smile, and a passion for skateboards, Child D would not be singled out from his age peers except intellectually. His parents have tried both Montessori and public schools, and have encountered the continuing problem of trying to find an appropriate educational environment for their budding natural scientist. The younger of two boys, (all of the other children, including the two yet to be described, are first-born males) Child D often finds himself at an intellectual advantage but physical disadvantage with the other males in the household. On the whole, though, there is a healthy forebearance and good-humored acceptance of the remarkable intellect and unusual interests of this child.

Whereas Child D shows signs of becoming a natural scientist (he is not far enough along to tell for sure), Child E seems clearly destined to become a writer. Having taught himself to read before age three (this he has in common with both Children C and D), Child E taught himself to type at age four and has been typing all manner of things since then with great gusto and facility. He writes short plays and stories, novels which he begins but does not finish, letters and newspapers. None of his works to date would be mistaken for an adult's writing, but they certainly could be taken for the works of a talented child at least twice his age. Child E attends a private "open" school in the Boston area, comes from a middle-class family like the other children in the study, looks like and is in many respects a typical six-year-old. His journalist father and teacher mother are older than most parents of a six-year-old first born, and their dedication to his education is remarkable. Indeed, the family moved to the Boston area largely to find resources appropriate to meet the needs of their child.

Rather small and birdlike in appearance, my initial impressions of the boy were that he enjoys his school and his classmates (it is not a school for gifted children, although my guess was that there are others there who would be so labelled). Since our meetings have been only brief ones, I cannot describe the boy in much more detail in these pages. There can be little doubt about his orientation toward the written word, however, even after knowing the child for as little as an hour or two. He plays with words, both in writing and orally, trying out detailed narratives, reciting long passages from plays and musicals, describing the activities of friends both real and imaginary with a relish and richness quite unique.

The third child I have been seeing recently was nearly three when I met him. His psychiatrist mother and biochemist father have put enormous energy into raising this child and providing for his education, expending a much greater proportion of their time than even the parents of the other prodigies. At our first meeting his parents reported that the child had a fairly extensive vocabulary in six different languages and was reading adult-level books. While an assistant and I did not see these feats with our own eyes, we did observe a truly exceptional child, one who exhibited an adultlike sense of humor and who leafed through a book on geometric solids, reading with comprehension descriptions of such strange forms as dodecahedrons.

Perhaps most impressive (and reassuring) was the childish, almost cherubic quality of this exceptionally gifted youngster. That his mind grasped meanings many years prematurely there is little doubt. At the same time, he showed himself to be a typical two-and-a-half-year-old in charming ways. It is impossible to know how much Child F's seemingly happy adjustment to life is due to the unstinting efforts of his parents to make him feel at home in any environment. Only time will tell how the wider community receives this phenomenal youngster, but undoubtedly it will require accommodation of all parties concerned.

All told, my coworkers and I have spent more than one hundred hours observing, interviewing, and studying the education of these six individuals. Other than the developmental measures on Children A, B, and C, no formal testing or evaluation has been done. Our findings to date, therefore, are more impressionistic than systematic. To say that we have done three years of pilot work is perhaps too strong a statement, but it is certainly true that our efforts have raised questions more than provided answers.

In the next section we will consider some of the issues that have been brought into focus by these informal and naturalistic observations of prodigious achievement in children. We will examine more systematically the nature of the mixture of child and adult qualities that seem to be characteristic of all prodigies. Are the adultlike qualities restricted to the child's special field or do they extend to others? Do the adult characteristics include emotional or interpersonal qualities as well as intellectual ones? Is it the case that our prodigies use formal operations, or are they simply very good at using concrete thought?

PRODIGIES AND COGNITIVE-DEVELOPMENTAL THEORY: LIKE ALL, LIKE SOME, LIKE NONE

Some years ago Clyde Kluckhohn and Henry Murray (1948) wrote that: "Everyone is in certain respects (a) like all other men, (b) like some other men and (c) like no other man" (p. 53). I would like to use Kluckhohn and Murray's wise observation as a point of departure from which to pursue my purpose, which is to show how the prodigy's mix of child and adult qualities is clarified by the universal-to-unique framework. Specifically, I will show that early prodigious achievement is: (a) like all other developmental phenomena, (b) like some other developmental phenomena and (c) like no other developmental phenomenon. Only with respect to (a) does existing developmental theory make predictions about prodigies. Some modifications of theory are needed to account for the other aspects of child prodigies, as we shall see.

Ways in Which Early Prodigious Achievement Is Like All Other Developmental Phenomena

The primary way in which early prodigious achievement is akin to the Piagetian stages of intellectual development—and therefore like all other developmental changes—is that both are achieved through a sequence of broad levels of mastery. Furthermore, in their general cognitive abilities prodigies resemble their age-mates much more strongly than one might expect. In those few instances where some kinds of psychological measures have been made (i.e. Revesz's prodigy, Baumgarten's nine cases, and my own subjects) it is clear that these extraordinary children do share general developmental qualities with their more average peers.

Data from a Preliminary Study of Early Prodigious Achievement. My assistant, Richard Bensusan, and I administered a battery of four cognitive-developmental measures in 1976 to the two eight-year-old chess players and the music composition student, who had turned ten in late 1975.[4] Our aim was twofold. First, we were interested in assessing the general developmental progress in each of these children in relation to his age peers. Second, we wanted to investigate the extent to which remarkable precocity generalizes across developmental domains. The available evidence about early prodigious achievement seems to present a strong challenge to Piaget's notion of décalage, almost a *reductio ad absurdum* of his assertions of synchronous development. The pattern of results for the three children we tested, presented in Table 5.1, illustrates why this is the case.[5]

Table 5.1 indicates that the performance of all three subjects fell well within the normal age range on each of the four measures. To be sure these children are all very bright and do well in school; likewise they did relatively well on the developmental measures we administered. But in none of these general developmental tests was their progress anywhere near the extraordinary levels they had achieved in their special fields. While these children have shown extreme prodigious achievement in chess and music composition, they fall within the typical range of variation in the more general developmental levels of logic, role-taking, spatial reasoning and moral judgment. Thus, in terms of Piaget's

[4]The four measures given were: (1) Inhelder and Piaget's (1958) five chemicals task, a test of the level of acquisition of various concrete and formal logical operations; (2) a role-taking task devised by John Flavell (1968) and his associates at the University of Minnesota; its aim is to test social/cognitive development by assessing the level of ability to take another's point of view; (3) a map-drawing exercise, an adaptation of Piaget and Inhelder's (1948) layout diagram task (Snyder, Feldman, & LaRossa, 1976) which gives a general estimate of the level of the coordination of spatial/logical reasoning; (4) a psychometric measure of level of moral judgment and reasoning prepared by James Rest (1974) based on Kohlberg's stages of moral development. See R. Bensusan. *Early Prodigious Achievement: A Study of Cognitive Development*, M.A. Thesis, Tufts University, 1976.

[5]It should be noted that in some of his more recent writings (e.g. *The development of thought: Equilibration of cognitive structures*) Piaget is more equivocal with respect to the issue of synchrony and less committed to "structures d'ensemble." Yet it is also true that Piaget has offered no substitutes to replace these ideas.

Table 5.1
Data Summary: Developmental Levels of Three Child Prodigies

Task	Subject A Composer (age 10:3)	Subject B Chess Player (age 8:7)	Subject C Chess Player (age 8:9)
1. *Map-Drawing* —six levels between ages 7 and 19: 10–11 year olds typically achieve level 3	Modal Level 3–4	Modal Level 2–3	Modal Level 2–3
2. *Moral Judgment*—* six levels from age 10 to adulthood. Level 1–2 typically achieved by 10-year-olds. Level 3–4 typically achieved by 13-year-olds.**	Modal Level 3	Modal Level 3	Modal Level 4
3. *Role-Taking*— Three scorable levels and one nonscorable category (N). Level 1 typically achieved by 7–9-year-olds; Levels 1-2 by 10–12-year-olds; levels 2–3 by 13–16-year olds.	Level 2	Level 1	Category N
4. *Five Chemicals*— Four levels from age 7 to adulthood. Level 1 typically achieved by 7–9-year-olds; Level 2, 9–12-year-olds; Level 3, 12–14-year-olds; Level 4, 14-year-olds and up.	Early Level 3	Level 2	Early Level 2

*Rest's instrument typically yields higher scores than the more standard Kohlberg interview.
**Rest's instrument not designed for use with children younger than 13 or 14.

universal stages they seem to be developing quite normally and unexceptionally. The two young chess players seem to be functioning at the late Concrete stage, while the ten-year-old composer shows signs of moving into a transition from Concrete to Formal reasoning.

A theoretical point arises here regarding synchrony in development which presents us with a conundrum: according to cognitive-developmental theory, to account for these children's adult-level performance in chess and music one would either have to argue that the cognitive development of these children was generally advanced beyond their years or that their extraordinary achievements were accomplished through the unusually facile use of immature cognitive structures (for example, Concrete Operations). Neither of these explanations seems plausible, but Piagetian theory cannot account in any other way for the observation that the prodigies studied show acceleration within a specific domain of thought while their general level of thinking seems to remain age-appropriate.

It should be noted that the three children we tested were chosen for study *precisely* because they had special talents in very specific domains. I wanted to demonstrate that there are instances of precocity that are difficult if not impossible to explain within existing cognitive-developmental theories. If the two chess players' performance at the game, for example, is at a level which unquestionably utilizes Formal Operational logic, then theory would require that these children have mental processes available to solve at least some other Formal Operations problems. We see that they do not, at least not with the measures used. Furthermore, the theory posits that certain tasks are more "resistant" to the application of various mental structures than others. If so, it follows that tasks which are less resistant should be solved earlier. Yet our prodigies violate these principles as well. They perform in a highly "resistant" domain at an advanced level long before they do so in any other. While their performance in general developmental domains is not markedly different from their age peers, in their chosen fields they have achieved a level of mastery characteristic of highly skilled adult practitioners. The existence of prodigies thus seems to violate Piagetian theory, particularly the notion of décalage, in that they advance rapidly within a single domain which should be very resistant to mastery.

Levels within Fields. If we accept the premise that prodigies tend to develop normally in terms of Piaget's universal stages of development, then we must account for the fact that they seem to outstrip their own stage to such an extent in their specific fields. This can be done if we imagine that achievement in specific fields, contrary to Piaget's expectation, is not dependent on achieving the most advanced stage of intellectual development but rather depends on advancing through levels of mastery of *a particular domain*. Although there are few data with which to examine this issue from an empirical position (cf. Turiel, 1977, 1979), I can offer some anecdotal evidence in support of the argument.

Chess may provide the most compelling case for levels existing within a domain of knowledge rather than within an individual. Chess players are rated on an elaborate system which yields a scale from 600 to over 2600 points. The scale is divided into several levels (e.g. "B player" = 1200–1400 points, "Grand Master" = above 2400 points). Although the specific transition points between levels are somewhat arbitrary, the levels themselves represent qualitative differences in competence. I have been told by a chess Master that players at one level can frequently tell the level of other players without knowing their point rating by simply observing how they play the game. The structure of chess—as reflected in the rating system—seems to be such that learning the game involves advancing through a number of discrete, qualitatively different levels of understanding and performance. As far as we know, no new player has ever started to play the game at an "A" (or even "B") level of competence, nor skipped levels along the way. These anecdotal observations seem to support the notion that progress *within* the field of chess is orderly and stagelike, even for child prodigies like Bobby Fischer and the two children in my own study.

Other supporting evidence is still more indirect. One of the most striking observations I have made of the three teachers who have participated in the study is that each one teaches in a way that is intended, at least in part, to recapitulate the history of the discipline, with a particular eye to the qualitative changes that have occurred in the structure of the field over time. The two chess teachers, despite radical differences in overall style, lead their charges through the great games of the great champions of the past, beginning with the same games by the same Masters from the early part of the last century and deriving similar principles about the changing game of chess. The composer takes his student back into medieval music and begins a trek through selected changes in musical composition that occurred over the succeeding centuries. In addition to taking an historical look at the field, all three teachers also introduce their students to its *frontiers*. In chess, games that have been played by the great Masters of the day at recent tournaments are poured over move by move. For the music teacher, concerts and recordings of major new works are analyzed and reanalyzed. Thus, the teachers create a tension between past and present and between past and future as well. Obviously not every change of structure in a discipline can be reexperienced by any one student, and the teachers are selective about what they choose to present. This selectivity seems to depend upon how the teacher perceives both his student's inclinations and the major changes in the discipline as well as upon what he aspires to achieve in the way of transmitting knowledge.

There is the fascinating possibility that each of the three teachers is trying, without necessarily knowing explicitly what he is doing, to conceptualize his discipline in terms of *developmental levels*. When asked if they see their domains as organized this way, all three confirmed that they did. Furthermore, each in his own way wondered how it could possibly be otherwise. Similarly, all three teachers agreed that their students were advancing through a set of levels that corresponded, roughly, to those constituting the history of the discipline itself. None of the teachers saw his young student as fundamentally different from any other individual who aspires to reach the highest levels of his field—what was distinctive about the three prodigies, according to their teachers, was the speed with which the children had progressed through the levels. Prodigious achievement, then, is like all other developmental achievements in that it occurs through a set of stages or levels.

Ways in Which Early Prodigious Achievement Is Like Some Developmental Achievements

Those achievements which have been typically referred to as *developmental* in the literature are abilities which all of us eventually acquire. Indeed, one of the most significant contributions of developmental theory and research, particularly the work of Piaget, has been to draw attention to those universal qualities. *However, the central premise of this chapter is that early prodigious achievement is also developmental, despite the fact that few of us experience the incredible rapidity of achievement, or even the passionate dedication that is the hallmark of the prodigy.*

I see in early prodigious achievement the qualities of the more general developmental changes, except for two: (1) early prodigious achievement is not a universally occurring phenomenon (although it does depend on the existence of certain universally acquired thought processes); (2) the achievement of precocious mastery is not "spontaneous" in the sense that Piaget tends to use the term. Early prodigious achievement will not occur in the absence of specialized resources and intensive efforts on the part of master instructors, i.e. it will not occur without education. In this respect, early prodigious achievement is similar to other nonuniversal developmental achievements.

The specific domains of nonuniversal achievement are less likely to be mastered by all as we move from the universal to the cultural and on to the unique regions of developmental advance (see Chapter 1). For cultural domains all members of a group are expected to reach at least an acceptable level of mastery of the different domains, i.e. to advance to a certain stage of development. Domains associated with the disciplined region of the continuum are more optional. These are typically mastered in their more advanced stages in adulthood as part of work or adult-level play. It is important to note that cultural and disciplined (as well as the other) domains of knowledge are not independent of each other. For example, in order to achieve the disciplined mastery of a mathematician, one must first learn some basic facts about numbers and their manipulation. This is an achievement of cultural knowledge. The mathematician goes beyond cultural mastery by using his knowledge of numbers in a qualitatively different way from those of us who can do little more than check restaurant bills or figure out which size can of applesauce is the best buy. It should be clear, though, that the mathematician could never function at a highly specialized, disciplined level if he had not first learned about the more basic properties of numbers.

For all regions of the universal-to-unique continuum other than the universal one, then, some form of intervention or instruction is essential. Domains in all regions, be they universal, cultural, or unique ones, however, seem to be structured so that individuals advance through qualitatively different levels (or stages) of achievement as they gain mastery over the domain. To illustrate the process of advance, let us examine how prodigies progress as they are prepared to practice their crafts.

The Education of a Prodigy. Folklore on child prodigies suggests that such children perform dazzling feats in their fields with very little instruction or practice. We read, for example, of the young Yehudi Menuhin who refused to play with a toy violin at the age of four, lamenting "But it does not sing!" (Magidoff, 1955). And in Vladimir Nabokov's novel *The Game,* loosely based on the life of chess Master Samuel Reshevsky, the eight-year-old protagonist is mesmerized the first time he sees chess pieces on a board. It is clear almost from his first confrontation with chessmen that this child was born to be a chess player, at least so Nabokov's story goes.

But contrary to this popular image of the child prodigy, it is clear that early prodigious achievement does not occur without extensive and often formal instruction. It is true that such children may reach a *relatively* high level of performance with *relatively* little instruction, but past a certain point either the child is provided with expert instruction or the promise of the prodigy is likely to remain unfulfilled.[6] One of the young chess players in my study asked his father to teach him to play chess after

---

[6]There is of course the danger of *too much* or *too intense* instruction with talented children. Stage mothers and fathers have probably contributed to the "early ripe, early rot" assumption many people still hold about prodigies.

watching televised coverage of the Fischer/Spassky World Championship Chess Matches in 1972. The child was four years old at the time of his request. His father knew just enough chess to teach the eager child the basic moves of the game, which were quickly learned. That summer the family took a membership in a swimming club and the boy swam some, but spent most of his time beating everyone who played chess at the pool. Before the age of five the child had achieved a level of play higher than that of the average New Jersey suburbanite. Here was a child who looked as if he'd been "born to play chess." And yet, while his performance was remarkable to be sure, it was still a far cry from tournament level chess.[7]

It was during this summer that the boy's parents realized that something extraordinary was happening with their child's chess playing. His parents began to search for a suitable teacher, enrolled the child in a chess club, and began the arduous process of educating a prodigy. The problem of finding adequate instruction and experience for the boy was, happily, reduced by virtue of the family's geographical location: they lived near New York City, where there is an active chess subculture. If my young subject had happened to have lived in some other area of the country (say, Hutchinson, Kansas, for example) the chances of finding appropriate instruction would have been considerably lower. In fact, the chances of a youngster getting the crucial chess instruction is reduced greatly outside metropolitan areas in New York or California. Most of the strong young players in the country come from around New York City or from Los Angeles or San Francisco. About fifty percent of the top chess players under age 13 come from one of these areas, which have only about ten percent of the population of the United States (cf. *Chess Life & Review,* December, 1977, p. 663).

The availability of instruction depends as much on the field itself as it does on the location of major centers of activity within the field. Early prodigious achievement simply will not occur unless a domain of knowledge is sufficiently evolved so that instruction is available in some reasonably efficient form to the "pretuned" potential prodigy. In this respect, prodigious achievement is not spotaneous in Piaget's sense, nor is it the consequence of developing a set of universal "natural concepts." It seems unlikely, for example, that there would be chess prodigies if chess were itself in such an early stage of its evolution that knowledge about the field could not be efficiently and systematically communicated. Chess has a technical language, as scholarly literature, and is even beginning to

[7]Parenthetically, it has been my experience that identifying a child prodigy is not difficult. As with this young chess player, a prodigy's talent asserts itself in the most obvious sorts of ways. With quite nominal exposure to the appropriate domain, the child with the proclivities for prodigious achievement will make such extraordinary progress that a parent would have to be truly oblivious not to recognize such exceptional talent.

evolve a pedagogy (Kane, 1974). Prodigies also seem to respond to early exposure to high level performance in their domains. For example, the two chess players in my study first saw the game played at World Championship level. Yehudi Menuhin was taken to the San Francisco Symphony Orchestra regularly before he was two years old. Likewise, the young composer I am studying heard classical music in his home virtually from birth. Once a child has been exposed to the higher reaches of the domain some means of effective instruction, including a pedagogy (or at least teachers who have individual pedagogies), seems necessary if the child is to move from passionate interest to high-level competence to unique expression.

With the children in my study it is too early to tell how they will relate to their domains as adults. We do not yet know whether these boys will eventually make unique contributions to their fields, or, indeed, whether they will even continue to pursue these fields as adults. Whatever else I have learned from my work in this field, though, of this I am sure: the road from extraordinary early mastery to the advanced levels of a domain is steep, treacherous, torturous, and above all, long—even for prodigies. Early prodigious achievement is a joint effort among dedicated individuals, of whom the prodigy is but one participant. In the case of Menuhin, for example, the entire family shared—indeed took as its primary task—the proper education of young Yehudi. In his case the enterprise was underwritten by a wealthy patron, and happily no expense or effort needed to be spared. The results speak for themselves (Magidoff, 1955), but a concordance of factors was necessary for Yehudi to realize his greatness: a dedicated family, a patron willing to pay for the education of the child, a child able to absorb all of the attention and still retain the humility necessary to accommodate distinction, the availability of appropriate educational opportunities, reasonably good health, family stability, etc. The experience of a prodigy is therefore in certain respects akin to the experience of anyone else who aspires to master a discipline. As we shall see, however, the prodigy's experience is also quite different in certain important respects.

Ways in Which Early Prodigious Achievement Is Like No Other Developmental Achievements

Early prodigious achievement is like no other developmental achievements in that the child prodigy represents an unusual (but not altogether discrepant) form of idiosyncratic expression. What distinguishes the prodigy from other children is that the selection of a disciplined body of knowledge is accomplished much earlier than is typical, and thus by definition the child who practices a discipline at an unusually advanced level does so in an idiosyncratic way. Recall from our earlier discussion that a combination of child and adult qualities is strikingly present in all descriptions of prodigies. Prodigious achievement is therefore idiosyncratic even when the child has as yet to achieve a distinctive style, specialty or *metier* that is more typically a natural outgrowth of mastery of the discipline itself. A mature style may be fashioned later, or it may not, but a prodigy can still legitimately be considered to have achieved idiosyncratic mastery of a disciplined body of knowledge. For some prodigies even basic cultural domains like reading and writing have not been mastered before the child has begun to explore the far reaches of his or her specially selected terrain. Such was the case, for example, with Erwin Nyiregyhazi, who was protected and guarded from the outside world (including the world of school) so that he could put all of his available energies into music performance and composition. The consequences of advanced work in one domain and limited experience in others seems likely to lead to performance that is a peculiar and very unusual combination of child and adult.

Therefore, what distinguishes the prodigy is not so much the fact of her or his achievement but the *timing* of that achievement relative to those in other regions of development. Typically, the performance of the prodigy is outstanding relative to other children, but less often is the achievement exceptional relative to mature practitioners in the same field. Thus, at six or seven years of age Bobby Fischer could defeat strong players twice his age, but until well into his teens he was no match for Grand Masters. Even the most remarkable of musical prodigies, Mozart, did not compose works that are now considered masterpieces until he was in his late teens and early twenties. What makes a prodigy so extraordinary, then, is the seemingly reciprocal relationship between a field or domain and the young child who aspires to master it. It takes most individuals decades to reach a level of mastery where expression can genuinely occur; the prodigy reaches this point much earlier. Reaching a level of mastery, however, is no guarantee that unique works will be forthcoming from the prodigy; it simply means that the early achiever has more time to find and use his "voice."

EARLY PRODIGIOUS ACHIEVEMENTS AS CO-INCIDENCE

The key difference between the developmental view of prodigies proposed here and other views of such children lies in how the phenomenon is conceptualized. Common sense tells us that a child prodigy occurs because of some *truly extraordinary characteristics of the child*. I think prodigious achievement is better conceptualized as a remarkable *co-incidence*, that is, of a fortuitous concordance of a specialized individual and a specialized environment (including a technology and pedagogy) during some period of time. During this time the conditions in the prevailing environment are such that it is possible for the individual to express this potential through a given medium, field, craft or discipline. This way of conceptualizing the problem, while it may seem obvious enough, has certain implications which seem to me far from obvious.

The idea of co-incidence is obvious in the sense that an individual must work *at* something or *in* some field to achieve prodigiousness. Suppose, for example, that Albert Einstein had been born fifty thousand years ago, or five thousand years ago, or even five hundred years ago; human morphological continuity over this time period has been such that this apparently could have happened (e.g., Washburn & Howell, 1960). Is it reasonable to suppose that Albert Einstein would have achieved the remarkable insights he did into the workings of the universe if he had been born before the era of science, or for that matter, of recorded history? Perhaps Einstein would have done something remarkable regardless of the age in which he was born, perhaps not. The point is that the transcendent quality of Einstein's achievement was as critically a function of the state of a field of knowledge at a particular point in its own history as it was a function of Einstein's talent.

Those familiar with Einstein's earliest years may be thinking that he was no child prodigy; he supposedly did not even speak until he was three or four years old. However, this example should serve to draw attention to the crucial importance for prodigious achievement of the state of development of a given body of knowledge, including its codability and communicability at a given moment in historical time. Of note in this connection is the fact that Einstein's field was physics, in which early prodigious achievement is (as yet) unheard of. The occurrence of remarkable achievement in a field by a young child (or for that matter, by anyone at all) depends on the existence and successful transmission of a highly evolved body of knowledge.

In early prodigious achievement, a child acquires vast amounts of knowledge in a very short time. The acquisition of this knowledge is facilitated when it is available in an organized and communicable form. Nonetheless, there is obviously something quite special about children who can do this. Taking chess as an illustration, the amount, abstractness and complexity of knowledge required to play master-level chess is enormous (Chase & Simon, 1974). The probability that an individual could be taught to play sophisticated chess games by the age of six or seven, as was the case for Bobby Fischer and for two of the children in my own study, is virtually nil. To deny the obvious gifts of such individuals requires massive distortion of the facts, but to ignore the importance of a highly distilled and communicable body of knowledge is equally shortsighted. Like my subjects, Bobby Fischer learned to play chess before he was six. From that time on, Fischer read hundreds of books about chess, had intensive formal instruction, and reached the rank of Grandmaster when he was fifteen—a remarkable achievement to be sure, but one which took more than nine years to accomplish (Collins, 1974).

Thus I see early prodigious achievement as the occurrence in time and space of a remarkably preorganized human being, born and educated during perhaps the optimal period and in a manner perhaps most likely to engage the child's interest and commitment to the mastery of a highly evolved field of knowledge. In other words, a "co-incidence" occurs, more remarkable even than the awesome talents which make it possible. This subtle, delicate coordination of elements of human potential and cultural tradition is to me even more dazzling than the abilities characteristically attributed to these children. The individual's abilities themselves will not lead to unique achievement or even necessarily to prodigious mastery of a field. Nonetheless, the current popular notion of prodigies still carries some of its ancient connotation of something out of the usual course of nature, of children who are somehow abnormal or monstrous. There is nothing "abnormal" or "monstrous" about co-incidence, however; it represnts an unusual but comprehensible occurrence brought about by a number of different forces that, in concert, produce prodigious achievement.

An optimal match of individual talent to environment is of course highly improbable; since the beginning of human history there are likely to have been many individuals who were preorganized for one specific purpose but born at a moment in time or at a place where their unique organizations had no appropriate environment through which to express themselves. It follows that when we see a natural experiment of the sort we typically refer to as a "child prodigy," what we are actually seeing is the successful occurrence of a co-incidence. As with any random process, early prodigious achievement is no more or less probable than any other combination of human and cultural factors mingling across a few moments of time. Since it seems to require a specially organized being and a highly evolved, accessible body of knowledge, however, instances of early prodigious achievement are actually rather rare.

Co-Incidence and Education

It is now possible to expand this view of co-incidence so that each human being may be viewed as a natural experiment in which an individual and his or her optimal environment "try to find each other." When such an experiment really works (in the sense of a remarkable match of child to field) it means that a fortuitous set of circumstances has prevailed. Our human progenitors have fashioned environments to receive and nurture the biological part of the "experiment" (that is, the child) based on traditions of knowledge and skill accumulated over the ages—including a crucial body of knowledge about how to educate the young. From time to time an individual comes along who seems to have been preorganized to derive full benefit from the hundreds of years of cultural preparation that preceded his appearance. In these cases, culture and nature seem to have been working in concert.

Early prodigious achievement indicates that occasional extreme reciprocity between an individual and traditions of knowledge is part of this continuing evolutionary process. The rare and remarkable match of child to craft, while riskier in the individual case, makes greater the likelihood of cultural adaptation to changed conditions over time. This is so because the prodigious achiever is more likely, if only in a statistical sense, to add to a culture's store of valued knowledge, to achieve a unique reorganization of a domain. By achieving the upper reaches of expertise at an early age prodigies have, if nothing else, more time to explore the intricacies and subtleties of their fields. Obviously, not all instances of precocious mastery lead to unique or creative changes in a body of knowledge; it is simply more likely that they will do so. And it is from among the contributions of prodigies and others that disciplined, cultural and universal achievements will eventually be selected (cf. Chapter 2).

The fact that there are not more examples of prodigious achievement suggests that, on the whole, Nature is a conservative gambler. I am not suggesting by this statement that Nature has a game plan, but rather that the few prodigies produced means relatively few chancey situations. Since the risks—as well as the likely payoffs—of producing a specialized organism are greater than the risks of producing a flexible one, and since a complex, subtle set of environmental forces is required for the pretuned organism to express its potential, it makes sense that relatively few astounding co-incidences of this sort would occur. To produce a large number of specialized individuals, limited in the range of environments to which they might respond, would seemingly go against the grain of evolution. Only with the security of numbers could such an improbable gamble pay off.

Sometimes, perhaps most times this gamble does not pay off; individuals may be preorganized for a domain with which they never connect. An implication of this dilemma is that some of these individuals may in some way be aware of their predicament. Although I have no systematic data to support this belief, I have encountered a number of individuals who feel that they have a significant contribution to make, but who seem unable to find something to do which expresses their unique preorganization, which satisfies the need to be really good at something. The desire to express an idea or to fulfill a need to communicate is one of the conditions for creativity. As Olga Korbutt, the remarkable Soviet gymnast, once observed in a television interview, "If gymnastics had not existed, I would have had to invent it!"

Looking at issues in this way points to the need to understand the reciprocal relations among intrinsic human talents, culturally evolved qualities of a field or craft or discipline, and traditions pertaining to the formal transmission of knowledge. Failing to recognize the contributions of any one of these factors is like watching a player piano: despite what it looks like, the piano does not play itself. Likewise, every great pianist is playing *music* which has a history too. To understand achievement one must understand the joint histories of all the participants, and this is especially true where truly remarkable achievement occurs.

The idea of co-incidence is thus intended to draw attention to the fact that prodigious achievement is only possible as a consequence of the most incredibly delicate interplay of forces, one set of which is the child's own unique qualities. These alone, however, will not produce a prodigy. They must be carefully coordinated with a number of other factors: a field of knowledge that is sufficiently evolved to serve as inspiration, resource, and challenge to the aspiring neophyte; a set of catalytic forces to assist the newcomer in traversing the byways and intricacies of the craft—educational forces in the broadest sense; and a few moments in time and space which permit all of the other forces to interact. Our tendency to be awed by the prodigy should not keep us from realizing that his or her achievements are all the more remarkable because of the incredibly improbable ballet of forces that must entwine if early prodigious achievement is to result.

About some of the forces that govern co-incidence there is as yet little more to say: children are more or less gifted in various domains; knowledge is more or less distilled and communicable; technologies are more or less evolved. Yet these forces not only can be better understood but perhaps even brought into more fruitful coordination with the other sets of factors that make up co-incidence. The forces that are of interest in the present context are, of course, those which bear on education.

If education is crucial for prodigies, and I have tried to show that it is, it is also true that prodigies are crucial for understanding and improving education. I have tried to indicate that co-incidence is not a notion that applies only to prodigies. In the view I have presented, the same sets of forces that interact and intertwine to produce prodigies also interact to produce all achievements. It is granted that co-incidence is a very broad notion and that its ability to guide observation is as yet limited. Nonetheless, it does attempt to draw all of development—universal as well a nonuniversal—into a single framework by invoking a common set of causal mechanisms. To understand the education of a prodigy is to begin to understand education in a way that transcends the specifics of prodigies themselves. It allows for the possibility of differential developmental progress in specific domains, accounting for the peculiar mix of adult and child qualities found in prodigies. It requires coordination and concordance, but not synchrony. This view does not render any less puzzling the fact that virtually no research on prodigies has appeared in the literature in the past forty years. But now, perhaps there are compelling reasons for learning more about early prodigious achievement within a framework where the existence of a prodigy makes sense and where understanding more about these unusual children may enrich our understanding of all development.

6
the chilò as craftsman*

In a book review that appeared in the *Phi Delta Kappan,* John Bremer, a former Commissioner of Education in British Columbia, wrote:

> If the world itself is elusive and ambiguous (and it seems increasingly to be so), then definitions should correspond; nothing would be more misleading than to present clear and distinct definitions in unequivocal terms. Some definitions are simply sloppy, and open education needs no more of them; but perhaps we would all profit from a definition if it were like a poem. A metaphor is "elusive and ambiguous" but it has its own kind of precision, and it requires for its completion, its fulfillment, the activity of the poet in each one of us. (1975, p. 719)

This chapter is a response to Mr. Bremer's request for a new poetic image to guide the educational process. The image to be explored springs from pressures for change in educational theory and practice from a source often referred to as "open education." Open or informal education, drawing largely from the model of the British Infant School, differently structures the learning environment so that the individual child has greater selection and choice over what he or she will do and greater control over what will be learned and how it will be learned.

The purpose of this chapter is to discuss and put into perspective images or views of the child that currently seem to reflect and guide educational practice, and also to show that crucial aspects of changing educational practice are not adequately represented in these images. My

*A version of this chapter appeared in the *Phi Delta Kappan,* 1976, *58,* 143–149. Reprinted by permission of the *Kappan.* I am indebted to Diane E. Levin of Wheelock College for her many substantive contributions to this chapter.

basic premise is that if education is to better fulfill its mission, the child's relationship to knowledge must be reconceptualized in a fresh image. The image I have in mind is suggested in the phrase "the child as craftsman."

It is not my intention to reject ideas that have guided generations of educators. In fact I will point out continued uses for each of these and argue for the preservation of certain of their aspects. My purpose is rather to draw implications from the developmental framework discussed in earlier chapters for discussions about education. I choose to put these observations in imprecise form because, following John Bremer's lead, it seems to me that precision in these matters is premature. My basic premise is that educational thinking has lost its sense of direction. "The child as craftsman" image is intended to suggest a possible banner behind which to regroup and pursue the elusive goal of educational excellence.

CURRENT IMAGES

There have, of course, been many images in educational thinking, but three, usually in combination, have contributed much meaning to policy and practice during this century. Each view has had a period of ascendance, a period of major influence, and periods when it has come under intense criticism. In order of ascendance, we may label them the "individual differences/trait tradition," the "environmental patterning tradition," and the "stage developmental tradition." In reaction to inadequacies in the first two, open or informal education has embraced the third. As should be clear already, I see even the traditional developmental view, improvement though it may be on earlier views, as having substantial limitations of its own.

Individual Difference/Trait Tradition

Deriving primarily from the works of Galton, Pearson and the other early correlationists, this view is one of a child with a certain set of essentially immutable traits, one or more of which determines both the speed and the amount he is able to learn. During the early years of the century there were few questions about what was appropriate for a person to learn; curriculum content was assumed to be rather unchanging and obvious. That the educational curricula of the day stressed classical Greek, Latin and Medieval poetry illustrates this point well. The idea was to take a child (in practice, many children) and to didactically present what was known to be valuable or "true." With the curriculum fixed in this way, it was only the child's traits or capabilities which would determine the extent to which he could absorb the knowledge presented by the teacher.

This is the guiding image of the child in the "traditional" class-room, where the responsibility for learning is placed on the child. Failure to learn in a traditional classroom is also the child's responsibility. The teacher, by virtue of having mastered the knowledge included in the curriculum did not need to demonstrate any special ability to teach. The responsibility of the teacher was to select what was taught, when and how. The presumption was, for the most part, that anyone who could do geometry could teach geometry; the question of whether geometry should be taught at all, or when a child should be able to learn it, was not perceived as a serious issue. The timing and sequencing of topics in the curriculum were set by the wisdom and experience of those who had been responsible for teaching long enough to have a sense of what worked and what did not. Thus curriculum development was based on accumulated wisdom from generations of trial and error.

Although this is an overly simplified account of the main features of the individual differences view, I think that it conveys a sense of the viewpoint fairly well. This view sees knowledge as acquired in units, one built upon the other. The ability to acquire knowledge is similarly understood in terms of one's capacity to learn relative to one's peers. The *amount* of knowledge gained is measured quantitatively, as is the amount of learning capacity. If a child is able to reproduce less than what a teacher has presented, then it is considered that the child's capability prevented him or her from learning all to be learned in a given period of time in a given classroom. Any student's ability and achievement may be measured on the basis of how much and how quickly material is assimilated relative to both the expectations of the teacher and to the other students in the class (or to some normative group).

Knowledge, from this point of view, is a stable body which exists independent from the individual who must acquire it. The extent to which an individual is capable of acquiring that body of knowledge is an indicator of the child's ability to learn. Both the manner in which the knowledge to be acquired is selected and the manner in which the child learns it are seen as essentially static and unchanging.

Environmental Patterning

The individual differences notion of the child as student worked fairly well as long as bodies of knowledge were believed to (and did) remain reasonably stable and as long as the responsibility for learning was placed primarily on the child. With the work of Watson, Pavlov, and especially E. L. Thorndike in educational psychology, the idea that the child was a vessel into which varying amounts of knowledge could be poured was fundamentally questioned. The questioning took more or less the following form.

If the basic mechanisms of learning are the same for all individuals (even for all organisms), then the amount that one learns should be a direct function of the kinds of experience in the environment one has had. If so, then it should follow that the *quality* and *amount* of experience will determine the quality and amount of material that is learned. Therefore, it is misleading to place the responsibility for learning on the child, who has only limited ways of knowing what is important to learn for survival and well-being. It is the responsibility of those who are more experienced to guide the learning process and select the information to be acquired.

The environmentalist view, or perhaps it is better labelled the *learning* view, thus removed responsibility from the shoulders of the overburdened child and placed it on the shoulders of the now overburdened teacher. No child was deemed too naive or dull to learn. Learning was a function of the environmental arrangements that a good teacher was able to make. In its extreme form, learning theory led to the ridiculous belief that "everyone is exactly the same as everyone else," to paraphrase Kurt Vonnegut. Without evidence to argue against the learning paradigm, however, it was very difficult to refute. And when refuted, it was usually with the individual differences notion just presented. Thus, for several decades, arguments seemed to seesaw between the two views.

The former, individual differences extreme, tended to characterize the child as having a set of essentially unchanging, built-in qualities that determined the amount that he or she could learn. Learning was to be done in the same time frame and with the same amount of exposure for all children. The process was assumed to involve acquisition of an essentially static body of knowledge up to the limits of the child's learning "capacity." The latter learning view saw the child as having virtually unlimited potential, and no significant differentiation among children's capabilities was acknowledged. In this view, if enough were known about how environments work, of the "contingencies of reinforcement" as Skinner puts it, all children would be able to learn in an effective step-by-step manner and all would eventually achieve equivalent mastery of designated bodies of knowledge.

Differences in achievement in the trait view are a function of the amount of learning ability in the child, whereas differences in the environmental patterning view are a function of the effectiveness of environmental engineering. In both, however, the child is the passive recipient of either a biological gift or a cultural one. His fate as a learner is in all important respects a function of forces beyond his own control.

Values of These Earlier Views

The inadequacies of the two views just outlined have become increasingly evident. Reaction to some of these limitations probably stimulated

English educators to create the many varieties of what we now call the British model, the open, or the free schools. Still, some valuable insights into both children and educational processes have been achieved as a result of these ideas about children and learning. Such insights and the wisdom that accrued from them should be preserved.

The individual differences notion of learning ability reminds us of the valuable fact that children *do* differ from one another in many ways, including in the quality and style of their learning. While the attempt to find a single comprehensive metric for the overall capability of a child (the IQ) has probably done as much harm as good, interest in the variety and diversity of intellectual and personal qualities has been a constructive expression of this view. Individuals do differ; they may not take in knowledge in the simple fashion that an individual differences view suggests, but children do learn at varying rates, use capabilities and skills uniquely, and react differently to various materials and to subtleties of teachers. It is folly to ignore these qualities, and the notion of individual differences helps draw attention to them.

The importance of careful analysis of subject matter is the most promising legacy of the environmental engineering or learning tradition. It is overly optimistic (in fact incorrect) to suggest that every individual is capable of learning every important body of knowledge and that each will learn it in the same way, but it has been demonstrated beyond doubt that careful arrangement of environmental conditions in and out of the classroom has substantial influence on the amount and quality of learning (cf. Skinner, 1968). To ignore the importance of the manner in which knowledge is best structured for transmission or the conditions under which rewards and punishments are effective is to ignore some of the more powerful and pervasive influences on human behavior. Thus, while it would certainly be misleading to place the entire burden for learning on the teacher or the "environmental engineer," there is no question that a *substantial* portion of the burden rests there. The danger, as has been amply illustrated in many overly mechanized "learning environments," is to assume that there are no significant factors *other* than the speed with which a student moves through a set of programmed steps.

The Stage-Developmental Tradition

The developmental view of childhood has been embraced with increasing enthusiasm by proponents of open education as well as by free school and deschool advocates. It is loosely based on the work of developmental theorists like Piaget, Bruner, Kohlberg, Werner, Loevinger and others. The child is seen as proceeding through a series of qualitatively distinct *stages*, each of which provides powerful rules for interpreting reality and guiding behavior. The source of these rules is the child's intrinsic tendency to interact with the environment in growth-inducing ways. The developmental view stresses that the child is involved in making choices and decisions about what is appropriate for his or her own development. The child, therefore, is a most significant agent in determining the pace, quality and pattern of his own growth.

While it differs from the individual differences and learning traditions in many ways, the developmental tradition also shares some of their characteristics. The developmental conception involves a set of hierarchically organized, invariantly sequenced, essentially inevitable stages through which the child passes. In this respect it has a strong nativistic bias, in common with the individual differences view. For the developmentalist, though, it is the universal sequence of stages of development that is biologically based, not the individual learning capacity of the child. According to this view the rate at which a child advances through the stages may vary, but the *sequence* is not subject to variation. In this respect it shares a premise with an environmentalist view.

The developmental view postulates a series of *universal* intellectual systems which all children acquire, and this is its distinctive quality. Each of these systems is qualitatively different from the previous one, as if the child traded in the computer that is his mind every couple of years on a state-of-the-art model, retaining some of the software from the old machine and salvaging whatever hardware could be integrated into the new model. As one system is integrated into the next, it provides the basic rules by which the child deals with the world. These rules may be of a cognitive nature (for example, those conceived by Piaget or Werner), social-emotional (like Erikson's or Loevinger's) or a combination (Kohlberg's moral judgment stages, for example). Sometimes the stages of one sequence are seen to be prerequisite to the stages of another; for example, Piaget's level of concrete operations is said to be prerequisite for Kohlberg's level of conventional moral judgment and reasoning (Kohlberg, 1971).

Thus, the developmental view is in some important respects very different in quality and substance from previous traditions. It posits a step-by-step, sequential, hierarchical set of changes that occurs universally, and it puts the child at the center of the process as an active participant in his own development, and therefore in his own education.

The Stage-Developmental View and Informal Education

Developmental theories have been constructed to give order and meaning to universal developmental phenomena. They are applied only with difficulty to many educational issues. The value of the developmental view for education is that it locates the basic source and direction of behavior within the child; it also provides a context within which to make diagnostic decisions (cf. Swap, 1974). But, granting that a broad developmental frame of reference is a way of telling generally where the child is, a conception of growth such as Piaget's does not lead to very clear specification of what to provide in the way of educational experience for the child on a given day, week or month (cf. Ennis, 1975). Piagetian theory (to take the view most familiar to me) deals with *inevitabilities* in development that occur over long periods of time, typically several years—inevitabilities which were selected for their universality. How this theory could have much to say about the process of instruction or the formation of curriculum is difficult for me to understand. Indeed, Piaget has never claimed to provide such guidance (Aebli, 1970; Piaget, 1972).

What is striking about development from this point of view is its pervasiveness, universality and inevitability. Only an extreme laissez-faire educational philosphy like that of A.S. Neill and other "free school" advocates would see education as guided by such a broad developmental framework. Paul Goodman hoped, for example, that all education would someday occur in the same way that children seem to learn to speak: informally, without pressure, without explicit tutoring by adults. The difficulty with this wish is that most of the knowledge and skill that a culture values and wishes to transmit to its young is *not* of such a universal, spontaneously acquired nature. While the attractiveness of a stage-developmental framework is evident and real, it has and should serve only as a very general backdrop for educational issues. The countless decisions of the teacher, curriculum maker, and administrator are—and must be—substantially ignored by stage-developmental views such as those described above.

Perhaps it is just as well that the developmental view be broad, for images and metaphors should not be unduly restrictive. At their best they should guide but not direct. And a case could certainly be made that the stage-developmental framework, so popular with those who advocate informal classrooms, offers a sufficiently rich image for this purpose. Yet, the open educator (or any educator) must deal with a group of real children—choosing materials, organizing activities, individualizing instruction, and trying to help each child integrate experience from conceptually distinct domains. To make these kinds of choices and decisions requires going well beyond a traditional stage-developmental frame of reference.

Some theorists (most notably Kohlberg) have tried to make a limitation of developmental theory into a strength by arguing that education should aim for improvement in what Piaget calls décalage (i.e. within-stage learning), since it seems unnecessary to aim for stage-to-stage improvement—which occurs inevitably anyway (Kohlberg, 1970; Kohlberg & Mayer, 1972). Thus, as Kohlberg and others have argued, the role of education should be to help the student apply his mental structures to as many new situations as possible. This seems to be similar to what some open educators have called "messing about" (Hawkins, 1974) or "horizontal experience" (Corwin & Levin, 1975).

Piaget, however, sees décalage as relatively unimportant to his general conception of intellectual development, leading one critic of Kohlberg's educational arguments to argue that he has "totally misunderstood" the meaning of décalage (Schrag, 1973). To Piaget, the specific constraints on applying one's mental operations to a particular object, in comparison to other objects, are referred to as "resistances." Birds are said to be more "resistant" to the application of a number scheme than are flowers (Piaget, 1971). This is obvious enough: birds flying around are hard to count because they are moving. Flowers, in contrast, sit sedately on the table and submit to the intention of the person trying to count them. However, the notion of resistances is about as far as Piaget goes in considering the factors responsible for décalage. What to Piaget is a minor matter, a blemish on an otherwise elegant formulation, is to Kohlberg the stuff of which educational practice is made.

Perhaps more troublesome to the educator than the question of whether or not one should aim to increase décalage is the fact that progress in intellectual development is guaranteed by Piagetian theory and beyond any significant influence of the teacher. The teacher's role is secondary in the sense that stage-to-stage movement is spontaneously achieved by the child and guaranteed to occur (see Chapter 1). Within this framework the best that teachers can hope to do is facilitate growth by providing stimulating activities from which children may choose. Control of the process comes from within the child, from the set of self-regulating mechanisms that Piaget describes in his equilibration model. To facilitate décalage is a disturbingly secondary role for teachers, however, and one they should not accept.

It seems to me that educators believe there is much more to education than facilitating the application of existing mental structures to new situations. But while it seems clear enough that there is more to education than logic, or science, or even intellectual development for that matter, it is not so clear just how to select a curriculum from among the many possibilities or to establish that curriculum within the traditional developmental framework.

THE DEVELOPMENTAL TRADITION AND
THE MATTER OF EDUCATIONAL GOALS

By assuming that the child is self-motivated and a relatively autonomous goal seeker and goal setter, much of the responsibility for deciding what to learn is left to the discretion of the child. Virtually any activity which engages students' interest and attention, which contributes to general growth trends and is aimed at a developmentally appropriate level is acceptable to a developmentalist or a teacher espousing a developmental view.

George Hein, for example, is an open educator who has expressed the situation well:

> The old argument was of the form that learning Latin was useful or that memorizing was good for the mind. What Piaget is saying is that any study is good for the mind, not because learning Latin is a particularly desirable activity or because memorizing is especially good training but because every intellectual task is good for developing the intellect. (1974, p. 10)

While it is obvious that not all things can be studied at all times, there is little in developmental theory *à la* Piaget to help *choose* what to teach and when to teach it. Given the rather limited usefulness of a developmental frame of reference for guiding specific educational decisions, why has it been so attractive to the open educator?

I think that the developmental metaphor is attractive partly because it makes the specific choice of subject matter or learning goal less relevant than the general developmental appropriateness of the activity. This, in turn, allows the educator to give over a substantial amount of choice to the student without feeling that he has evaded responsibility. While the concern with providing stimulating experiences is certainly a defensible one, there appears to be more to this attraction than a well-motivated decision based on the explicit or implicit principles of the stage model itself.

Although it is impossible to establish with certainty the extent to which decisions are actually influenced by this motive, I think that a substantial impetus for embracing a stage-developmental view is that it side-steps questions for which educators currently have no satisfactory answers. These questions have to do with educational objectives, goals, and values—ends toward which the educational process is aimed and means toward achieving them. The developmental view is therefore attractive both for what it does and for what it does not encompass.

But surely the time will come when educators will seek a framework within which to synthesize the traditional belief that they have a crucial role to play in the education of the young with the more recent acknowledgement that their students also have an active part to play in these decisions. It is toward that end that the remainder of this chapter is aimed.

TOWARD ANOTHER IMAGE

It should be evident from the discussion thus far that, first and foremost, a satisfying view of the roles of both teacher and child must include those aspects of the educational process which are either ignored or inadequately captured in existing images. Perhaps the most important of these aspects is a reasonable notion of what the future will be.

For the educator's work to have meaning it must be guided by a vision of the future as well as a sense of the connection between that future and the educational preparation designed to meet its challenges. If educators find themselves preparing students for a future which no longer exists, or for a future which will *never* exist, the consequences for the student—and eventually for his society—will be disastrous. Thus it is of immense importance that a plausible notion of the future be contained within any image that aspires to guide educational thought. And yet the future is harder than ever to predict; growing consensus within many of the academic disciplines, including physics and philosophy, suggests that the future is in principle unknowable; indeed, it is even altered by every attempt to comprehend it.

One of the reasons for adopting a developmental view is that it leaves open the issue of precisely where the educational process is going, yet it avoids the utter chaos of the unknown. The theory essentially guarantees that every child will achieve formal operations, the final stage of logical throught in Piaget's system, and this is perhaps enough. In this light informal education may be seen as an adaptive response within the educational community to a time of uncertainty and lack of direction. It is also a valid response to increasing recognition that children are complex beings, somewhat differently motivated and organized than adults, and are capable of making many more decisions about their own lives and education than we had thought.

I would point out, however, that it is unwise to continue to ignore indefinitely a limitation of the developmental framework—that it does not specify *educational* ends—a conclusion that has even been reached by some who are identified with informal education (Corwin & Levin, 1975; Hawkins, 1974). Developmental theory sets such a broad goal for education that every child will achieve it—whether or not there are educators, schools, curricula or even books.

Development and Educational Practice

The stage-developmental framework is thus too far removed from day-to-day educational decisions to be altogether relevant to much of what happens in classrooms and schools. It is like having a map of the United States when the problem at hand is to get from Newark, Delaware to Princeton, New Jersey by the most scenic route. The scale is simply too large, the ability to guide only useful at a very general level, and most of the critical information simply not there. David Hawkins writes:

> But when it is considered analytically as a mode of abstraction, the developmentalist scheme is inadequate to the deepest and most central con-

cerns of education. It is inadequate because it buries under a metaphor just that level of interaction between "development" and "learning" without which our species would lack its most distinctive characteristics. (Hawkins, 1974, p. 237; see also Feldman, 1971, 1974)

This distance between the developmental framework and the practice of education leads spokesmen for open education such as George Hein to vacuous invocations like the following: "So, in order to have intelligence develop, it is necessary to have lots of experience, lots of active engagement, and especially, to have many varieties of experience" (1974, p. 10). Hein's message seems to be: if everything is educational, then let us have lots of everything.

In sum, a new framework is needed to respond to two sorts of educational concerns. First, it should help discriminate among the virtually infinite number of possible futures for a given child that can be accommodated by the stage-developmental image. Second, it should suggest ways to help decide among the tremendous number of tasks, materials, activities, bodies of knowledge, etc. that could be selected as "educational" at any grade, age, or level of preparation.

The Child as Craftsman

The image I have chosen for the purposes above—while certainly not the only one possible—is that of the *child as craftsman*. I will try to convey a general sense of what I mean by this image, and then consider some specific educational issues using this view as a guide.

To see the child as a craftsman means to see him or her as a person who wants to be good at something. It suggests that the child continually wishes to take pride in accomplishment and build a sense of integrity about his own work, regardless of the actual level of the work produced. The notion is somewhat akin to Robert White's (1959) effectance motivation, except that White's notion implies more of a need to feel mastery over what seem to be uncontrolled forces in the environment. The inclination toward craftsmanship no doubt is influenced by effectance motivation which leads to a sense of competence, but the craftsman image is intended to go beyond this to include a more direct link to specific fields of endeavor and to suggest why some activities are so much more compelling to a given child than others.

The image of the craftsman is not intended to suggest that young children are predestined to find satisaction within a single, particular craft or field or discipline. It simply emphasizes that one of the aims, perhaps the principal aim of education, should be to *engage* the child in pursuit of mastery of a satisfying craft or crafts, and to find work to do that is likely to bring adult satisfaction, fulfillment and expression. This image also does not imply that each of us necessarily has some of the poet or artist in him; it leaves open the question of just what it is that will engage the interest and enthusiasm of a child at a given point in time. What it does suggest is that there are ways that children can be engaged in activities that bear directly on their future as workers in various fields.

It should be obvious that the selection of a lifetime's work may be a dangerous one to make too early. And this is not at all—or at least not necessarily—what I have in mind with the craftsman image. I suggest the image primarily as a way to think about the child and his relationship to knowledge at any point during his educational life. By thinking of the child as actively trying to find satisfying work to do and trying to become good at something, the current aims of the educator and the educational process become somewhat altered. The image includes the recognition that, at his own level, the school-aged child is already intent on becoming a craftsman, even if he is not yet sure of what his life's work will eventually be. *Perhaps the most important implication of this image is to suggest that the main purpose of education may well be to provide conditions under which each child can pursue and achieve more advanced levels of mastery within a chosen field or fields of work.*

I should point out that my conception of the variety of possible crafts that one might pursue is a very inclusive one. Edgar Friedenberg has written that "You have to be really good in America to make it for long as a physicist, a rock musician or a parent; but for the rest, Spiro T. Agnew is probably good enough" (Friedenberg, 1970). While Mr. Agnew's fall from power may raise some questions about the currency of Friedenberg's remark, the sense of it is clear and still is true—few fields in this culture seem to genuinely demand excellence and still fewer really value it. When I use the term "craft" in the present context, I mean it to include as many kinds of work as society offers to its members: basketweaving, oratory, mathematics, chess, mechanics, salesmanship, pantomime—the full range of activities that enrich and sustain social and intellectual life. And I would also hope that the idea of craftsmanship leads to greater valuing of diverse occupations as well as standards of excellence that tend to bring forth the best efforts of each of us. To me, valuing excellence and appreciating diversity are two swatches cut from the same cloth.

The notion of the child-as-craftsman includes the view that the child has the capability (although not unlimited) to choose his or her own pursuits. This is similar to, but not the same as, the assumption of Piagetian theory that the child possesses self-regulatory mechanisms which govern development. The decision to master a particular craft or to become involved in activities that might lead to such mastery is not the same as exercising or even constructing universal cognitive structures, although self-regulatory mechanisms are no doubt involved in both. To try to master a craft is a many layered task, and making the choice to study a particular body of knowledge means meeting a series of challenges linked to the specific content and structure of the field. Oftentimes the student is not even aware of these links. Indeed, the craftsman idea suggests that the sensitive eye of a teacher must direct and help select the activities of the child, because the teacher can often better appreciate the relationship between a specific activity the child is exploring and a more general domain of knowledge and skill.

The concept of *engagement* in intended to capture the intensity of the relationship that should exist between student and subject matter; it demands that the final arbiter of an educational decision is the enthusiasm, commitment, and productiveness of the child at his work. Thus, educators might in the future become detectives, sleuths who, armed with knowledge of the structure and levels of various fields, search for activities that engage the energies of the child and lead to sustained effort. I am obviously simplifying a very subtle and demanding process by this characterization; frankly, we know little about how such sleuthing can be done successfully, except, of course, we know that great teachers have been doing it for generations. However, if the child-as-craftsman image strikes a responsive cord, then the likelihood of learning more about the processes of engagement and of the structure and sequence of levels of mastery increases, because this knowledge would become instrumental to the achievement of valued educational objectives.

Curriculum

What would be the implications of the child-as-craftsman idea for curriculum formation? First, a renewed emphasis on subject matter would be called for, although not because the study of certain classical subjects "disciplines" the mind; the return to an emphasis on subject matter would *not* be with the idea that everyone ought to study any particular subject. The emphasis follows instead from the fact that introduction to and guidance within a field is a prerequisite to real engagement. Rather than introducing a "general" sort of mental discipline, the child-as-craftsman view leads to a notion of discipline through the acquisition and mastery of challenging work in a field. It is implied in the view here that specific ways of thinking are acquired as part of learning a craft and that a "generally disciplined" mind is not necessarily a desirable, or at least a preeminent goal for education (cf. Salomon, 1979).

Little is actually known about the psychological demands that various fields make on those who aspire to practice them. The curriculum reform movement of the late '50s and '60s represented one attempt to clarify these issues. This movement was inspired by Jerome Bruner's call to learn better how to transmit what we know:

Perhaps the task of converting knowledge into a form fit for transmission is, after all, the final step in our codification of knowledge. Perhaps the task is to go beyond the learned scholarship, scientific research, and the exercise of disciplined sensibility in the arts to the transmission of what we have discovered. Surely no culture will reach its full potential unless it invents ever better means for doing so. (Bruner, 1971, p. 19)

With the enhanced acuity of hindsight we know now that attempts to reform curricula confused the *logic* of a discipline with its developmental levels. Thus, physics and biology and mathematics were broken down into their principles and theories, but not studied in terms of the ways in which individuals move from initial encounter to engagement, from engagement to mastery of early levels, from apprentice to journeyman, and so on. In other words, the *developmental* aspects of these fields were generally not incorporated into the curricula. Nor were relationships between the capabilities of children and the demands of these disciplines transmitted to teachers in ways they could use.

To see the child as a budding craftsman leads to formal considera- tion of the relationship of the proclivities of a child to the structure and sequence of knowledge acquisition in a field, particularly to the levels of mastery of that field. Curriculum formation becomes a joint function of child, field, and their continuing relationship under the guidance of teachers who understand development within domains.

CULTURAL VERSUS INDIVIDUAL CHOICE

We are led to consider an important distinction between those skills and knowledge required of *all* individuals in a society versus those which are more optional. To the extent possible, we might hope that the former will be acquired through pursuit of the latter, but, of course, this cannot be guaranteed. It is legitimate for society to expect its citizens to read, to write, to be able to count, to perform basic arithmetic functions, and to have some sense of the system of government and proper codes of behavior.

It must be acknowledged that the goal of craftsmanship tends to shift the current emphasis on "basic skills" as the "core" of curriculum to a somewhat more peripheral role. Some might argue that if students are encouraged to pursue their own interests to a much greater extent than they do now, at some point these interests may conflict with the crucial task of preparation for adult life in society, i.e., students would not learn the basic skills. The view here suggests that the balance could be shifted substantially in the direction of work within a field without seriously jeopardizing the stability of the social order. Presumably, children would be asked to demonstrate their mastery of culturally required skills and knowledge through some form of competency testing. A premise of the craftsman image is that much of what is required of a citizen for full participation in the social life of the culture would be acquired naturally and as a matter of course as one moved through the levels of one's craft. For example, an architect who is successful must be able to deal with people effectively, understand business, comprehend government regulations, etc., in addition to designing buildings.

Instruction

Another distinction which has been implicit in the discussion until now should be made explicit. This is the distinction between the *stages* of general cognitive developmental theory and the *processes* it postulates to account for developmental change; this distinction is particularly critical when considering instruction. When I argue that the Piagetian notion of developmental stage is useful but inadequate for guiding educational theory and practice, I make this argument only for the systems of thought represented by each of the stages. The processes by which one achieves any developmental advance may well be similar for all developmental changes, including those that are much more fine grained and specific than the broad Piagetian levels. Since instruction is intended to facilitate developmental advance, the process of instruction seems well guided by the developmental framework. In contrast to most curricular decisions which lack a formal basis in theory, the instructional process I envision to encourage craftsmanship is one that has richly elaborated underpinnings drawn from developmentalists such as Piaget. The child-as-craftsman notion may add to but does not replace existing guides to instruction. Still, there are some aspects of instruction that seem somewhat altered when this new image is invoked.

The matter, for example, of *how much* a child can learn is not a meaningful issue unless considered (a) in relation to a field of endeavor and (b) in relation to the extent to which the child and the field are well matched. The impliction is that a fair estimate of a child's capability makes sense only *after* he or she has become engaged in serious attempts at mastery of a domain. Prior to the presence of clear evidence of such engagement, it is as likely that a poor *match* of child to field acounts for variable performance as much as the presence or absence of a set of qualities in the child. For example, a child who is believed to have a "poor memory" in school may be able to remember enormous amounts of technical information about engines and engine parts if his passion is automobiles. While it is no doubt true that some individuals have good "general memory" abilities, the craftsman idea implies that this may not matter all that much for most purposes. "Can the child remember the lines from Act III?" may be a more fruitful question to ask than "Does the child have a large digit span?"

Related issues concern *when* and *how* teachers introduce the child to various fields. The idea of the child-as-craftsman, as mentioned earlier, suggests that the primary role of the teacher is to discover the propensities and proclivities that the child exhibits, then to organize resources to further the child's mastery of these interests. During the very early years this would of course be a less specialized process (except for child prodigies). Many of the same preschool activities are applicable to several fields of endeavor, but the decisions would be expected to become more focused with time.

I would argue that if the goal of craftsmanship is to be applied to early education we will have to pay closer attention to how to help children get beyond surface encounters so that they may experience the sense of satisfaction from mastery which the image implies. Products which arise out of brief encounters with materials are not likely by themselves to contribute to a feeling of craftsmanship, since they involve primarily exploring the novel aspects of experience. Initially getting to know something is only a first and a prior step to the process of deep engagement.

It follows that we need to study how children become engaged once the initial novelty of an experience or material has worn off, and how educators can foster such extended involvement (Levin, 1978). Deep engagement is unlikely to occur in a completely open or unstructured school situation, since engagement occurs only when continuous, sustained, supervised participation in a field is available. But while we know something about the conditions which do *not* regularly stimulate such commitment to work, we know very little about the conditions which do. What sorts of mentors or models, for example, are appropriate for young children? How beneficial is exposure to the most mature forms of a field, such as great works of art or brilliant musical works? For child prodigies, early exposure to great works in one's field seems to be a catalyst to engagement; is this also true for other children? Obviously we have only begun to consider the many issues that are raised, but not resolved, by the craftsman image.

As the child reaches the elementary school years channeling of effort into fewer activities pursued with more intensity would seem to be a sensible educational strategy. Presumably at this time the child will begin to seek greater skill and depth in instruction within a field, and teachers cannot be experts at everything. This in turn leads to the possibility that expert practitioners be available as mentors for providing needed sophistication in instruction. What I have in mind is not, strictly speaking, an apprentice relationship between novice and master. This relationship implies too little choice on the part of the student and too much power on the part of the expert. There is an apprenticelike quality to the educational relationship I have in mind, but mentor seems to express this relationship better than master.

Progress and the Future

Changing lenses to a wider angle, we must ask if the child-as-craftsman view leads to a conception of educational progress that makes sense for an uncertain future. The image does draw attention to the fact that achieving mastery of basic cultural tools alone leaves too much undone, and that it is not sufficient to expound maxims like "every child should be able to achieve his or her unique potential." Without a clear sense of the manner in which that uniqueness is to be identified, nurtured and expressed, perhaps the traditional educational aim of "preparation for adulthood" is as precise an expression of educational purpose as we can muster; the child-as-craftsman view though, leads me to suggest a plausible notion of how progress in education may be measured.

Assuming for the sake of discussion that the primary aim of education is to be engagement which leads to some sort of apprenticeship for students who aspire to master a field, how might progress toward these valued goals be assessed? We have accepted that the future is unknowable in any precise sense, yet the idea of progress seems to demand a clear vision of the future. Given that we would accept the basic idea of the child-as-craftsman image, under what circumstances, then, could we judge education to be successful?

The craftsman notion suggests to me that progress be gauged in terms of two criteria. The first is simply a restatement of the educational aim of engagement in a more precise form: to the extent that *greater numbers* of individuals find fields to pursue, find work that engages their energies and through which they derive satisfaction, education can be considered to be making "progress." The matter of how "satisfaction" and "fulfillment" are to be measured is of course a problem of great difficulty, but in principle it seems to me no more so than the problem of devising, say, economic indicators. Indeed, some have suggested "quality of life indicators" are not so very different from this first criterion of educational progress. In any event, if the criterion of engagement makes sense, I think it is only a technical problem—although a most challenging one—to produce ways of measuring it.

The second criterion of educational progress follows from my thoughts about creativity (Feldman, 1974, 1975; see also Chapter 4). This way of looking at creativity suggests that if education is done well, creative contributions will tend to take care of themselves. In other words, an education which fosters sustained commitment, satisfaction and joy in accomplishment will naturally lead to occasions that require one to go beyond the limits of one's craft. To reach the limits and find yet another problem to be solved, a goal to be achieved, an idea to be expressed, a technique to be worked out—these are the conditions which favor creativity.

Therefore, I submit that the twin signs of progress toward a fruitful education for the future are: (1) an increasing number of individuals engaged and committed to pursuit of mastery of their fields, and (2) the number of novel, unprecedented, or unique contributions that occur in these fields. This notion of progress does not specify in detailed terms just what the ends of education should be, nor does it require a certain body of knowledge to be acquired at a certain pace. It is a notion of educational progress which is appropriate for a world in which basic assumptions have been challenged and where uncertainty about the goals of education is very deep. It is also consistent with the broader view of development presented in earlier chapters in this book.

Individuality

I would like to close this chapter with a note about individuality. The importance of expressing one's uniqueness as a human being is something that the traditional stage developmental view has seemed to all but ignore (Tyler, 1978). Perhaps more than anything else the craftsman image speaks to that desire in each of us to leave our mark, to have done something that is of lasting value. It should be clear by now that developmentalists have of late been almost exclusively concerned with those aspects of change that make us all part of the human family. This emphasis has certainly been beneficial for many purposes, but it has also become clear that it has severe limitations.

Knowing that each person shares certain universal qualities and that each of us will experience certain developmental achievements does not satisfy the need to express our singularity in some way. There have never been two human beings with identical physical characteristics. It may also be that each unique human organism has something to express that has never been expressed in quite the same way before.

The idea of craftsmanship seems to capture the desire for individual expression that is a part of the heritage of every human being. I am not suggesting that the desire for expression implies that young children be given totally free rein to do whatever they please. This is not what I mean by individuality at all. I do believe, however, that those who are responsible for preparing children to enter society should recognize that a substantial challenge lies in being able to help each child acquire the attitudes and skills of craftsmanship in a domain pleasing to them and valuable to their culture.

At the risk of being repetitious, let me say once more that the craftsman image does not imply that each person will necessarily do what is conventionally called "creative work" in a field. But simply because major new contributions to knowledge cannot be produced by everyone does not mean that we should all despair of leaving some mark in our chosen fields of endeavor. All of us can contribute our best efforts to our work—whatever it may be—in a way which carries the stamp of our own individuality. If young children were prepared for a future of craftsmanship it might be possible to strike a better balance between the inculcation of basic skills and the encouragement of human expression; a balance, I hope, that does full justice to the universal and to the unique in each of us.

afterword

David Feldman and I are good friends and I feel more comfortable calling him by his first name—especially as I plan to argue with him. When David asked me to write a postscript for his book I was both flattered and alarmed: flattered because I admire him and his work, alarmed for the same reason. I knew the book (which I had not yet seen) would be highly original, and I knew enough about myself to realize that my way of assimilating new ideas is to use them, explore them, argue with them. So I warned David that he might find his book ending with an argument. To his credit, he welcomed the opportunity to have his book open a dialogue within its covers. Here goes.

I found *Beyond Universals in Cognitive Development* easy to read, not because it is conceptually simple, but because it pursues a fascinating argument. At the same time, I had trouble classifying its subject matter. It is not exactly about *ontogeny,* the study of the species-typical course of development of individuals who are members of the same species: this is the main subject of Piaget's oeuvre. It is not exactly about what might be called *personogeny,* the study of the development of the unique configuration of charactertistics describing each individual human being: this is the main subject of Leona Tyler's recent book, *Individuality, Human Possibilities and Personal Choice in the Psychological Development of Men and Women.* It is not exactly about the parallels or other relationships between ontogeny and phylogeny: this is a subject approachable only in fields where there is enough useful knowledge and understanding both of individual development within species and of evolution from species

175

to species, as treated in Stephen Jay Gould's masterly synthesis, *Ontogeny and Phylogeny*.

To my surprise. I find myself believing that David has written a book about *phylogeny* itself. As a psychological novelty moves from being an original, unique response toward becoming a universal characteristic of all members of the species, it comes to typify the species. Understanding the incorporation of such novelties into the species-typical repertoire or competence is an important aspect of phylogenetic theory. But of course, David does not approach his subject by interspecies comparisons in the manner of an evolutionary theorist. He is interested in the psychological transitions that occur within our own species. The transitions which concern him are of two main kinds, corresponding to his two main conceptual aims.

The connecting link is the idea that the same processes which can be observed in the ordinary course of individual development are also at work in cases of great creativity, i.e., in the production of unique ideas and works. What is rare and difficult in the individual who produces a unique response becomes easier and more frequent, until everyone can and does develop it. Some unique responses exhibit this historic movement from unique to universal because the environment, within which all psychological development occurs, itself evolves. There is nothing in this argument requiring that all creative responses have a similar history of U-to-U movement. But some do, and those become the universals dealt with in developmental theories more conventional than David's.

These ideas are important and, for me, difficult. I have felt the need to restate the argument in the form of eight propositions. The first five are intended as paraphrases of David's argument. The next two are, I think, extensions compatible with his argument and necessary for it. The eighth proposition introduces a theoretical alternative which may be incompatible with David's argument. (I say 'may be' advisedly, because it is never easy to sort out the necessary interconnections and legitimate pathways within the maze of a complex argument.) This alternative deals with the differences between ordinary development and creative work, a question which has long concerned me.

Proposition 1. Unique creative thoughts and universally shared ideas are constructed by individuals using the same processes for both, especially those processes outlined in Piaget's disequilibration theory.

Proposition 2. Some environments are especially favorable for the initial production of certain novelties.

Proposition 3. Some individuals are specially tuned (whether by heredity or previous experience) to be the first to construct certain ideas, make certain creative achievements.

Proposition 4. The fortunate conjunction of the favorable environment and the tuned individual provide the circumstances in which novelties are produced.

Proposition 5. Variations in environmental circumstances, analogous to selection pressures in the theory of evolution, determine which initially unique ideas will spread through a population.

A corollary of Proposition 5 is the following:

Proposition 6. Non-tuned individuals come to construct the same ideas that tuned individuals have previously done; moreover, they may come to do so under environmental conditions that are no longer the same as those prevailing at the time of first creation.

We may ask, how might the environment have changed so that Proposition 6 is the case? Two major possibilities come to mind.

Proposition 7. Whatever historical trends first produced the environment favoring the particular innovation in question then continue, become deeper and more widespread. In other words, the environment becomes more favorable to the particular discovery. Hence, less well-tuned individuals now become capable of the same discovery.

Proposition 8. The initial creative production itself fundamentally changes the environment for other individuals. They live and grow and work in a world where that product already exists. They do not have to produce it, only to *reproduce* it.

Propositions 7 and 8 are not mutually exclusive, but they are quite different from each other. Proposition 7 and David's Proposition 1 are compatible with each other: the later producers of an idea and the first ones work in the same way. Proposition 8, however, is intended to propose an alternative that may be incompatible with Proposition 1. The first creator of an idea cannot imitate any one else; neither can he or she be taught the idea via direct instruction. If imitation and learning from instruction are different from creative work, then the later constructors of an idea may do so by different means from the first creator.

I hasten to add that imitation and learning from instruction are by no means passive processes. As Piaget has long insisted, they require active construction by the individual. Intuitively, nevertheless, imitation and learning do not seem to me to be identical with the process of creative work. Let us now look a little more closely at the relation between creativity and ordinary development.

David's application of Piaget's disequilibration model both to ordinary development and to creativity is a good place to start. For each step in both kinds of process, we may well find a causal factor in some discrepancy between the desired and the actual states of affairs. But just at this point an important difference appears, because creativity is purposeful work and ordinary development is not.

Interesting creative processes almost never result from single steps, but rather from the concatenation and articulation of a complex set of interrelated moves. If only a single step or stroke were involved, theories of creativity that rely heavily on single great insights or on chance alone would be more plausible. If only a single step were involved, creative achievement would not be so rare, and creative products once made would be immediately seen by everyone as absolutely unarguable. In reality, of course, the most important creations are both very rare and often the occasion of great controversy. The picture we need is not one of the final placing of the keystone in an arch making a stable structure stand forth for all to see. The creative person struggles through many stages of his work and sets it before the world; then we, his co-inhabitants, must begin our struggle to assimilate what the creative person has done, to change ourselves a little so that we can experience things in the same new way, relive the creator's struggle at least a little.

In some measure, then, both the creative process and its incorporation by others—its move toward universalization—share this quality of protracted struggle within a complex web of relationships. This is quite different from the resolution of a single discord depicted in David's version of the disequilibration model.

For the creative person, this struggle is regulated and its diverse aspects orchestrated by a sense of purpose. The creator knows what he or she is trying to do. As David himself has pointed out, Picasso's first image guides the whole work. Of course, the image and the purpose may evolve as the work proceeds, but they still function as internally constructed regulators of the process as a whole. Rudolf Arnheim (1962) has brought this out beautifully for the case of Picasso's mural *Guernica*. The same sense of directed struggle toward a goal pervades Darwin's notebooks of 1837-38. There are surprises, unintended consequences, and self-discoveries of previously unrecognized motives and potentialities. But the process as a whole is purposefully directed. If Darwin had suddenly stumbled onto the discoveries of his contemporaries, Michael Faraday in electricity or even Gregor Mendel in genetics, they might have seemed to him like interesting curiosities or annoying mosquitoes: to make *those* discoveries was not part of his system of purposes.

The disequilibrium model, then, takes us only a small distance into the creative process. It was designed to deal with single steps in the process of intellectual growth, not to account for directionality. To understand creativity and invention we need to introduce the idea of the organized, purposeful working through of a complex array of difficulties standing between the creator and the goal.

The universal childhood developmental processes described by Piaget, on the other hand, proceed without the governance of intentions toward remote goals. This does not mean that ordinary growth is undirected. But we must look elsewhere to understand its regulation. The child in Piaget's account wants only to make an interesting sight happen again; an act is repeated and the child unintentionally discovers the principle of causality. The regulating mechanisms that guarantee that all children will go through the same developmental sequence is external to the child's intentions. It is an omnipresent feature, or set of features, of the physical-social environment. No matter what the child's intentions may be, he or she will undoubtedly discover the idea of object permanence. The regularity and predictability of the universal stages of psychological development are guaranteed not by the child's intentions but by the structure of the world.

David has made a very useful distinction between the *stages* of development of a work or of an idea and the series of psychological *states* through which an individual passes. I simply add here the point that the pre-existence, in the physical-social environment into which each child is born, of certain products of past struggles *externalizes the goal-state*. The adults around the child share a common understanding. The child, in moving toward the common understanding, moves toward something that already exists. Its very existence governs the child's movement.

There is another very important difference between creativity and ordinary development which dances into view at just this point in the discussion. Developmental movement toward universally shared ideas, the common understanding, *diminishes* the psychological distance between the child and those around him. The development of the creative person has an almost opposite effect. The more he succeeds in constructing a new point of view which governs the look of all problems and possibilities, the more he increases the distance between himself and others. He must fashion ways of coping with this distance, accept a sort of existential loneliness. The distance is not only a necessary consequence of creative work, it is a valuable tool—preventing the creative person from sinking back into banality.

The maintenance of this distance carries with it a new sense of personal identity, a feeling of specialness. "I am different. Let this not upset you," wrote the medieval philospher Paracelsus. Now if all the creative person needed to do was to maintain his distance and sense of specialness, his work would be easier, but for us the task of distinguishing creativity from psychosis would become impossible. The distinction, however, is implicit in the plea of Paracelsus. He *recognizes* that there is a difficulty, that he is looking at the world from a special place, that others see things differently. His words are not only a mark of recognition of his own plight, but also of the plight of those around him.

To be effective, the artist must be able to step back from the canvas and ask, what have I made? How does this look, not only from my position one paintbrush-length away from the work, but also from other viewing distances? This ability to take the point of view of another begins to develop in early childhood. By the age of 7 or 8 the child can perform the rather simple perspective-taking transformations required for Piaget's three-mountain problem, imagine himself standing in another place. But the creative person must carry this development several orders of magnitude further. He must see the world with different eyes, and yet remember to look at it, from time to time, with ordinary vision. He cannot be effective if he is simply and permanently estranged from his fellow creatures.[1]

This obligation to move back and forth between radically different perspectives produces a deep tension in every creative life. In the course of ordinary development similar tensions begin to appear. What we mean by such terms as *adaptation* and *adjustment* is the resolution of these tensions. But that is not the path of the creative person. He or she must safeguard the distance and the specialness, live with the tension.

David is not the only scientist who has thought about the problem of individuality. The special value of his thought lies in his struggle to forge the link between the unique and the universal. In thinking these thoughts stimulated by his book, I have enjoyed thinking of him simply as David. I have had in mind another David who with very simple means, a sling and a stone, decisively ended an argument. David Feldman, also working with simple means, also has done something memorable. He has opened a much needed discussion.

HOWARD E. GRUBER
Institute for Cognitive Studies
Rutgers University

---

[1] "I always feel as if my books came half out of Lyell's brain . . . the great merit of the *Principles* [Charles Lyell's *Principles of Geology*] was that it altered the whole tone of one's mind, and therefore that, when seeing a thing never seen by Lyell, one yet saw it partially through his eyes." Charles Darwin in a letter, Aug. 29, 1844.

a final word

As always, I am instructed by discussions with Howard Gruber, and as usual he has gone to the heart of the matter. I was fascinated by his characterization of my book as dealing with issues of phylogeny, as I had not thought of it exactly that way myself before. I agree with Howard that the major point of the book is the nature of the relationship between different types of transitions—those characteristic of "normal" cognitive development and those which characterize creative advances. He is correct in pointing out that much of my discussion of universal and nonuniversal hangs on there being some similarity between creative works and developmental advances of a less ambitious nature, but it is in discussing this relation that I think he has taken my arguments a bit afield.

While Howard suggests that one of his Propositions may be incompatible with my framework, I found all eight of them to fit comfortably within the view set forth in these pages. To be sure, he has made a real contribution by clarifying the issues, making explicit some of the implications of the universal-to-unique continuum and exploring processes that are presumed to account for its existence and evolution. However, I think that Howard may be suggesting differences between our views that are not really there. I think the problem begins with Howard's Proposition 1. Proposition 1 reads:

> Unique creative thoughts and universally shared ideas are constructed using the same processes for both, especially those processes outlined in Piaget's disequilibration theory.

181

I have indeed argued that the achievement of creative contributions shares basic transition processes with achievements that are more mundane and common, but I did not imply (at least I did not intend to imply) that they necessarily shared *all* of the same qualities. Coal and diamonds are both made of carbon, but they are not the same thing.

It should not be surprising that Howard, whose contributions to our understanding of creativity have been so seminal and so important, would go on to emphasize the differences between great creativity and more ordinary achievements. My own discussion of creativity was not aimed to denigrate in any way the uniqueness (or the anguish) of creativity writ large, but simply to suggest that both the processes of creative work and developmental advances may be illuminated by those processes of change that they share. I believe that we may best enhance our comprehension of the seemingly mysterious process through which creative work is done by recognizing that it is not a wholly distinct enterprise from other efforts at reorganizing one's thinking.

Creativity (in the sense of the production of major original works) comes about when an individual has mastered a discipline and has reached the limits of knowledge in that field. After a long journey from universal to unique reorganizations, through acts of great courage and at some risk, the creator transcends the barriers of ignorance, plunges into the unknown, and transforms both his own mental organization and the world's store of knowledge by these efforts. To achieve this kind of result (as Howard has shown in his work on Darwin) requires an overall mission or sense of purpose which is marked by periods of lonely sustained effort, many small advances in addition to a few earthshaking insights, reversions, and stalemates. While Howard is right in saying that the very young child is less aware of his "mission" or "plan" for constructing more sophisticated mental scaffolding, it is also true that creative individuals are often themselves unaware of their purposes and goals, or at best only dimly so (cf. Ghiselin, 1952). In this respect, Darwin seems to have been an exception.

One final point. An original mind is most clearly distinguished by its ability to see connections that are important but not obvious. Howard showed just this cast of mind in *Darwin on Man* when he demonstrated that it is possible to study Charles Darwin as an adult by using Piaget's genetic epistemology, despite the enormous differences between the great evolutionist pursuing his theory and the child discovering the principles of logical thought. But having once seen this connection, Howard left unspecified its nature, choosing instead to let the case speak for itself. The work presented in my book is an attempt to, among other things, identify some of the landmarks along the route between unique achievements like Darwin's and universal ones like those of the normally developing child, making the connections more obvious in the process. Thus, Howard's Propositions 7 *and* 8, which have to do with the environmental conditions that catalyze change, are not at all incompatible with the universal-to-unique framework.

Mapping the terrain between universal and unique may seem to some to lessen the "specialness" of great accomplishment by demonstrating that it shares kinship with other developmental processes, but I must say that this has not been the result for me. I find myself more rather than less awed by achievements great and small because I understand better the complex and delicate conditions under which they are brought about. It may seem that by emphasizing the continuities among intellectual achievements I have diminished the more rare and valuable ones; I believe that the opposite is actually the case. New distinctions that highlight the specialness of great achievement are also suggested by the universal-to-unique framework, and much of this book is at pains to draw them forth. Howard Gruber has elegantly extended these distinctions and continuities in his Afterword.

D.H.F.

BIBLIOGRApHY

Aebli, H. Piaget, and beyond. *Interchange,* 1970, *1*, 12–24.

Albert, R. Genius: Present-day staus of the concept, and its implications for the study of creativity and giftedness. *American Psychologist,* 1969, *24*, 743–753.

Anastasi, A. Heredity, environment and the question "How?" *Psychological Review,* 1958, *65*, 197–208.

Arbuthnot, J. Modification of moral judgment through role playing. *Developmental Psychology,* 1975, *11*, 319–324.

Antrobus, J. (Ed.). *Cognition and affect.* Boston: Little Brown & Co., 1970.

Aries, P. *Centuries of childhood: A social history of family life.* New York: Knopf, 1962.

Arnheim, R. *The genesis of a painting: Picasso's Guernica,* Berkeley: University of California Press, 1962.

Arnheim, R. *Art and visual perception.* Berkeley: University of California Press, 1969 (1954).

Atkinson, R. Computerized instruction and the learning process. *American Psychologist,* 1968, *23*, 225–239.

Ausubel, D. *The psychology of meaningful verbal learning.* New York: Grune & Stratton, 1963.

Ausubel, D. *Educational psychology: A cognitive view.* Toronto: Holt, Rinehart & Winston, 1968.

Barbe, W. (Ed.). *Psychology and education of the gifted: Selected readings.* New York: Appleton-Century-Crofts, 1965.

Barlow, F. *Mental prodigies.* New York: Greenwood Press, 1969 (1952).

Barron, F. Complexity-simplicity as a personality dimension. *Journal of Abnormal and Social Psychology,* 1953, *48*, 163–172.

Barron, F. The disposition toward originality. *Journal of Personality and Social Psychology,* 1955, *51*, 478–485.

Barron, F. The dream of art and poetry. *Psychology Today,* 1968, *2*, 19–23.

Bart, W., & Airasian, P. Determination of ordering among seven Piagetian tasks

185

by an ordering-theoretic method. *Journal of Educational Psychology*, 1974, *66*, 277–284.

Bart, W., & Smith, M. An interpretive framework of cognitive structures. *Human Development*, 1974, *17*, 161–175.

Baumgarten, F. *Wunderkinder psychologische untersuchungen.* Leipzig: Johann Ambrosius Barth, 1930.

Beilin, H. Learning and operational convergence in logical thought development. *Journal of Experimental Child Psychology*, 1965, *2*, 317–339.

Bem, S. The role of comprehension in children's problem solving. In P. Sears (Ed.), *Intellectual development.* New York: Wiley, 1971.

Bereiter, C. Educational implications of Kohlberg's cognitive-developmental view. *Interchange*, 1970, *1*, 25–32.

Bereiter, C., & Engelmann, S. *Teaching disadvantaged children in the preschool.* Englewood Cliffs, N.J.: Prentice-Hall, 1966.

Blatt, S. & Kohlberg, L. Effects of classroom discussion upon children's level of moral judgment. In L. Kohlberg & E. Turiel (Eds.), *Recent research in moral development.* New York: Holt, Rinehart & Winston, 1973.

Bloom, B. *Stability and change in human characteristics.* New York: Wiley, 1964.

Brainerd, C. Neo-Piagetian training experiments revisited: Is there any support for the cognitive-developmental stage hypothesis? *Cognition*, 1973, *2*, 349–370.

Brainerd, C. Cognitive development and concept learning: An interpretive review. *Psychological Bulletin*, 1977, *84*, 919–939.

Brainerd, C., & Allen, T. Experimental inductions of the conversation of 'first-order' quantitative invariants. *Psychological Bulletin*, 1971, *75*, 128–144.

Brearley, M. *The teaching of young children: Some applications of Piaget's learning theory.* New York: Schocken Books, 1970.

Bremer, J. Review of B. Spodek and H. Walberg, *Studies in open education. Phi Delta Kappan*, 1975, *57*, 718–719.

Brim, O., Glass, D., Neulinger, J., & Firestone, I. *American beliefs and attitudes about intelligence.* New York: Russel Sage Foundation, 1969.

Brown, R. *A first language.* Cambridge, Massachusetts: Harvard University Press, 1973.

Bruininks, R., & Feldman, D. H. Creativity, intelligence and achievement among disadvantaged children. *Psychology in the Schools*, 1970, *7*, 260–264.

Bruner, J. S. Freud and the image of man. *American Psychologist*, 1956, *11*, 463–466.

Bruner, J. S. *The process of education.* New York: Vintage Books, 1960.

Bruner, J. S. The conditions of creativity. In H. Gruber, G. Terrell, & M. Wertheimer (Eds.), *Contemporary approaches to creative thinking.* New York: Prentice-Hall, 1962.

Bruner, J. S. The course of cognitive growth. *American Psychologist*, 1964, *19*, 1–15.

Bruner, J. S. The growth of mind. *American Psychologist*, 1965, *20*, 1007–1017.

Bruner, J. S. *On knowing.* New York: Atheneum, 1968 (1962).

Bruner, J. S. *Toward a theory of instruction.* New York: Norton, 1968 (1966).

Bruner, J. S. *The relevance of education.* New York: Norton, 1971.

Bruner, J. S. The nature and uses of immaturity. *American Psychologist*, 1972, *27*, 1–22.

Bruner, J. S. *Beyond the information given.* New York: Norton, 1973.

Bruner, J. S., & Olson, D. R. Learning through experience and learning through media. In D. R. Olson (Ed.), *Media and symbols.* Chicago: University of Chicago Press, 1974.

Bruner, J. S., Olver, R., & Greenfield, P. M. *Studies in cognitive growth*. New York: Wiley, 1966.

Bunge, M. Levels: A semantical preliminary. *The Review of Metaphysics*, 1960, *13*, 396–406.

Campbell, D. Evolutionary epistemology. In P. Schilpp (Ed.), *The philosophy of Karl Popper*. Vol 14, I & II. *The library of living philosophers*, La Salle, Ill.: Open Court Publishing Company, 1974.

Campbell, D. On the conflicts between biological and social evolution and between psychology and moral tradition. *American Psychologist*, 1975, *30*, 1103–1126.

Caplan, J., & Nelson, S. On being useful: The nature and consequences of psychological research on social problems. *American Psychologist*, 1973, *28*, 199–211.

Card Rotations Test. Princeton, N.J.: Educational Testing Service, Copyright 1962.

Case, R. Structures and strictures: Some functional limitations on the course of cognitive growth. *Cognitive Psychology*, 1974, *6*, 544–573.

Cavalli-Sforza, L., & Feldman, M. Cultural versus biological inheritance: Phenotypic transmission from parents to children (A theory of the effect of parental phenotypes on children's phenotypes). *American Journal of Human Genetics*, 1973, *25*, 618–637. (a)

Cavalli-Sforza, L., & Feldman M. Models for cultural inheritance I. Group mean and within group variation. *Theoretical Population Biology*, 1973, *4*, 42 55. (b)

Chase, W., & Simon H. Perception in chess. *Cognitive Psychology*. 1974, *4*, 55–81.

Chittenden, E. What is learned and what is taught. *Young Children*, 1969, *25*, 12–19.

Chomsky, N. *Syntactic structures*. The Hague: Mouton, 1957.

Chomsky, N. *Language and mind*. New York: Harcourt, Brace, Jovanovich, 1968.

Clarke, B. The causes of biological diversity. *Scientific American*, 1975, *233*, 50–60.

Clarke-Stewart, K. A. Interactions between mothers and their young children: Characteristics and consequences. *Monographs of the Society for Research in Child Development*, 1973, *38*, Serial No. 153.

Cole, M., Gay, J., Glick, J., & Sharp, D. *The cultural context of learning and thinking*. New York: Basic Books, 1971.

Collins, J. *My seven chess prodigies*. New York: Simon & Schuster, 1974.

Conkling, H. *Poems by a little girl*. New York: Frederick A. Stokes, 1921.

Corwin, R., & Levin, D. *The educational application of some aspects of cognitive development*. Cambridge, Mass.: Lesley College Graduate School, 1975 (mimeo).

Cowan, P. *Piaget: With feeling*. New York: Holt, Rinehart & Winston, 1978.

Crockenberg, S. Creativity tests: A boon or boon-doggle for education? *Review of Educational Research*, 1972, *42*, 27–45.

Cronbach, L. J. The two disciplines of scientific psychology. *American Psychologist*, 1957, *12*, 671–684.

Cronbach, L. J. Intelligence? Creativity? A parsimonious reinterpretation of the Wallach-Kogan data. *American Educational Research Journal*, 1968, *5*, 491–511.

Cronbach, L. J., & Furby, L. How should we measure "change"—or should we? *Psychological Bulletin*, 1970, *74*, 68–80.

Cropley, A. A five year longitudinal study of the validity of creativity tests. *Developmental Psychology*, 1972, *6*, 119–124.

Dart, F., & Lal Pradhan, P. Cross-cultural teaching of science. *Science,* 1967, *155,* 649–656.

Dasen, P. Cross-cultural Piagetian research: A summary. *Journal of Cross-cultural Psychology,* 1972, *3,* 23–39.

Dawkins, R. *The selfish gene.* New York: Oxford University Press, 1976.

Deci, E. *Intrinsic motivation.* New York: Plenum, 1975.

De Groot, A. *Thought and choice in chess.* The Hague: Mouton, 1965.

Dewey, J. *Experience and education.* New York: Collier Books, 1963 (1938).

Dobzhansky, T. *Mankind evolving: The evolution of the human species.* New Haven: Yale University Press, 1962.

Dobzhansky, T. *Genetics of the evolutionary process.* New York: Columbia University Press, 1970.

Dobzhansky, T. *Genetic diversity and human equality.* New York: Basic Books, 1973.

Dodwell, P. Children's understanding of spatial concepts. *Canadian Journal of Psychology,* 1963, *17,* 141–161.

Duckworth, E. The having of wonderful ideas. *Harvard Educational Review,* 1972, *42,* 217–231.

Dunn, L. *Peabody Picture Vocabulary Test.* Circle Pines, Minnesota: American Guidance Service, 1965.

Durost, W., Bixler, H., Hildreth, G., Lunk, D., & Wrightstone, J. *Directions for administering Metropolitan Achievement Tests, Elementary Battery.* New York: Harcourt, Brace, & World, 1959.

Eiseley, L. *The immense journey.* New York: Vintage Books, 1957 (1946).

Eisner, E. *A comparison of the developmental drawing characteristics of culturally advantaged and culturally disadvantaged children.* Project No. 3086, Contract No. OE-6-10-027, Stanford University, 1967.

Elkind, D. Piaget and Montessori. *Harvard Educational Review,* 1967, *37,* 535–545.

Elkind, D. *Child development and education: A Piagetian perspective.* New York: Oxford University Press, 1976.

Ennis, R. Children's ability to handle Piaget's propositional logic: A conceptual critique. *Review of Educational Research,* 1975, *45,* 1–41.

Erikson, E. H. *Childhood and society.* New York: Norton, 1963 (1950).

Feldhusen, J., Treffinger, D., & Bahlke, S. Developing creative thinking: The Purdue creativity program. *Journal of Creative Behavior,* 1970, *4,* 85–90.

Feldman, D. H. *A study of a fixed sequence of skill and concept acquisition requisite to performance of a common school task: Map drawing.* Paper presented at the Annual Meeting of the American Educational Research Association, Los Angeles, February 1969.

Feldman, D. H. *The fixed-sequence hypothesis: Individual differences in the development of school related spatial reasoning.* Paper presented at the Annual Meeting of the American Educational Research Association, Minneapolis, March 1970.

Feldman, D. H. Faulty construction: A review of Wallach and Wing's *The talented student. Contemporary Psychology,* 1970, *15,* 3–4.

Feldman, D. H. Map understanding as a possible crystallizer of cognitive structures. *American Educational Research Journal, 1971, 8,* 485–501.

Feldman, D. H. *Crystallizing experiences and education.* A proposal submitted to the Spencer Foundation, Chicago, August 1973. (a)

Feldman, D. H. *Psychology 1973/74 Text.* Guilford, Ct.,: Dushkin Publishing Group, 1973. (contributing author). (b)

Feldman, D. H. Problems in the analysis of patterns of abilities. *Child Development,* 1973, *44,* 12–18. (c)

Feldman, D. H. Universal to unique: A developmental view of creativity and education. In S. Rosner & L. Abt (Eds.), *Essays in creativity.* Croton-on-Hudson, New York: North River Press, 1974.

Feldman, D. H. Review of *Darwin on Man* by H. E. Gruber and P. H. Barrett. *Phi Delta Kappan,* 1975, *57,* 56–57.

Feldman, D. H. The child as craftsman. *Phi Delta Kappan,* 1976, 58, 143–149. (a)

Feldman, D. H. *Early prodigious achievement: A developmental perspective.* Invited Address presented at the Sixth Annual Symposium of the Jean Piaget Society, Philadelphia, June 1976. (b)

Feldman, D. H. The mysterious case of extreme giftedness. In H. Passow (Ed.), *The gifted and the talented: Yearbook of the National Society for the Study of Education.* Chicago: University of Chicago Press, 1979. (a)

Feldman, D. H. Toward a nonelitist conception of giftedness. *Phi Delta Kappan,* 1979, *60,* 660–663. (b)

Feldman, D. H. Stage and sequence: Getting to the next level. *The Genetic Epistemologist,* 1980, in press.

Feldman, D. H., & Markwalder, W. Systematic scoring of ranked distractors for the assessment of Piagetian reasoning levels. *Educational and Psychological Measurement,* 1971, *31,* 347–362.

Feldman, D.H., & Sears, P. Effects of computer assisted instruction on children's behavior. *Educational Technology,* 1970, *10,* 11–14.

Feldman, D. H., & Snyder, S. *Structure/content relations in developmental transitions.* Paper presented at the Biennial Meeting of the Society for Research in Child Development, New Orleans, April 1977.

Feldman, D. H., Marrinan, B., & Hartfeldt, S. Transformational power as a possible index of creativity. *Psychological Reports,* 1972, *30,* 335–338.

Finley, C. A comparison of the California Achievement Test, Metropolitan Achievement Test and Iowa Tests of Basic Skills. *California Journal of Educational Research,* 1963, *14,* 79–88.

Flavell, J. H. *The developmental psychology of Jean Piaget.* New York: Van Nostrand, 1963.

Flavell, J. H. Concept development. In P. Mussen (Ed.), *Carmichael's manual of child psychology.* New York: Wiley, 1970.

Flavell, J. H. Comments on Beilin's "The development of physical concepts." In T. Mischel (Ed.), *Cognitive development and epistemology.* New York: Academic Press, 1971. (a)

Flavell, J. H. Stage-related properties of cognitive development. *Cognitive Psychology,* 1971, *2,* 421–453. (b)

Flavell, J. H. *Cognitive development.* Englewood Cliffs, N.J.: Prentice-Hall, 1977.

Flavell, J. H., & Wohlwill, J. Formal and functional aspects of cognitive development. In D. Elkind & J. H. Flavell (Eds.), *Studies in cognitive development.* New York: Oxford University Press, 1969.

Flavell J. H., Botkin, P., Fry, C., Wright, J., & Jarvis, P. *The development of role-taking and communication skills in children.* New York: Wiley, 1968.

French, J., Ekstrom, R., & Price, L. *Manual for kit of reference tests for cognitive factors.* Princeton, N.J.: Educational Testing Service, 1963.

Freyberg, P. Concept development in Piagetian terms in relation to school attainment. *Journal of Educational Psychology,* 1966, *57,* 164–168.

Friedenberg, E. Educational testing and the social system. *Change Magazine,* January/February, 1970.

Furth, H. *Thinking without language: Psychological implications of deafness.* New York: Free Press 1966.

Furth, H. *Piaget for teachers.* Englewood Cliffs, N.J.: Prentice-Hall, 1970.

Gagné, R. Contributions of learning to human development. *Psychological Review,* 1968, *75,* 177–191.

Gardner, H. *The arts and human development.* New York: Wiley, 1973.

Gardner, H., Howard, V., & Perkins, D. Symbol systems: A philosophical, psychological and educational investigation. In D. R. Olson (Ed.), *Media and symbols.* Chicago: University of Chicago Press, 1974.

Gardner, J. (Ed.). *Readings in developmental psychology.* Boston: Little-Brown, 1978.

Geertz, C. *The interpretation of cultures.* New York: Basic Books, 1973.

Gelman, R. Conservation acquisition: A problem of learning to attend to relevant attributes. *Journal of Experimental Child Psychology,* 1969, *7,* 167–187.

Gelman, R., & Gallistel, C. R. *The child's understanding of number.* Cambridge, Mass.: Harvard University Press, 1978.

Gerard, R. The biological basis of imagination. *The Scientific Monthly,* June 1946. In B. Ghiselin (Ed.), *The creative process.* New York: Mentor, 1955 (1952).

Getzels, J., & Csikzentmihalyi, M. *The creative vision: A longitudinal study of problem finding in art.* New York: Wiley, 1976.

Getzels, J., & Jackson, P. *Creativity and intelligence: Explorations with gifted students.* New York: Wiley, 1962.

Ghiselin, B. *The creative process.* New York: Mentor, 1955 (1952).

Ginsburg H., & Opper, S. *Piaget's theory of intellectual development: Second edition.* Englewood Cliffs, N.J.: Prentice-Hall, 1979.

Golomb, C. Children's representation of the human figure: The effects of models, media and instructions. *Genetic Psychology Monographs,* 1973, *87,* 197–251.

Golomb, C. *Young children's sculpture and drawing.* Cambridge, Mass.: Harvard University Press, 1974.

Goslin, D. *The search for ability.* New York: Science Editions, 1966 (1963).

Goss, A., & Nodine, C. *Paired-associates and learning: The role of meaningfulness, similarity, and familiarization.* New York: Academic Press, 1965.

Gruber, H. E., & Barrett, P. *Darwin on man: A psychological study of scientific creativity.* New York: E. P. Dutton, 1974.

Gruber, H. E., & Vonèche, J. (Eds.). *The essential Piaget.* New York: Basic Books, 1978.

Guilford, J. P. Creativity. *American Psychologist,* 1950, *5,* 444–454.

Guttman, L., & Schlesinger, I. Systematic construction of distractors for ability and achievement test items. *Educational and Psychological Measurement,* 1967, *27,* 569–580.

Haddon, F., & Lytton, H. Teaching approach and the development of divergent thinking abilities in primary schools. *British Journal of Educational Psychology,* 1968, *38,* 171–180.

Harvard Educational Review, 1969, *39,* No. 1, 1–123; No. 2, 273–356; No. 3, 449–631.

Hatano, G., Yoshio, M., & Binks, M. Performance of expert abacus users. *Cognition,* 1977, *5,* 47–55.

Hawkins, D. *The informed vision: Essays on learning and human nature.* New York: Agathon, 1974.

Heath, T. *Aristarchus of Samos: The ancient Copernicus.* London: Oxford University Press, 1959.

Hein, G. *Piaget, materials, and open education.* Newton, Mass.: Educational Development Center, 1975 (1973).

Henle, M. Fishing for ideas. *American Psychologist,* 1975, *30,* 795–799.

Hilgard, E. Issues within learning theory and programmed learning. *Psychology in the Schools,* 1964, *1,* 129–140.

Hilgard, E. Creativity: Slogan and substance. *Centennial Review,* 1968, *12,* 40–58.

Hollingworth, L. *Children above 180 IQ.* New York: Arno Press, 1975 (1942).

Horton, R. African traditional thought and Western science: Part I: From tradition to science. *Africa,* 1967, *37,* 50–71. (a)

Horton, R. African traditional thought and Western science: Part II: The closed and open predicaments. *Africa,* 1967, *37,* 155–187. (b)

Hunt, D. A conceptual level matching model for coordinating learner characteristics with educational approaches. *Interchange,* 1970, *1,* 68–81.

Hunt, J. McV. *Intelligence and experience.* New York: Ronald Press, 1961.

Hunt, J. McV. The psychological basis for using pre-school enrichment as an antidote for cultural deprivation. *Merrill-Palmer Quarterly,* 1964, *10,* 211–248.

Inhelder, B., & Chipman, H. (Eds.). *Piaget and his school.* New York: Springer-Verlag, 1976.

Inhelder, B., & Piaget, J. *The growth of logical thinking from childhood to adolescence.* New York: Basic Books, 1958.

Inhelder, B., & Sinclair, H. Learning cognitive structures. In P. Mussen, J. Langer, & M. Covington (Eds.), *Trends and issues in developmental psychology.* New York: Holt, Rinehart & Winston, 1969.

Inhelder, B., Sinclair, H., & Bovet, M. *Learning and the development of cognition.* Cambridge, Mass.: Harvard University Press, 1974.

Jackson, P., & Messick, S. The person, the product, and the response: Conceptual problems in the assessment of creativity. *Journal of Personality,* 1965, *33,* 309–329.

Jensen, A. How much can we boost IQ and scholastic achievement? *Harvard Educational Review,* 1969, *39,* 1–123.

Johnson, P. Some psychological aspects of subject matter structure. *Journal of Educational Psychology,* 1967, *58,* 75–83.

Johnson, P., Cox, D., & Curran, T. Psychological reality of physical concepts. *Psychonomic Science,* 1970, *19,* 245 –247.

Kagan, J. *Change and continuity in infancy.* New York: Wiley, 1971.

Kagan, J., & Gardner, H. *Cognitive Development.* New York: Harper & Row, 1972 (film).

Kane, G. *Chess and children.* New York: Charles Scribner's & Sons, 1974.

Keating, D. (Ed.). *Intellectual talent: Research and development.* Baltimore: The Johns Hopkins University Press, 1976.

Kellogg, R. *Analyzing children's art.* Palo Alto: National Press Books, 1969.

Kessen, W. "Stage" and "structure" in the study of children. In W. Kessen & C. Kuhlman (Eds.), Thought in the young child. *Monographs of the Society for Research in Child Development,* 1962, *27,* 53–70.

Klein, R., Hale, G., Miller, L., & Stevenson, H. Children's paired associate learning of verbal and pictorial material. *Psychonomic Science,* 1967, *9,* 203–204.

Kluckhohn, C., & Murray, H. Personality formation: The determinants. In C. Kluckhohn and H. Murray (Eds.), *Personality: In nature, society and culture.* New York: Knopf, 1961 (1948).

Koestler, A. *The act of creation.* New York: Dell Publishing, 1964.

Kofsky, E. A scalogram study of classificatory development. *Child Development,* 1966, *37,* 191–204.

Kogan, N. *Creativity and sex differences.* Paper presented at a Symposium on Sex Differences in Play, Imagination, and Creativity: Current Research and Implications, Eastern Psychological Association, Boston, March, 1972.

Kogan, N., & Pankove, E. Longterm predictive validity of divergent-thinking tests: Some negative evidence. *Journal of Educational Psychology*, 1974, *66*, 802–810.

Kohlberg, L. Cognitive stages and preschool education. *Human Development*, 1966, *9*, 5–17.

Kohlberg, L. Early education: A cognitive-developmental view. *Child Development*, 1968, *39*, 1013–1062.

Kohlberg, L. Stage and sequence: The cognitive-developmental approach to socialization. In D. Goslin (Ed.), *Handbook of socialization theory and research.* New York: Rand McNally, 1969.

Kohlberg, L. Reply to Bereiter's statement on Kohlberg's cognitive-developmental view. *Interchange*, 1970, *1*, 40–48.

Kohlberg, L. From is to ought: How to commit the naturalistic fallacy and get away with it in the study of moral development. In T. Mischel (Ed.), *Cognitive development and epistemology.* New York: Academic Press, 1971.

Kohlberg, L. The claim to moral adequacy of a highest stage of moral development. *Journal of Philosophy*, 1973, *70*, 630–646.

Kohlberg, L., & Gilligan, C. The adolescent as a philosopher: The discovery of the self in a postconventional world. In H. Kraemer (Ed.), *Youth and culture: A human-development approach.* Belmont, Calif.: Brooks/Cole, 1974.

Kohlberg, L., & Mayer, R. Development as the aim of education. *Harvard Educational Review*, 1972, *42*, 449–496.

Kohlberg, L., & Turiel, E. Moral development and moral education. In G. Lesser (Ed.), *Psychology and educational practice.* Glenview, Illinois: Scott, Foresman, 1971.

Kohnstamm, G. Experiments on teaching Piagetian thought operations. In J. Helmuth (Ed.), *Cognitive studies 1.* New York: Brunner-Mazel, 1970.

Kris, E. *The neurotic distortion of the creative process.* Lawrence, Kansas: University of Kansas Press, 1958.

Kuhn, D. Mechanisms of change in the development of cognitive structures. *Child Development*, 1972, *43*, 833–844.

Kuhn, D. Inducing development experimentally: Comments on a research paradigm. *Developmental Psychology*, 1974, *10*, 590–600.

Kuhn, D. Relation of two Piagetian stage transitions to IQ. *Developmental Psychology*, 1976, *12*, 157–161. (a)

Kuhn, D. Short-term longitudinal evidence for the sequentiality of Kohlberg's early stages of moral judgment. *Developmental Psychology*, 1976, *12*, 162–166. (b)

Kuhn, T. *The structure of scientific revolutions.* Chicago: University of Chicago Press, 1962.

Labov, W. The logic of non-standard English. In F. Williams (Ed.), *Language and poverty.* Chicago: Markham, 1970.

Langer, J. Disequilibrium as a source of development. In P. Mussen, J. Langer, & M. Covington (Eds.), *Trends and issues in developmental psychology.* New York: Holt, Rinehart & Winston, 1969. (a)

Langer, J. *Theories of development.* New York: Holt, Rinehart & Winston, 1969. (b)

Langer, J. Interactional aspects of cognitive organization. *Cognition, 1974, 3,* 9–28.

Laurendeau, M., & Pinard, A. *The development of the concept of space.* New York: International Universities Press, 1970.

Lenneberg, E. *Biological foundations of language.* New York: Wiley, 1967.

Levin, D. *Peer interaction as a source of cognitive developmental change.* Ph.D. Thesis, Tufts University, 1978.

Levi-Strauss, C. *The savage mind.* Chicago: University of Chicago Press, 1966 (1962).

Loevinger, J., & Wessler, R. *Measuring ego development I.* San Francisco: Jossey-Bass, 1970.

Lombroso, C. *The man of genius.* New York: Charles Scribner's & Sons, 1898.

Lord, F., & Novick, M. *Statistical theories of mental test scores.* Reading, Mass.: Addison-Wesley, 1968.

Lowenfeld, V., & Brittain, W. *Creative and mental growth.* New York: Macmillan, 1975.

Luquet, G. *Les dessins d'un enfant.* Paris: F. Alcan, 1913.

Lynch, K. *The image of the city.* Cambridge, Mass.: M.I.T. Press, 1961.

Mackinnon, D. Personality and the realization of creative potential. *American Psychologist,* 1965, *20,* 273–281.

Magidoff, R. *Yehudi Menuhin: The story of the man and the musician.* New York: Doubleday, 1955.

Markwalder, W. Stage mixture and cognitive development. *The Southern Journal of Educational Research,* 1972, *6,* 219–225.

Mayr, E. *Populations, species and evolution.* Cambridge, Mass.: Harvard Univesrity Press, 1970.

McClearn, G. Genetic determination of behavior (animal). In L. Ehrman, G. Omenn, & E. Caspari (Eds.), *Genetics, environment and behavior: Implications for educational policy.* New York: Academic Press, 1972.

McLuhan, M. *Understanding media: The extensions of man.* New York: McGraw-Hill, 1964.

Mischel, W. *Personality and assessment.* New York: Wiley, 1968.

Mischel, W. Sex typing and socialization. In P. Mussen (Ed.), *Carmichael's manual of child psychology.* New York: Wiley, 1970.

Montour, K. William James Sidis, the broken twig. *American Psycchologist,* 1977, *32,* 265–279.

Murray, F. The acquisition of conservation through social interaction. *Developmental Psychology,* 1972, *6,* 1–6.

Nabokov, V. *The defense.* New York: Putnam, 1964.

Nicholls, J. Creativity in the person who will never produce anything original and useful: The concept of creativity as a normally distributed trait. *American Psychologist,* 1972, *27,* 717–527.

Olson, D. R. *Cognitive development: The child's acquisition of diagonality.* New York: Academic Press, 1970.

Olson, D. R. On a theory of instruction: Why different forms of instruction result in similar knowledge. *Interchange,* 1972, *3,* 9–24.

Olson, D. R. What is worth knowing and what can be taught? *School Review,* 1973, *82,* 27–43.

Olson, D. R. (Ed.). *Media and symbols: The forms of expression, communication, and education.* Chicago: University of Chicago Press, 1974.

Olson, R. (Ed.). *Science as metaphor.* Belmont, Calif.: Wadsworth, 1971.

Olton, R., & Crutchfield, R. Developing the skills of productive thinking. In P. Mussen, J. Langer, & M. Covington, (Eds.), *Trends and issues in developmental psychology.* New York: Holt, Rinehart & Winston, 1969.

Paivio, A., & Yuille, J. Word abstractness and meaningfulness, and paired-associate learning in children. *Journal of Experimental Child Psychology,* 1966, *4,* 81–89.

Pascual-Leone, J. A mathematical model for the transition rule in Piaget's developmental stages. *Acta Psychologica,* 1970, *32,* 301–345,

Pascual-Leone, J., & Smith, J. The encoding and decoding of symbols by children: A new experimental paradigm and a neo-Piagetian model. *Journal of Experimental Child Psychology,* 1969, *8,* 328–355.

Phillips, D., & Kelly, M. Hierarchical theories of development in education and psychology. *Harvard Educational Review,* 1975, *45,* 351–375.

Piaget, J. The mission of the idea. In H. E. Gruber & J. Vonèche (Eds.), *The essential Piaget.* New York: Basic Books, 1978 (1915).

Piaget, J. *The language and thought of the child.* New York: New American Library, 1974 (1923).

Piaget, J. *The moral judgment of the child.* Glencoe, Ill.: Free Press, 1948 (1932).

Piaget, J. *The origins of intelligence in children.* New York: Norton, 1963 (1952).

Piaget, J. *The construction of reality in the child.* New York: Basic Books, 1954.

Piaget, J. *Logic and psychology.* New York: Basic Books, 1960.

Piaget, J. *Six psychological studies.* New York: Random House, 1967.

Piaget, J. Piaget's theory. In P. Mussen (Ed.), *Carmichael's manual of child psychology.* New York: Wiley, 1970.

Piaget, J. *Structuralism.* New York: Basic Books, 1970 (1968).

Piaget, J. The theory of stages in cognitive development. In D. Green, M. Ford, & G. Flamer (Eds.), *Measurement and Piaget.* New York: McGraw Hill, 1971.

Piaget, J. Intellectual evolution from adolescence to adulthood. *Human Development,* 1972, *15,* 1–12.

Piaget, J. *The child and reality.* New York: Grossman Publishers, 1973.

Piaget, J. *The development of thought: Equilibration of cognitive structures.* New York: Viking, 1977 (1975).

Piaget, J., & Inhelder, B. *The child's conception of space.* New York: Norton, 1967 (1948).

Piaget, J. & Inhelder, B. *The psychology of the child.* New York: Basic Books, 1969.

Polanyi, M. *Personal knowledge.* Chicago: University of Chicago Press, 1974 (1958).

Popper, K. *The logic of scientific discovery.* New York: Basic Books, 1959.

Reese, H., & Parnes, S. Programming creative behavior. *Child Development,* 1970, *41,* 413–423.

Resnick, L. (Ed.). *The nature of intelligence.* Hillsdale, N. J.: Lawrence Erlbaum Associates, 1976.

Rest, J. *Manual for the defining issues test: An objective test of moral judgment development.* Minneapolis: University of Minnesota, 1974. (mimeo)

Rest, J., Turiel, E., & Kohlberg, L. Level of moral development as a determinant of preference and comprehension of moral judgments made by others. *Journal of Personality,* 1969, *37,* 225–252.

Revesz, G. *The psychology of a musical prodigy.* Freeport, N. Y.: Books for Libraries Press, 1970 (1925).

Riegel, K. Dialectical operations: The final period of cognitive development. *Human Development,* 1973, *16,* 346–370.

Roe, A. *The making of a scientist.* New York: Dodd Mead, 1953.

Rohwer, W., Jr. Learning, race and school success. *Review of Educational Research,* 1971, *41,* 191–210.

Salomon, G. What is learned and how it is taught: The interaction between media, message, task and learner. In D. R. Olson (Ed.), *Media and symbols.* Chicago: University of Chicago Press, 1974.

Salomon, G. *The interaction of media, cognition and learning.* San Francisco: Jossey-Bass, 1979.

Sameroff, A. Can conditioned responses be established in the newborn infant? *Developmental Psychology,* 1971, *5,* 1–12.

Sarason, S. B. *Individual psychology: An obstacle to comprehending adulthood.* Invited Paper, Vermont Conference on Early Prevention of Pscyhological Stress, Burlington, June 1978.

Scarr-Salapatek, S. An evolutionary perspective on infant intelligence: Species patterns and individual variation. In M. Lewis, (Ed.), *The origins of intelligence.* New York: Plenum, 1975.

Scarr, S., & Weinberg, R. Performance of black children adopted by white families. *American Psychologist,* 1976, *31,* 726–739.

Schaie, K., & Strother, C. A cross-sequential study of age changes in cognitive behavior. *Psychological Bulletin,* 1968, *70,* 671–680.

Schmidt, O. Darwinism and continental socialism. In R. Olson (Ed.), *Science as metaphor.* Belmont, Calif.: Wadsworth, 1971.

Schrag, F. A response to Kohlberg and Mayer. *Harvard Educational Review,* 1973, *43,* 309-311.

Schwebel, M., & Raph, J. *Piaget in the classroom.* New York: Basic Books, 1973.

Scott, J. Critical periods in behavioral development. *Science,* 1962, *138*: Warner Modular Publication Reprint 754, 1973, 1–10.

Scribner, S., & Cole, M. Cognitive consequences of formal and informal instruction. *Science,* 1973, *182,* 553–559.

Sears, R. Sources of life satisfactions of the Terman gifted men. *American Psychologist,* 1977, *32,* 119–128.

Silverman, I. W., & Geiringer, E. Dyadic interaction and conservation induction: A test of Piaget's equilibration model. *Child Development,* 1973, *44,* 815–820.

Simon, H., & Newell, A. Human problem solving: The state of the theory in 1970. *American Psychologist,* 1971, *26,* 145–159.

Simpson, G. G. Review of *Darwin on Man* by H. E. Gruber & P. Barrett. *Science,* 1974, *186,* 133–134.

Skinner, B. F. *The technology of teaching.* New York: Appleton-Century-Crofts, 1968.

Smedslund, J. The acquisition of substance and weight in children V: Practice in conflict situations without external reinforcement. *Scandinavian Journal of Psychology,* 1961, *2,* 203–210.

Smedslund, J. Patterns of experience and the acquisition of the conservation of length. *Scandinavian Journal of Psychology,* 1963, *4,* 257–264.

Snyder S. S., Jr., & Feldman, D. H. Internal and external influences on cognitive developmental change. *Child Development, 1977, 48,* 937–943.

Snyder, S. S., Jr., Feldman, D. H., & La Rossa, C. A manual for the administration and scoring of a Piaget-based map drawing exercise. In O. Johnson (Ed.), *Tests and measurements in child development: A handbook (II).* San Francisco: Jossey-Bass, 1976. (abstract)

Staats, A. *Child learning, intelligence and personality: Principles of behavioral interaction approach.* New York: Harper & Row, 1971.

Stanley, J., Keating, D., and Fox, L. (Eds.). *Mathematical talent: Discovery, description and development.* Baltimore: The Johns Hopkins University Press, 1974.

Stenhouse, D. *The evolution of intelligence.* London: George Allen & Unwin Ltd., 1973.

Stephens, J. *The process of schooling.* New York: Holt, Rinehart & Winston, 1967.

Stevenson, H., Hale, G., Klein, R., & Miller, L. Interrelations and correlates in children's learning and problem solving. *Monographs of the Society for Research in Child Development,* 1968, *33* (whole No. 7).

Strauss, S. Inducing cognitive development and learning: A review of short-term training experiments I: The organismic developmental approach. *Cognition*, 1972, *4*, 329–357.

Strauss, S., & Rimalt, I. Effects of organizational disequilibrium training on structural elaboration. *Developmental Psychology*, 1974, *10*, 526–533.

Sullivan, E. The issue of readiness in the design and organization of the curriculum: A historical perspective. *Educational Technology*, 1970, *1*, 439–448.

Swap, S. Disturbing classroom behaviors: A developmental and ecological view. *Exceptional Children*, 1974, *41*, 163–171.

Taylor, J. *Development of musical concepts and a discussion of music education.* Unpublished manuscript, Yale University, 1972.

Terman, L., & Merrill, M. *Stanford-Binet Intelligence Scale, Form L-M.* Boston: Houghton-Mifflin, 1960.

Thorndike, E. L. *Selected writings from a connectionist's psychology.* New York: Appleton-Century-Crofts, 1949.

Thrower, N. *Maps and man.* Englewood Cliffs, N. J.: Prentice-Hall, 1972.

Thurstone, T., & Thurstone, L. *Examiner's manual for the Primary Mental Abilities Test.* Chicago: Science Research Associates, 1963. (a)

Thurstone, T., & Thurstone, L. *Primary Mental Abilities Test for grades four through six.* Chicago: Science Research Associates, 1963. (b)

Torrance, E. *Guiding creative talent.* Englewood Cliffs, N.J.: Prentice-Hall, 1962.

Torrance, E. *Torrance tests of creative thinking (Research Edition).* Princeton, N. J.: Personnel Press, 1966.

Tuddenham, R. Theoretical regularities and individual idiosyncracies. In D. Green, M. Ford, & G. Flamer (Eds.), *Measurement and Piaget.* New York: McGraw-Hill, 1971.

Turiel, E. An experimental test of the sequentiality of developmental stages in the child's moral judgments. *Journal of Personality and Social Psychology*, 1966, *3*, 611–618.

Turiel, E. Developmental processes in the child's moral thinking. In P. Mussen, J. Langer, & M. Covington (Eds.), *Trends and issues in developmental psychology.* New York: Holt, Rinehart & Winston, 1969.

Turiel, E. Conflict and transition in adolescent moral development. *Child Development*, 1974, *45*, 14–29.

Turiel, E. Distinct conceptual and developmental domains: Social convention and morality. In C. B. Keasey (Ed.), *Nebraska Symposium on Motivation.* Lincoln, Nebraska: University of Nebraska Press, 1977.

Turiel, E. *Social/cognitive development.* Invited Paper presented at the Ninth Annual Symposium of the Jean Piaget Society, Philadelphia, June 1979.

Tyler, L. *Individuality.* San Francisco: Jossey-Bass, 1978.

Underwood, B., & Schulz, R. *Meaningfulness and verbal learning.* Philadelphia: Lippincott, 1960.

Uzgiris, I. Situational generality of conservation. *Child Development*, 1964, *35*, 831–842.

Van den Daele, L. Qualitative models in developmental analysis. *Developmental Psychology*, 1969, *1*, 303–310.

Van den Daele, L. Infrastructure and transition in developmental analysis. *Human Development*, 1974, *17*, 1–23.

Van Lawick-Goodall, J. *In the shadow of man.* Boston: Houghton-Mifflin, 1971.

Vygotsky, L. *Thought and language.* Cambridge, Mass.: MI.T. Press, 1962 (1934).

Waddington, C. Genetic assimilation of an acquired character. *Evolution*, 1953, *7*, 118–126.

Waddington, C. *The strategy of the genes.* London: Allen & Unwin, 1957.

Waddington, C. *Principles of development and differentiation.* New York: Macmillan, 1966.

Walker, D. *What curriculum research?* Paper presented at the Annual Meeting of the American Educational Research Association, Chicago, April 1972.

Wallach, M. Review of *Torrance Tests of Creative Thinking. American Educational Research Journal,* 1968, *5,* 272–281.

Wallach, M. Creativity. In P. Mussen (Ed.), *Carmichael's manual of child psychology.* New York: Wiley, 1970.

Wallach, M. *The creativity-intelligence distinction.* New York: General Learning Press, 1971.

Wallach, M., & Kogan, N. *Modes of thinking in young children.* New York: Holt, Rinehart & Winston, 1965.

Wallach, M., & Wing, C. *The talented student: A validation of the creativity-intelligence distinction.* New York: Holt, Rinehart & Winston, 1969.

Wallas, G. *The art of thought.* New York: Harcourt, Brace, 1926.

Washburn, S., & Howell, F. Human evolution and culture. In S. Tax (Ed.), *The evolution of man, Vol. 2.* Chicago: University of Chicago Press, 1960.

Werner, H. The concept of development from a comparative and organismic point of view. In D. Harris (Ed.), *The concept of development.* Minneapolis: University of Minnesota Press, 1957.

Werner, H., & Kaplan, B. *Symbol formation.* New York: Wiley, 1963.

White, R. W. Motivation reconsidered: The concept of competence. *Psychological Review,* 1959, *66,* 297–333.

Williams, G. *Adaptation and natural selection: A critique of some current evolutionary thought.* Princeton, N. J.: Princeton University Press, 1966.

Wilson, E. O. *Sociobiology.* Cambridge, Mass.: Harvard University Press, 1975.

Witty, P., & Lehman, H. Nervous instability and genius: Poetry and fiction. In W. Barbe (Ed.), *Psychology and education of the gifted.* New York: Appleton-Century-Crofts, 1965.

Wohlwill, J. The age variable in psychological research. *Psychological Review,* 1970, *77,* 49–64.

Wohlwill, J. The place of structured experience in early cognitive development. *Interchange,* 1970, *1,* 13–27.

Wohlwill, J. *The study of behavoral development.* New York: Academic Press, 1973.

Wolfle, D. Intellectual resources. *Scientific American,* 1951, *185,* 42–46.

Zender, M., & Zender B. Vygotsky's view about the age periodization of child development. *Human Development,* 1974, *17,* 24–40.

Zervos, C. Conversation with Picasso. In B. Ghiselin (Ed.), *The creative process.* New York: Mentor, 1955 (1952).

author index

Page numbers in *italics* indicate where complete references are listed.

199

201

subject index